D0795156

EIGHTH EDITION

Start Up and Run Your Own Business

JONATHAN REUVID

HERTFORDSHIRE LIBRARY SERVICE

WITHDRAWN FOR SALE

Pleas

Ren
Enqui
Textr

KoganPage

LONDON PHILADELPHIA NEW DELHI

Publisher's note

Every possible effort has been made to ensure that the information contained in this book is accurate at the time of going to press, and the publishers and authors cannot accept responsibility for any errors or omissions, however caused. No responsibility for loss or damage occasioned to any person acting, or refraining from action, as a result of the material in this publication can be accepted by the editor, the publisher or any of the authors.

First published in Great Britain in 2003
Second edition 2003
Third edition 2004
Fourth edition 2006
Fifth edition 2007
Sixth edition 2007
Reprinted 2008
Seventh edition 2009
Eighth edition 2011

Apart from any fair dealing for the purposes of research or private study, or criticism or review, as permitted under the Copyright, Designs and Patents Act 1988, this publication may only be reproduced, stored or transmitted, in any form or by any means, with the prior permission in writing of the publishers, or in the case of reprographic reproduction in accordance with the terms and licences issued by the CLA. Enquiries concerning reproduction outside these terms should be sent to the publishers at the undermentioned addresses:

120 Pentonville Road	1518 Walnut Street, Suite 1100	4737/23 Ansari Road
London N1 9JN	Philadelphia PA 19102	Daryaganj
United Kingdom	USA	New Delhi 110002
www.koganpage.com		India

© Kogan Page Limited, Jonathan Reuvid and individual contributors, 2003, 2004, 2006, 2007, 2009, 2011

The right of Jonathan Reuvid and the individual contributors to be identified as the author of this work has been asserted by them in accordance with the Copyright, Designs and Patents Act 1988.

ISBN 978 0 7494 6060 0
E-ISBN 978 0 7494 6113 3

British Library Cataloguing-in-Publication Data
A CIP record for this book is available from the British Library.

Library of Congress Cataloging-in-Publication Data
Reuvid, Jonathan.
    Start up and run your own business : the essential guide to planning, funding and growing your new enterprise / Jonathan Reuvid. – 8th ed.
       p. cm.
    Includes index.
    ISBN 978-0-7494-6060-0 – ISBN 978-0-7494-6113-3 (ebk)
    1. New business enterprises–Management. 2. Small business–Management. I. Title.
    HD62.5.R475 2011
    658.1'1–dc22
                                      2010045360

Typeset by Saxon Graphics Ltd, Derby
Production Managed by Jellyfish
Printed and bound in Great Britain by CPI Antony Rowe

Brief Contents

Contents

Do you need free legal advice on starting up or running a small business?

The Law Socie[ty]

Legal pitfalls have been the downfall of many promising businesses. Through the *Lawyers For Your Business* scheme the Law Society offers you:

- access to business-related legal advice
- a free half-hour initial consultation with a solicitor in your area

Call a *Lawyers For Your Business* member for advice on a range of legal issues, including:

- Finance
- Taxes
- Insurance
- Cash flow
- Company structure

- Franchising
- Employment
- Business premises
- Contracts
- Health & safety

For a list of solicitors in your area who are members of *Lawyers For Your Business*

call: 020 7405 9075
e-mail: lfyb@lawsociety.org.uk
www.lawsociety.org.uk/lfyb

The Law Society

Lawyers For Your Business

Setting up in business should be an exciting process, but without the right advice it can also be a minefield, particularly where legal issues are concerned.

Often businesses do not consult with a solicitor for fear of large legal bills, by which time any remedy still available is likely to be expensive. Early consultation is advisable if there is legislation to be complied with or important legal documents, such as contracts, to be signed.

Lawyers For Your Business is a network of 1,000 solicitor firms in England and Wales offering specialist advice to small and medium-sized businesses.

To help firms access business-related legal advice, *Lawyers For Your Business* offers a free half-hour initial consultation with a solicitor in your area who is a member of the scheme. Advice could be sought on a range of legal issues including finance, taxes, employment law, contracts, company structure and health & safety.

The initial *Lawyers For Your Business* consultation is free, however, it is important that you clarify estimated costs at the outset before you decide to proceed. You should ask for a forecast of how costs will change in various eventualities, for example, if a matter goes to court.

For a list of solicitors in your area who are members of *Lawyers For Your Business*.

call: **020 7405 9075**
e-mail: **lfyb@lawsociety.org.uk**
www.lawsociety.org.uk/lfyb

advertisement feature

List of Figures

List of Tables

Acknowledgements

This book would not be possible in its present format without the contributions of my three long-standing collaborators in the fields of business finance, taxation and employment.

Kevin R Smith, Managing Director of AWS Structured Finance Ltd, the international financial consultants and a partner of Aspen Waite Accountants, has updated his chapters on funding alternatives and raising capital with practical advice relevant to the difficult business environment of 2011.

Paul Waite, Managing Partner of Aspen Waite, the accountancy and taxation advisers, has revised his two taxation chapters in light of the new Chancellor's Emergency Budget of 22 June 2010 and its far-reaching implications.

Nathan Donaldson, a Partner in law firm DWF LLB, has provided a comprehensive review of the current legislation in respect of employment law and human relations, the third key area in which entrepreneurs need to rely on professional expertise.

Once again, my sincere thanks to all three for their generous participation.

Jonathan Reuvid

Introduction

At first sight 2011 might not seem the best of times to set up and start a new business. With consumers suffering from increased taxation and benefits reductions, and the expenditure budgets of both the private and public sectors cut back severely, we could expect that demand for the delivery of services or manufactured goods by new suppliers would be in sharp decline.

However, there is another logic at play, at least for B2B customers and potential suppliers. On the one hand, the new government has introduced the most savage cuts in public expenditure for at least 30 years in order to address the structural deficit of £156 billion in the nation's finances, as the Conservative–Liberal coalition warned when it took office in May 2010. Moreover, the reductions in government departmental budgets are not a one-year wonder but are sure to persist for at least three years with a continuing emphasis on driving down state expenditure as a proportion of GDP. On the other hand, while the increased burden of personal taxation is expected to continue for a similar period, the Chancellor also moved swiftly in his emergency budget of 22 June 2010 to reduce company taxation and put in place new incentives to stimulate business so as to accelerate the recovery from recession.

The combined effect of these measures on the business environment is significant and has actually opened up fresh opportunities for small businesses generally and those with an entrepreneurial spirit who may be encouraged to start up on their own. The reason is that Government departments, previously insulated from the ravages of recession, have had to rethink their priorities and the ways in which they carry out their functions more cost effectively. This is not just a matter of cutting outsourced programmes, halting recruitment, encouraging early retirement or shedding staff through redundancy programmes in order to work within reduced budgets for a year or two. Both central and local government now have to look at ways of restructuring or downsizing their organizations to continue performing essential functions. In this context, outsourcing at lesser cost to private business has become a highly attractive alternative.

The private sector had already embarked on restructuring as a reaction to the 2008–09 recession and this will be a permanent process as industry strives to remain competitive in markets both home and abroad, particularly in Europe, that will return to growth slowly. Therefore, there are also continuing opportunities for innovative new entrepreneurial businesses in the private sector.

In rewriting *Start Up and Run Your Own Business* for its eighth edition I have refocused on the essential elements for success in exploiting these opportunities while retaining and updating all the chapters that have permanent relevance to new business entrepreneurs. Part One takes readers from concept to the actual start-up, with the emphasis on creating a lean business and testing the marketing strategy to verify that it generates sales before taking the plunge. Part Two covers the fundamentals for running any small business, with cash management, pricing and costing and sales and customer relations in the forefront. Use of the internet is also highlighted as the most cost-effective tool for any small business. Part Three is for entrepreneurs who have succeeded in growing a profitable, robust small business and now seek to plan forward development into a more substantial organization. Export management and more sophisticated management accounting and reporting tools that are not essential for those starting up are included. At the same time, this final part offers a foretaste of the future for those who are starting out on their journey and may succeed.

Building a business is not an adventure to be undertaken lightly; it demands determination, dedication and self-discipline. Employing others demands qualities of leadership, which are largely a matter of inborn character, and management skills that can be acquired through training and experience. This book does not attempt to offer management training in those areas. However, I have tried to provide in *Start Up and Run Your Own Business* and its companion volume *Working for Yourself* the basic advice and tools for anyone planning to create their own business or entering self-employment.

Jonathan Reuvid

Ten top tips for a

1. Write a business plan.

Many businesses seem to get by without a plan, and so might yours. On the other hand, preparing and presenting an effective business plan can make all the difference between success and failure. Besides being a great way of capturing the long-term objectives and financial goals for your business, your business plan can be used to demonstrate to prospective lenders, investors and customers that you have thought through your ideas and that they are dealing with a business which has good potential. It also gives you a benchmark to monitor your progress, so if something starts to go off track you can take prompt action to put it right.

2. Learn all you can about your chosen industry.

If you have never worked in your business sector before, get some work experience. Make sure you know the laws you need to comply with as there is a considerable amount of red tape to deal with. For example, talk to HM Revenue & Customs about tax issues before you start. If your industry has a trade association, it might be worth getting in touch to see if they can help you understand any special regulations you might need to comply with.

3. Understand everything you can about your customers.

Before you get started, it pays to talk to the people you'll be looking to sell to. Unless your product or service is completely revolutionary, your customers will already be buying it from someone else. By communicating with them, it will help you to understand what might make them buy from you instead.

4. Listen to advice.

As well as advisors at Lloyds TSB Commercial, there are lots of sources you can get guidance from. Talk to people who'll be honest about your business idea and listen to what they say.

5. Dip your toe in the water first.

It's possible to run many businesses on a part-time basis from home. An effective way to see if your business idea is viable is to stay in full-time employment, while managing your business in the evenings and at weekends. This will allow you to check if your idea is viable before taking the big step of losing your regular income. Even if you are just 'trying out' your business, open a business account as soon as possible – it will help in the long run to keep both your personal and business accounts separate.

6. Keep money in reserve and keep costs down at the outset.

Keep expenditure down as much as possible when starting up. Do you really need new premises or could you work from a spare room in your house? Don't plough every penny you have into the business unless you have absolutely no choice. No matter how well you plan, most people find they need a bit more money for something after a few months.

Free business banking includes cheques, standing orders, cash, Direct Debits, deposits and withdrawals. All we ask is that you operate your account in credit or within agreed limits.

Calls may be monitored or recorded. Lloyds TSB Commercial is a trading name of Lloyds TSB Bank plc and Lloyds TSB Scotland plc and serves customers with an annual turnover of up to £15m. Authorised and regulated by the Financial Services Authority.

successful start.

7. Make use of free publicity and networking.
It's easy to waste money on ineffective marketing, so think hard about anything you spend. Word of mouth is often the best form of advertising, so something as simple as asking satisfied customers to tell their friends about you can have a big impact. And learn to network – talk to as many people as you can about your business. You never know where those conversations might lead.

8. Set up books and records as soon as possible.
It can cost a lot of money to have an accountant sort out messy records further down the line, so get book-keeping systems set up properly before you start trading. Make sure you keep all business receipts – even from before you start trading if they relate to your business – you might be able to use them to offset tax. Having a good book-keeping system will also mean you can keep track of your business progress from day one.

9. Prepare your support network.
Starting a business is hard work. You're going to need to devote a lot of time to it for at least the first year and probably well beyond that. Make sure those closest to you understand the size of the task and the sacrifices you'll need to make to ensure your business is a success.

10. Be resilient, adapt and change.
There will be times in the first few months when things don't go your way. Maybe you will lose an important order, or an employee will let you down. Whatever that may be, learn from it and keep going. Be prepared to adapt. One great advantage for start-up businesses is that they can evolve and change direction much faster than larger more established ones. Be prepared to refine your business plan if the right opportunity presents itself.

We understand how daunting starting your own business can be, that's why we'll give you a named manager to support you, a range of free guidance services to get you off on the right foot, and 18 months' free day-to-day banking; so you can spend less time worrying about your banking and more time building your business.

For more information visit us at www.lloydstsb.com/business or call
0800 328 6101.

THE FDs'
EXCELLENCE
AWARDS
2010 WINNER
BANK OF THE YEAR

Winner 2005-2010

WE'VE BEEN VOTED THE UK'S MOST SUPPORTIVE BANK FOR BUSINESS.

At Lloyds TSB, we believe in offering you support throughout your business journey. It's why we have Relationship Managers who get to know your business and can give you the guidance and support you may need, through the good times and the bad. Our ability to offer this support is one of the reasons we were voted Bank of the Year at the Finance Directors' Excellence Awards, for the sixth year in a row.

To find out how we can help your business, visit us at www.lloydstsb.com/business, in branch or call 0800 328 6101.

Lloyds TSB | for the journey...

Bank of the Year 2005 – 10 FDs' Excellence Awards in association with the ICAEW and supported by the CBI & Real Business.

Part One
From Concept to Starting

PART ONE CONTENTS

Chapter One
Identifying the Opportunity

Where you are now

The first question for you to answer is: where are you coming from? Why are you thinking about starting your own business now and why are you reading this book?

In previous editions I have suggested that everyone in employment should carry a 'Plan B' in their backpack in the expectation that sometime in mid-career you will be faced with an opportunity or driven to consider the possibility of starting up in business on your own as a result of:

- premature retirement;
- inadequate pension;
- restructuring of your employer's business that limits your career prospects;
- frustration with your job;
- losing your job;
- leaving school or university with no job prospects;
- joining a family business.

The circumstances differ widely and so, probably, will your motivations. Let's review them individually.

Premature retirement and inadequate pension

Perhaps you have taken early retirement on favourable terms as a part of your employer's programme to reduce staff. Perhaps your employer has changed the company pension plan so that you will no longer enjoy a defined benefit related to final salary or that your pension contributions have been raised, and this prompts you to walk away with your accumulated pension rights. In either case your pension income, if you are eligible, is unlikely to be adequate and you will have a clear idea of the additional income that you need to generate to maintain your and your family's standard of living. Earned income now is probably more important than the future capital value of a new business. Alternatively, if you are already a pensioner you may find that you cannot manage on an income whose purchasing power is reduced.

Limited career prospects or frustration with your job

You have two options: soldiering on while looking for better and more satisfying employment, or striking out on your own. If you have an entrepreneurial itch, you will examine the latter while looking for a new appointment.

Losing your job

Whatever the circumstances, redundancy or disagreement with your employer, you are now unemployed and the experience will be unsettling. The good news, if you have handled your exit skilfully, is that you will have received a lump sum in cash. That cushion will give you a little time to plan your future.

Do not take a Micawber attitude that 'something will turn up' and rely on finding another job quickly. In today's employment market, finding a new job is more likely a matter of luck rather than judgement. You must focus on self-employment alternatives, including starting your own business.

Leaving school or university without a job

You may have begun to plan for starting your own business before you left school or while still at university. With the poor job outlook, you would have been wise to do so and, hopefully you will find much in the first two parts of this book to help you start that process.

Joining the family business

You are in a different category from those in the other situations described above. However, you may have similar reservations in taking up the opportunity to those who are fed up with their current jobs, and prefer to explore the alternatives rather than making such a family commitment. Perhaps you dislike the kind of business in which the family is engaged or see no long-term future for it; perhaps you do not relish the idea of working under a dominant member of your family. Again, if you are a self-starter and have inherited an entrepreneurial gene, starting your own business may be more attractive.

As you begin the evaluation process, you need to decide at quite an early stage whether the way forward for you is self-employment as a sole trader (a 'one-person business'), forming a partnership with one or more colleagues, or starting up and running a company. The decision you take will be partly a function of your business experience, particular skills and qualifications, and partly a reflection of your personal preferences and ambitions. We will return to this question shortly in the context of the type of business that you have in mind.

The small business start-up scene in the UK

Whatever your motivation for wanting to strike out on your own, you should be aware of the overall small business start-ups and closures record before beginning to plan your own venture. The most recent statistics are reported in the November 2009 Bulletin of the Office for National Statistics (ONS) for the births, deaths and survivals of enterprises in 2008.

Of the 2.4 million businesses completing VAT returns in 2008, new businesses accounted for 11.6 per cent. This birth rate was the same as for 2006 but below those for all other years since 2002. Conversely the death rate of businesses failing was 9.4 per cent, at 219,000, also the same as in 2006 and lower than every year since 2000. Taking births and deaths into account, the total number of small businesses increased each year by between 31,000 (2000 and 2001) and 58,000 (2006).

At the time of writing there are no official statistics available for 2009, but we know already that the fallout from the financial crisis and recession has impacted business births strongly. In July 2009, a spokeswoman for Bureau van Dijk, the electronic data publisher reported that 395,327 new businesses had been registered at Companies House. This rate of more than 1,000 new businesses a day is higher than any year in the last 25 years except for 2006–07, the high point of the last boom. It is also significantly higher than the rate over the similar period of the last recession in 1992.

The possibility of launching businesses on the internet has also been a key factor, enabling entrepreneurs to build and run businesses from attics and spare bedrooms.

The chances of survival

More interesting than the absolute numbers are the records for one-year to five-year survival rates of business that were born between 2003 and 2007. Table 1.1 shows the following survival rates from this database.

Somewhat depressingly, it appears that at least a third of all business start-ups fail within three years and, on more limited evidence, more than half are likely to close within five years. According to insolvency practitioners BDO Stoy Hayward, more than 26,000 first year businesses failed in the year 2008–09.

TABLE 1.1 Survival rates of new businesses

Births	2003	2004	2005	2006	2007
One year survival	92.6	94.2	94.3	96.5	95.5
Two year survival	78.0	78.7	79.8	80.7	–
Three year survival	63.6	65.3	64.7	–	–
Four year survival	54.3	54.7	–	–	–
Five year survival	45.6	–	–	–	–

Small businesses are important

At the beginning of 2008 there were 4.7 million business enterprises in the UK of which 91 per cent employed fewer than 5 people. Table 1.2 analyses their contribution to employment (7.8 million) and sales turnover of the private sector.

Timing

Above all, timing is crucial. There will be one or more times in your life when events and circumstances conspire to create real opportunity. As long ago as 2003, the Household Survey of Entrepreneurship commissioned by the Department of Business, Innovation and Skills (BIS), then the Department of Trade and Industry (DTI) Small Business Service (SBS), found that almost a quarter of adults in England are either already involved in entrepreneurial activity (13 per cent) or thinking about it (11 per cent).

If you are on the verge of start-up in 2011, review your timing carefully having regard to:

- funding requirements for the first two years;
- the current activity level of the market you intend to enter.

If your start-up requires bank-loan or overdraft funding and you have not completed arrangements with your bank, make certain

TABLE 1.2 Small businesses in the private sector

No. employees	Enterprises (per cent)	Employment (per cent)	Turnover (per cent)
Self-employed	74.1	16.8	7.7
One	4.0	1.9	1.0
Two to four	12.9	8.1	7.0
Five to nine	4.7	6.7	5.9
Fewer than 10	95.7	33.5	21.6

that funds are available. (As we go to press, high street banks continue to offer little encouragement to business start-ups or small businesses generally.)

If your funding is in place, be sure that your cash flow requirements are covered through to at least the end of 2012. Additional funds may not be available if you have to go back for more in 12 months time.

If the market you are entering is already depressed or likely to be affected by the economic slowdown in the near future, you may be wise to delay your start-up for a year or more. For example, this would be a poor time to start an estate agency. Similarly, if you intend to open a health club or fitness centre, even if local competition is weak, consider that, as family budgets are stretched by rising mortgage interest and food and fuel prices, leisure activities are likely to be curtailed at least temporarily. The same argument applies to the restaurant trade, garden centres and most of the retail trade except for online shops offering branded clothing at discount prices.

Of course, too much deliberation can result in inaction. Brutus in Shakespeare's *Julius Caesar*, one of literature's more misguided decision makers, declared: 'There is a tide in the affairs of men that taken at the flood leads on to fortune,' but do not confuse indecision with deliberate delay. If your original business concept is sound, the market opportunity will probably be there again when conditions improve. If not, then your decision to wait has a longer-term justification.

At the same time, be as sure as you can that the business activity in which you are about engage has a long-term future – 'sustainability', to adopt the current idiom. For example, those who decided to set up as service providers of Home Information Packs (HIPs) for people selling their homes and paid for expensive training made a bad decision. Well before the 2010 general election the two parties now governing had made it clear that they would abolish HIPs, as they did on taking office.

Profiling business start-up entrepreneurs

The age factor

Studies of the reasons why entrepreneurs start up their own businesses were made by several of the banks engaged in the provision of finance to small businesses before the 'credit crunch'. Attempts were made to distinguish between the motivations of younger and older entrepreneurs, often defined as those aged under and over 50. Significantly, the three main reasons were the same for both age groups: 'freedom' (cited by 93 per cent), 'challenge' (89 per cent) and 'the urge to make more money' (86 per cent). For the over 50s the third reason is compounded with retirement from a previous job. National statistics confirmed then that self-employment was more common among older workers (19 per cent) than among those under 50 (15 per cent) when they took early retirement or needed to supplement their pensions at normal retirement age.

There was also a counter-trend to the 'ageism' in employment that became prevalent in the 1980s and persisted until only a few years ago. The government is actively encouraging those in employment to defer retirement past age 65 and employers to raise retirement ages in order to allay the pension funding crisis, and a growing preference for employing older staff was noted in the various surveys.

Research also revealed that 65 per cent of Britain's small business bosses would rather employ older staff because they were considered to work harder and to be more reliable. These findings suggested that, as start-up businesses become successful and expand, they are likely to recruit a growing proportion of older staff, which might help to further the goal of a higher average retirement age.

A counter-factor to this trend was the influx of young jobseekers from the member states that joined the EU from 1 May 2004. This group, as well as pensioners, is also more likely to accept the statutory minimum wage that many employers offer.

Entrepreneurial urges

From its Household Survey of Entrepreneurship 2003, the DTI confirmed that men were twice as likely as women to be involved in entrepreneurial activity or to be thinking about it. While young people were more likely to be thinking about starting their own business, they were less likely to be entrepreneurs than older people. There were low levels of entrepreneurial activity among the Black population, but ethnic minority groups were more likely overall to be considering starting a business.

The same survey segmented the population into three main groups: Thinkers, Doers and Avoiders:

- Thinkers are those who are thinking about starting their own businesses.
- Doers are those who are already running their own business or are self-employed.
- Avoiders are those who are not currently engaged in entrepreneurial activity or thinking about doing so.

The findings of the 2003 survey were that 11 per cent of the population aged 16–64 are Thinkers, 13 per cent are Doers and 76 per cent are Avoiders. The main deterrent to becoming a Doer was identified as an aversion to risk and a heightened fear of debt.

'Risk takers' in the 2003 survey were found to be:

- 59 per cent male;
- 26 per cent aged 25–44;
- 39 per cent graduates or more highly qualified;

- 27 per cent in socio-economic group AB;
- 45 per cent in group C1.

In today's age of austerity, most of us have debt problems of varying orders of magnitude and necessity has become the mother (and father) of invention. Risk becomes unavoidable and more of us – school leavers, final year undergraduates, those facing redundancy or planning early retirement and underfunded pensioners – are driven to set aside inhibitions and explore self-employment or business start-up opportunities. But, if you are reading this book, I am 'preaching to the converted'.

Women in business

Although discrimination is still an issue for women in business, women business owners now account for a third of business start-ups. The proportion is reported to be rather lower for women aged over 50 but above 40 per cent for businesses started by those under 50. As long ago as October 2004 in a news release, Barclays Bank revealed that entrepreneurial activity among women in the UK had grown by 28 per cent since 2000. Barclays Bank also identified that more female singletons were setting up in business, with 26 per cent of the total being single, divorced or widowed, an increase of 11 per cent since 2000.

Motivations for starting their own business were found to be similar among women and men. However, factors such as more control or a better lifestyle may be rated higher among women than earning more money. Decisions on timing their start-ups are more affected by family and domestic issues, with children as a much stronger influence.

The top 10 activities in which women started up their own businesses included: hairdressing and beauty salons, retail clothing, other specialist non-food retailing, health and physical well-being, takeaway food shops and stalls, licensed and unlicensed restaurants and bars, cleaning services and management and business consultancy, including public relations and events management.

Defining your business

It is worth trying to position yourself within the profiles of start-up entrepreneurs and their businesses that you have read about – particularly those you know to have been successful. In order to make comparisons, you should first define your business concept and subject it to rigorous analysis. Given that the business you plan to start will probably employ fewer than 10 persons in its early stages, it will be classified as a 'micro-firm' in both the BERR and European Commission definitions of SMEs (2001).

Whatever the product or service at the core of your business idea, the first question to be asked that will test its strength is: 'Who will want to buy the product or service I plan to sell?' The viability of your business idea will depend crucially on the answer to this question. There are three elements to the question: 'What is the market for my product or service?', 'What are the barriers to entry?' and 'What price should I charge?' You need to answer all three parts of the question at the outset.

The market for your product or service

Confirming whether there is a strong potential or existing demand for your product or service, even in the best of times, requires some rigorous, objective evaluation, and poses still more questions:

- Are any others selling anything like it?
- How are they doing?
- Is there room for another business?
- Is there anything special about your product or service that makes it better?

If your past business experience has been working for a company that offers a similar product or service, you may be in a stronger position to answer these subsidiary questions. Experience will tell you whether the product or service you propose to sell is better than the product you have experience of, or whether your proposed service is superior (does it respond to product defects or customer complaints?). But don't assume that your past experience of a market is comprehensive. Many companies operate in a blinkered environment, living on an established customer base and strong brand, without exposure to the more competitive marketplace that faces a newcomer. Confirm that your perception of a market conforms to today's reality.

You can gather facts and figures about your target market from websites, by contacting trade associations and from their publications, or from your local library. Business Link, Chamber of Commerce and Enterprise Agency are also useful sources. Some banks provide a range of concise publications that may help you with starting and maintaining your market research. From this preliminary research you should be able to develop a clearer picture of the competition you'll face and be able to confirm whether you are offering something special. Just offering good service and after-sales care may be enough to provide you with a unique selling proposition (USP).

If there is no direct comparison to your business idea or no competitors in the marketplace offering your product or service, you may have to carry out a limited market survey to satisfy yourself (and anyone whom you ask to back your business idea) that there really is a market. Guidance on undertaking market research yourself to a professional standard is given in Chapter 2.

What are the barriers to entry?

Some possible barriers to entering a market relate to your personal circumstances such as:

- capital cost of equipment that is beyond your financial resources and unlikely to be fundable by bank borrowings or leasing;

- professional or trade qualifications that you don't have and cannot acquire quickly, for example as a Chartered Surveyor if you have in mind setting up a real estate agency for commercial property (you may be able to get by as an estate agent for residential property without qualification).

Some trade qualifications can be acquired quite quickly. For example, a young local farmer whom I know decided to become a plumber and went to a local college for six months where he gained the necessary qualification. However, that change of occupation took planning and preparation. You may not have the time to become qualified before you need to start work, and will have to take up lower-paid temporary work elsewhere while you are studying.

There are other kinds of barrier relating to the structure of the industry you intend to enter, and it is worth looking at the evidence available that indicates the industry sectors in which small businesses employing fewer than 10 people account for a greater or lesser share than the average 95.7 per cent share of total businesses identified in Table 1.2. Evidence based on government statistics for 2008 is summarized in Table 1.3.

TABLE 1.3 Industries where there are more or fewer than average small businesses (fewer than 10 employees)

Industry	Above average	Average or below
Agriculture, forestry and fishing	–	95.7
Mining, quarrying and utilities	97.0	–
Manufacturing	–	89.6
Construction	98.0	–
Wholesale, retail and repairs	–	93.5
Hotels and restaurants	–	88.1
Transport, storage and communication	96.6	–
Financial intermediation	–	94.3
Real estate, renting and other business	96.6	–
Other community, social and personal services	98.0	–

The first point to note is that the variations about the average are rather small, although no doubt there are wider differences between the segments within each sector. However, the barriers to entry for small businesses appear to be highest in manufacturing, hotels and restaurants, and higher in financial intermediation and the wholesale, retail and repair sectors; they are lowest in construction and in community, social and personal services. Nothing very surprising here, you may think, but the statistics suggest three conclusions:

- Whatever sector you choose to enter, the competition from other small businesses will be high.

- Your business needs to have a USP that differentiates it from competitors, for example being the only tapas bar in town.

- If your business is one where small business competition is lower, you may have an advantage if you can find a differentiated product or service offering that larger companies have difficulty in matching, such as home pizza or curry deliveries or low-cost contract cleaning.

What price should you charge?

The more competition there is, the more pressure there will be on the prices you could charge and, for your business to succeed, the price for your product or service must give you a decent profit. Your basic research will identify what the market prices are for comparable products or services and what your strongest competitors charge. If you do carry out formal market research, be sure to include questions about price.

All you need to do at this stage is to identify what price your market will bear and to see if it looks likely that you will make sufficient money from selling your product or service to cover your personal financial needs. Instruction on how to make profit and cash flow forecasts for business planning are given in Chapter 3 and in more detail in Chapter 8.

What sort of business structure do you want?

From the outset of your deliberations, it is a good idea to start thinking about how you will organize your business. The right structure for you will depend on your plans for the future as well as the nature of the product or service you will provide. The alternative structures are: sole trader, partnership, limited liability partnership (LLP) or limited liability company.

Sole trader

If you intend to work on your own for the foreseeable future, by operating as a sole trader you will avoid all the regulations that apply to limited companies; you just need to inform the income tax and social security authorities that you are working for yourself.

Remember also that if your business is to have a name other than your own, you must also put your own name on your headed paper. If in doubt about the approved use of your premises, you should also check with the local Planning Officer that your workplace is suitable.

Partnership

If there are two or more of you who will be running the business, you may want to form a partnership. Before doing so, be sure that you understand the full implications – each partner is personally liable for any debts incurred by the business even if they were run up by another partner – and first of all agree among yourselves how the business is to be run, how profits are to be shared and what will happen if you need to wind it up. All these matters should be covered in a legally binding partnership agreement to be drawn up before the business starts.

Limited liability partnership

If you expect that there will be more than two partners or you intend to hire more than secretarial staff, it is probably worthwhile to form a limited liability partnership, which as the title implies will limit your personal liability. This involves submitting an incorporation document (form LLP2) to Companies House and an annual return subsequently. You should have a solicitor draft a more formal partnership agreement.

Limited liability company

If you intend to run your business as a private limited company, you will need help from an accountant or solicitor to complete all the formalities of setting up the company before you start trading. Given the complexities of employment legislation and the implied risks of litigation, the limited company is probably more appropriate if you expect to employ more than one or two non-family members of staff.

Advantages other than the protection of limited liability include: a more credible identity, lower tax rates, better access for raising funds, and ease of disposal should you want to sell the whole or part of your business in the future.

Analysing your business needs

Having identified that your business idea is viable in market terms, subject to more detailed research, it is time to put some flesh on the skeleton by defining the resources that you will need to get started. Generally, the three most immediate resources you will need to consider are start-up funds, staff and location.

Start-up funds

Even if no investment in assets or significant pre-start-up expenditure is required, most new businesses have to wait a little time before income from sales starts to come in. Therefore, you will need to have cash available to pay wages or buy supplies in the opening months. The preliminary cash flow forecast will be sufficient to give a clear idea of the cash needed for this opening period. If your own savings are not enough to cover the cash requirement, you will need to use someone else's money.

There may be grants available to you as a start-up business, and information will be available from local agencies via Business Link and Chambers of Commerce, or check the Business Grant Finder Service on www.anbusiness.com. Funding alternatives and the whole process of raising capital are addressed in Chapters 4 and 5.

In general, there has been a trend among SMEs to move from overdraft finance to loans, encouraged by the banks, with technological change generating an increase in leasing finance. Equity finance, in the various forms discussed in Chapter 4, is only slightly more popular than in the past. As Kevin Smith points out in Chapter 4, you will certainly have to provide equity capital yourself for the start-up, and bank finance in these straightened times, if negotiable at all, may involve your providing security by way of a legal charge on your assets, most probably your home. Before going much further, you would be wise to consult your spouse or partner to be certain that you are both prepared to take on this element of personal risk.

Employing staff

Employing staff from your first day of trading will add greatly to your operating costs and is to be avoided unless the type and size of your business demand it. For entrepreneurs who start up as sole traders but need some administration backup, your first recourse in today's conditions should be to your family and any available time they have.

If you do have to employ staff at the outset, there are immediate employment law requirements, and you will need to involve yourself in PAYE and National Insurance administration and to have employer's liability insurance in place. The whole area of employment regulations and human relations good practice is a complex minefield to which Chapter 12 is devoted.

Even if you are employing individuals on a casual or one-off basis only, you should be aware of the national minimum wage provisions that apply to all employees. These came into being in April 1999 and have been revised regularly since. From 1 October 2010, the standard rate is £5.93 per hour for those aged 21 and above, rising from £5.80 previously, and for those aged 18 to 21 it is £4.92 from 1 October 2010, rising from £4.83 previously. Workers aged 16 to 17 now have a minimum hourly wage rate of £3.64, up from £3.57 prior to 1 October 2010. There are exemptions for apprentices under the age of 19 and those over 19 who are in their first year of apprenticeship; their minimum hourly rate is only £2.50.

The location for your business

If your business does not involve face-to-face contact with customers or clients on site and you are starting as a sole trader, then location will not matter. You should consider running your business from home if there is sufficient space, your family will accept the arrangement and you will not contravene any restrictions imposed by your mortgage lender, landlord or local authority on the work you can carry out. You may be subject to business rate council tax or capital gains tax if you sell the property, although the latter can normally be avoided.

Otherwise, if you must have separate business premises, you may be in an area where there are special grants for start-up businesses or where the local authority offers low-cost small business premises or workspaces. Convenience for staff and suppliers may be a consideration in the choice of premises, as will the nature of the area if your business will depend on attracting passing trade.

Some guidance on real estate assets is given in Chapter 16, but be sure to take professional advice on any lease or rental agreement that you take out. Ensure that you have the flexibility to adapt to unexpected changes in your level of trading. If the business does well you will probably want to move out into larger premises during the period of your tenancy agreement.

How others started

At an early stage you should spend time talking to as many friends and acquaintances as you can who have set up their own businesses in the past few years, preferably businesses in a similar field or with a similar character to your own planned enterprise. Input from those who have made it (or failed) goes beyond the market research described in Chapter 2, but will help you to design your research around the factors that others have found key to success.

Your first SWOT analysis

Once you have answered the basic questions surrounding your business idea, and before you get into the numbers, it is time to apply the well-worn but reliable management tool of a SWOT analysis, which is the acronym for the assessment of a business in terms of its present condition and future prospects from opposing standpoints:

- strengths;
- weaknesses;
- opportunities;
- threats.

List all the features or factors that you can think of objectively under each heading, and ask any member of the family, or a business friend with whom you have discussed your business concept, to review them. At this stage, before you carry out your market research and business planning, the lists of strengths and opportunities should be taken as provisional, but you should not wait to address weaknesses and threats.

Spend as much time as you need in deciding how to correct the more serious weaknesses where you can. Develop and articulate a strategy for pre-empting or combating each threat. If you cannot see how to overcome weaknesses or to draw up a contingency plan for addressing the threats, you should revisit your basic business idea. This may be the first moment of truth when you decide to abandon the original business idea or amend it significantly.

The same SWOT analysis should be repeated at the end of the business planning process (See Chapter 3) and can be applied at any stage in the development of your business to check progress and identify any limitations to future growth.

Inherent weaknesses and threats

The SWOT analysis will certainly reveal the inherent problems in your business concept – those that are inbuilt and an integral part of the concept. For example, if your proposed business is the mail order sale of fashion garments, which you have to hold stocks of and market through catalogues, success depends upon your flair in choosing seasonal stock ahead of time and your skill in contracting with reliable suppliers who respond rapidly to new designs and deliver on time. The element of flair in judging market demand is an unavoidable risk at the core of your business, and only you can make that judgement, but the identification and management of suppliers will call for a set of skills that you can hire or develop.

If your business is a telephone call centre, then a key element is the availability of operators who are readily trainable, as is an ability to retain staff. For that business, choice of location is paramount, since the right location will help provide a local supply of well-educated, articulate staff without too much competitive employment. In addition, your ability to train staff and your people skills in building a working environment that encourages loyalty will be essential ingredients. Interestingly, the recent experience of large service providers that outsourced their call centre activities to parts of Asia has not been entirely successful. The inability of obviously foreign operators to provide more than 'formula' responses to queries inevitably causes customer dissatisfaction. As a consumer you will surely have experienced the frustration of dealing with your bank's or internet server's Asian call centres.

What is crucial in confronting inherent weaknesses is to work out in detail how to overcome them, to identify the resources needed, and to build them into your business planning.

At the heart of your decision making is your own resourcefulness, initiative, imagination, determination and resilience – the personal qualities that are fundamental to success and without which any limitations to the growth of your business are likely to prove insuperable.

If you are unsure of your personal strengths and weaknesses, try carrying out a mini-SWOT on yourself in the form of a balance sheet, being as objective as you can. Show the result to business colleagues whose judgement you respect and to your family and ask for their candid opinions. Don't ask for their opinions before constructing a first draft – your nearest and dearest may not want to be too critical until they see that you can accept criticism. Of course, if they are being candid they may come up with personal flaws that you had ignored or of which you were unaware ('If only we could see ourselves as others see us'). Self-awareness is a great virtue in embryo entrepreneurs.

Choosing collaborators

Limitations in skills are less serious than limitations in personal qualities. Most management skills can be acquired through self-education or formal training, and technical or specialist knowledge and expertise can be added to your business through selective recruitment. Limitations in personal qualities can sometimes be compensated for by association or partnership with others who are strong in the qualities you lack, and perhaps, weaker in those attributes where you are strong. However, the most compatible partners may be those who share the same weaknesses as yourself, and such combinations are generally fatal to the business. The analogy of drowning men (or women) clinging to each other is not inappropriate.

Facing up to entrepreneurship

In the eleventh year of the millennium it is clear that the trends towards increased self-employment and business start-ups that gathered pace in the 1990s are set to continue. Changes of government, future membership of the European Monetary Union (not within the life of the present parliament), opt outs or not from parts of the Lisbon Treaty are unlikely to affect this socio-economic sea change. Indeed, the after-effects of the recession and the Coalition Government's commitment to a leaner public sector seem certain to accelerate the process for some years ahead.

For those in mid-career who had no inclination to leave the corporate fold or public service, the imminent prospect, in many cases the probability, of leaving secure employment may be depressing. Converting the threat to a promise of future opportunity demands a mindset adjustment and it makes sense to begin that process by scoping an alternative future for yourself now – as soon as possible.

Those with professional qualifications, such as lawyers and accountants, or with skills, such as graphic designers, IT and software specialists and quantity surveyors, may have a better prospect than others of self-employment as service providers. However, there is a distinction between those with specialist skill sets of any kind who can contemplate 'going it alone' and those in more general line and staff management positions or professionals in large firms who would have to set up an actual business organization, however small, employing other people.

A new career in your own business entails becoming an entrepreneur from the outset and it is for people in that situation that the following chapters are intended. Face up to the reality that your life will never be the same.

Checklist

- Be aware of the current small business start-up experience. In 2008, 11.6 of VAT-registered businesses were start-ups. In 2008–09 more than 1,000 new businesses registered each day – higher than in any of the last 25 years except for 2006–07.

- At least a third of all new business start-ups fail within three years and more than half within five years.

- Small businesses with fewer than five employees account for 91 per cent of all UK enterprises.

- Make sure you have covered funding requirements for the first two years before you start.

- Review your timing in relation to the current activity level of the market you are entering.

- Be sure that the business activity you select has a long-term future.

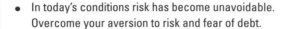

- In today's conditions risk has become unavoidable. Overcome your aversion to risk and fear of debt.

- One-third of start-up businesses have women owners. Their start-up decisions are more affected by family and domestic issues than those of men.

- Test the strength of your business idea by asking the questions:
  - 'What is the market for my product or service?'
  - 'What are the barriers to entry?'
  - 'What price should I charge?'
  - Together, the answers will tell you 'Who will buy the product or service I plan to sell?'

- Evaluate your market and competition objectively. If you have been working in a similar business, don't rely on experience alone. Use available information sources and carry out a limited market survey if necessary.

- Think about how you will structure your business. Registering as a private limited company has many advantages.

- Analyse your business needs: start-up funding, staffing requirements, where you will locate your business.

- Talk to as many people as you can who have set up their businesses in recent years, and identify the key factors that are likely to be crucial to your success.

- Carry out your first SWOT analysis. Address any weaknesses and threats. If you cannot see how to overcome them, amend or abandon your original business concept.

- Test your personal strengths and weaknesses through self-assessment by involving friends and family. Address the question: 'What limitation does my involvement impose on the likely success and growth of the business?'

- Take care in your choice of partners: make sure that they complement your capabilities and don't add to the problems.

- Face up to becoming an entrepreneur. You life will never be the same.

Chapter Two
Researching the Market

In Chapter 1 we discussed the core task of defining your business in terms of the market for your product or service, and referred to the dangers of relying on past experience of the industry, however well you think you know the business or the territory, without carrying out basic research to confirm your belief that your core business idea is marketable.

At this stage, it is possible that there is sufficient information available from publications, business agencies, trade associations, providers of finance and, of course, internet websites to give a clear picture of the competition and enable you to affirm that your business idea has a USP. However, if your product or service is truly distinctive, you will probably need to do more to convince yourself and any potential financial backer of the market opportunity.

Different types of research

Broadly, there are two types of market research: desk research and field research. Desk research is the process of tapping into information sources of the kinds described, and can be carried out from home by accessing published information and interrogating sources by telephone, fax and, increasingly, via the internet. The aim is to develop a profile of the market you are seeking to enter, and the past history and product offerings of market leaders who serve it.

Field research, as its name implies, involves person-to-person research 'in the field' – either by face-to-face or telephone interview, or sometimes, and usually less successfully, by fax or e-mail questionnaire. (The resistance to floods of incoming junk mail has hardened resistance to time-consuming questionnaires.) Field research is conducted with potential customers and suppliers, or with product users in the case of research into new product design or packaging.

Of course, professional market research can be purchased from a market research agency, but this is not an expense you would wish to incur while your business is in the design and planning stage. However, you can achieve much by carrying out the research yourself, provided that you follow the basic rules for researching objectively and thoroughly.

One research avenue you should not neglect is established competitors in the same line of business but operating in locations outside the territory you have chosen. You will find that most people are happy to talk about how they have developed their businesses, and their current problems and opportunities, provided that they do not view you as a direct competitor.

Research objectives

The starting point is to construct your research brief, specifying the information you need to evaluate your target market and the opportunity for you to gain entry – the same brief as you would give to a market research agency to develop its proposal.

The following are 10 key questions that you need to answer:

1 What is the value of the market you propose to enter?
2 Is the market growing or shrinking?
3 What and where is the main competition?
4 What are the market shares of your main competitors?
5 Are your competitors profitable?
6 What are consumers/customers looking for?

7 Where in the market should you position your product/service?

8 What is the profile of your average target customer and what market share could you capture?

9 How can you fulfil consumer/customer demand profitably?

10 How can you promote yourself economically to your target audience?

Depending on the nature of the business and its scope, there will be more or less information that you can gather by desk research before you begin to consider how to survey the target market yourself through field research.

Carrying out desk research

Let's consider two completely different kinds of business, both service industries, one a specialized form of consumer retailing, the other a service to industrial and commercial clients. Business A is the operation of a local fitness centre, of which you have no prior experience except as a keep-fit enthusiast. Business B is a consultancy to audit health and safety (H&S) standards in businesses and to advise on remedial action and the installation of H&S routines to conform with government regulations and national standards. (Suppose that before deciding to work for yourself you were a qualified H&S officer in an industrial area.)

For Business A, desk research will enable you to answer just a few of the 10 key questions on a national basis. You will be able to identify the overall value of consumer expenditure at fitness centres and on fitness products, and to confirm the rate of growth of the overall market. Local competition is readily identifiable – but not market share or profitability. There are a few listed companies engaged in fitness centre operations; they are obliged to file detailed accounts, and an inspection of these will provide some indications of how profitable these activities may be and whether their profitability is increasing or declining. However, in the context of planning a local business, desk research alone will not provide answers to the last seven questions.

For Business B, your prior work experience will help you to conduct desk research and to answer more of the 10 key questions. You should not rely on your experience only to answer Question 6 (What are consumers/customers looking for?) or Question 7 (Where in the market should you position your product/service?), although it may provide strong pointers as to the range of services you should offer and the market sector you should target, which can be tested at the next stage.

Indeed, there are two possible markets for your proposed H&S consultancy services: as an outsource provider of H&S management, or assisting clients to set up their own H&S functions in-house to best practice standards and training new or reallocated staff. Within the latter market, there are probably a number of niches in terms of size of companies and the nature of their products or services. You will have to check out both markets by direct contact in your field research.

Engaging in field research

Field research is only useful if it is completely objective. There is a great temptation, particularly if you are enthusiastic about your business concept, to wander round asking a few questions of possible customers and suppliers, perhaps people who know you quite well, and to fool yourself that you have conducted a useful research exercise. Worse still, you may phrase your questions so that the response you are hoping for is clearly evident, and people who know you and want to encourage you are likely to give you the answers you are looking for.

The best way to avoid these traps is to discipline yourself to draw up a representative sample of the market you are researching and to prepare formal questionnaires, whether you will be interviewing face to face or by telephone. It also helps to condition yourself to conduct interviews as if you were a professional researcher carrying out the assignment for clients rather than on your own behalf.

Sampling

A truly representative sample that accurately reflects the total market in terms of income and social groups, age groups, occupations and purchasing profiles is the ideal that researchers strive for when surveying consumer markets. But this is probably impossible to achieve. Instead, professional market research agencies often design 'quota' samples, and instruct their researchers to interview fixed numbers of respondents whose circumstances and buying habits conform to various templates. (The preliminary questions of each interview are used to establish into which quota definition the respondent falls.)

Alternatively, the research agency may decide to adopt 'random' sampling. For example, if a survey of 100 households were commissioned in a neighbourhood of 1,000 houses, interviewers would be instructed to call on every tenth house. A random sampling approach might be more appropriate in our Business B example, where you decide to interview potential clients for H&S consultancy or outsourcing among a range of selected industries located within your local region. A simple way to pick your sample would be to refer to the telephone *Yellow Pages* or *Thomson Local directory*, and pick your interview targets according to the size of sample and number of companies listed in each business category.

What size of sample should you pick? Statistically, you might think the bigger the sample the better. In practice, a sample of 100 is normally sufficient for consumer products or services if the sample is chosen carefully. For industrial products, as few as 30 interviews may suffice.

In the case of Business A, it should be possible to survey your local fitness centre market and produce unambiguous findings from 100 interviews of customers leaving local fitness centres, selected on a random basis. If there are two or three centres in serious competition, you should split interviewing between them.

For Business B, a quota of five or six extended telephone interviews in each of, say, six targeted industry sectors should give a clear picture of the market for your H&S services. If the findings are ambiguous, you may need to extend interviewing selectively.

Questionnaire design

Most of us have been interviewed from time to time in the street, in shopping centres, or at railway or bus stations – often when we're short of time and don't want to be stopped; so we know what the standard market research interview involves. Try to organize your questionnaire in a similar way to conventional interviewing techniques. Here are a few tips that may help you:

- Use short introductory phrases for each question to 'lead in' your respondents, such as 'I can see that you're a fit person – how often do you visit a fitness centre?'

- Arrange the topics for your questions in a logical order – proceed from the general to the particular. For example, in the case of research for Business A:
  - frequency of fitness centre visits;
  - weekend/weekday sessions;
  - with/without family or partner;
  - range of services and fitness products purchased;
  - seasonal variations in your fitness routines;
  - other fitness centres used;
  - other sources for fitness products;
  - customer spend per visit (range/average).

- Always position questions about money towards the end of the interview (they may be 'turn-offs' and cause the respondent to terminate).

- Try to ask questions in an open-ended form first so that they cannot be answered just by 'Yes' or 'No', before offering structured alternatives: for example, 'Which other fitness centres do you visit regularly?' before 'Which of these other local fitness centres, a, b and c, do you visit regularly, sometimes or never?'

- Include a few personal questions at the end of the interview to establish the demographic identity of the respondent (eg age group, occupation, residential neighbourhood, size of family).

Other field research

Of course, you will want to carry out other fieldwork in addition to interviewing prospective customers or clients. For Business A, you will need to visit each competitor location, examine the layout, range of equipment, quality and pricing, ancillary services such as sauna and massage, clothing, point-of-sale material and promotional offers, and observe the customer traffic. You will also need to approach equipment suppliers to check the availability, lead times, prices and credit terms that you could negotiate. For Business B, you may want to sample the quality of the H&S management that potential clients currently have, in order to assess their needs for outsourcing or training consultancy.

Using your market research findings

At this stage the market research you carry out yourself might throw up attractive niche market opportunities that you had not identified previously, or cause you to modify or extend your product or service offering. It will also deepen your understanding of the business opportunity, and provide much of the background data needed to support your business case at the next stage when you are seeking finance.

The Business B example differs from Business A in an important respect. Interviewing by telephone may establish your first list of actual business prospects among those who register a demand for the services that you intend to offer – in this case, H&S management consultancy. The same outcome is likely in the case of most business consultancy services you may research. You will be able to follow up on the prospect list later when your plan is complete, funding is in place and you are ready to launch your business.

The final test of objectivity, if your market research findings are negative in any important respect, is to decide whether you can overcome any weaknesses or threats to your business concept that they reveal. It is a good idea, in any case, to write up your research succinctly and to show the report to an adviser or friend who will give you an unbiased second opinion. As we counselled at the end of Chapter 1, if you are in any serious doubt, abandon the original concept and go back to the drawing board. The research exercise has not been wasted. It will stand you in good stead next time.

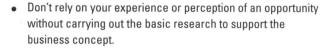

Checklist

- Don't rely on your experience or perception of an opportunity without carrying out the basic research to support the business concept.

- Define your research objectives first in terms of the key questions you need to answer.

- Carry out desk research first from home by accessing published information and the internet, interrogating sources by telephone, fax and e-mails.

- Don't neglect others in the same line of business but operating in a different location. Unless you are competing directly, they will probably be informative.

- Visit your competitors' locations and investigate their product range, quality, pricing and activity levels. Approach potential suppliers.

- Field research should be completely objective. Discipline yourself to draw up a representative sample of the market and to prepare formal questionnaires.

- Arrange the topics for your questions in a logical order. Always leave questions about money until the end of the interview.

- Ask questions in an open-ended form first so that they cannot be answered just by 'Yes' or 'No'. Then ask them in a structured form.

- Include a few personal questions at the end to establish demographic identity.

- If your research findings are negative, restructure the business concept – or abandon it and try again.

Chapter Three
Developing Your Business Plan

KEVIN R SMITH AND JONATHAN REUVID

Once a business opportunity has been identified and market research carried out, you need to start developing your formal business plan. The planning process will bring together all the exploratory work that you have carried out so far, demonstrate that your business concept and strategy are valid, and identify the financing needs to start up and run the business. There are many steps to this process, but the most critical will be the financial projections, which are essential to the capital raising activities discussed in Chapter 5. However, prospective investors will also want to study a complete business plan that defines clearly your business objectives, the marketplace in which you will be operating, your products or services, and the strategy and resources you will deploy in order to achieve the planned results.

The advice given in this chapter applies equally to genuine new business start-ups, management buyouts, ventures where an employer subcontracts a part of its business (usually services) to a group of employees as an alternative to redundancy, or where managers decide to break away from their employer and start trading in the same field.

Elements of the business plan

Writing a good business plan is not only the first step towards converting concept to reality but also the most important one. The business plan is the first real contact that the new business will have with potential funders, and not only will it say a lot about the business, but its presentation will also say a lot about the management and yourself. For any new business, funders are at least as interested in the management team as in the business. The plan will demonstrate how clearly the managers have thought through their business idea and how methodical and detailed their approach to the business is likely to be.

The following is a summary of the sections of your business plan, each of which must be articulated in detail in order to develop a cohesive and convincing plan:

- Concept and background
  Define your business concept and, if the business already exists, provide a history. Describe the industry (size, major participants, growth potential, barriers to entry, outside influences, etc). If your business is to be focused on a differentiated segment of the industry, describe that sector more thoroughly.

- Market
  Demonstrate that a market exists for your product/service in the general market or market niche that you have identified, estimate market share, assess the competition and outline your competitive advantages. Define the unique selling proposition (USP) of your business offering.

- Product/service
  Describe the product or service and its advantages compared with existing providers, outline future development and detail any patent or other intellectual property issues. Outline production/delivery issues and expected future requirements and premises. Identify the role of future research and development (R&D) and innovation in growing the business.

- Business strategy
  Demonstrate deep understanding of the market and business in the proposed strategy. This should be demanding but realistic. Outline areas such as capital expenditure and staff

recruitment. Profile the customer groups to which you will be marketing your products or services, define your business proposition, your channels to market and how you will gain sales. Timed action plans (who does what and over what intervals of time) may usefully be included in an appendix to your plan.

- Management team
  Identify key management and their roles, outline their backgrounds and skills. Identify any weaknesses in the team and how they will be addressed. Key directors or managers will be expected to demonstrate their financial commitment to the project. Include the CVs of key managers as an appendix to the plan.

- Financial planning
  Demonstrate careful thought in the financial projections and the assumptions but be concise (use appendices where necessary). Provide external corroboration of forecasts and assumptions where possible and, for an existing business, include historic accounts. The specific projections that you will need to include are:
  - profit and loss forecasts for three years: monthly for Year 1 and quarterly for Years 2 and 3;
  - cash flow forecast: again monthly for Year 1 and quarterly for Years 2 and 3;
  - pro-forma balance sheets: opening statement and at each year end;
  - capital expenditure plan for each year.

You should also add a sensitivity analysis that shows what happens if your assumptions are varied, for example if only 80 per cent of budgeted sales are achieved, if margins are shaved by 5 per cent, if fixed expenses increase by 10 per cent. Choose your alternatives carefully to include corrective actions that may lessen the unfavourable impact of change.

Cash flow projections

Of the formal financial planning documents, the cash flow projections are the most important. They will define funding requirements and allow prospective investors and lenders to evaluate the financial risk and the viability of the business. Having developed the assumptions on which the plan is based, it is sensible to write the cash flow projection first, from which the profit and loss estimates can be readily derived. The only elements of the profit and loss account that are excluded from the cash flow are depreciation, which is a non-cash expense item, and provisions for bad and doubtful debts, future taxation or other liabilities that do not occur during the period of the cash projection.

There is more on cash management in Chapter 8, but for planning purposes a common layout of a cash flow forecast that most banks and investors will find acceptable is included here as Figure 3.1.

Refined SWOT analysis

It is now timely to rewrite the SWOT analysis that you made earlier at the beginning of your business planning. This time it will provide a critique of your formal business plan and, if you include it as an appendix to the business plan, you need to ensure that you have fully described the strengths and opportunities in other sections of the plan and how you will exploit them. Again, you should concentrate on identified weaknesses and threats, describing your tactics for avoiding them and contingency plans should they occur. Be sure that any experienced person who studies your plan in detail will ask those questions and expect cogent answers. We have already addressed issues of inherent weaknesses and threats in Chapter 1.

FIGURE 3.1 Simple cash flow forecast

	Unit £												
	Month	1	2	3	4	5	6	7	8	9	10	11	12
RECEIPTS													
Cash sales													
Cash from debtors													
Capital injection													
Total receipts (A)													
PAYMENTS													
Payments to creditors													
Salaries/wages													
Rent/rates/water													
Heat/light/power													
Insurance													
Maintenance and repairs													
Postage/printing/ stationery													
Telephone/fax/ broadband													
Professional fees													
Capital payments													
Interest and bank charges													
VAT													
Total payments (B)													
Net cash flow (A – B)													
Opening bank balance													
Closing bank balance													

NOTE: Sales are scheduled by the actual month when customer payment is to be received. Expenses, including prepayments, are scheduled by the month when they are forecast to be paid.

Executive summary

If the business plan is the most important document, the two-page executive summary, which you write as the final planning step and place at the front of the document, may be crucial in gaining favourable attention. Banks and equity investors are bombarded with business plans, and many potential fund providers will not read further than the executive summary unless it grabs their attention. If it does not, all the time and effort that you put into developing the rest of the plan will be wasted.

In this overview, describe the key elements of the business, the market in which it will operate, key reasons for success and barriers to entry. Identify risks and how they will be managed, outline strategic objectives and potential for growth, state key strengths of the management team and past successes, present headline financial projections and, lastly, indicate how much finance is required and what it will be used for.

If you follow these guidelines your business plan should be well presented and logical; as suggested earlier, if a lot of detailed information is to be included this is often best done by using appendices. If the plan is muddled, has gaping holes in the information provided, has many typing or grammatical errors or anything else that undermines the professional feel of the document, this can often be enough for it to be rejected irrespective of the quality of the underlying business proposal; the reader will have lost confidence in the management team.

Taking advice

Most likely you will not have written a formal business plan of such complexity before and you will probably need help. At the least, even if you write the first draft yourself, you should seek an experienced second opinion to review the draft and suggest changes that will enhance it. If you have already appointed an accountant to advise you or another professional financial adviser to assist you in the fund-raising exercise, they will certainly be able to tell you whether your plan is sound, where it is weak and what improvements could be made.

It will also be a good idea to show your plan to someone you respect who has already been through the fund-raising process for their own business and successfully overcome any obstacles. They will have an experienced eye for detecting any holes in your plan on which finance providers may focus, and can help you frame answers in advance of any awkward questions. You should expect that your original draft will be revised and refined several times before you have a final document with which you and your advisers are completely comfortable.

Checklist

- Financial projections are the most essential part of your business plan in raising finance.

- Potential funders will also look for a comprehensive plan demonstrating that you have thought through your business idea thoroughly.

- The sections of your plan, in sequential order, should include:
  - business concept and background;
  - market;
  - product or service;
  - business strategy;
  - management team;
  - financial plan;
  - a SWOT analysis.

- The financial projections should include:
  - profit and loss and cash flow forecasts for three years;
  - pro-forma balance sheets;
  - a capital expenditure plan for each year.

- Cash flow forecasts (monthly for Year 1) are the most important element of the business plan. Add a sensitivity analysis that shows what happens if your assumptions about sales and costs prove too optimistic.

- The refined SWOT analysis attached to your business plan must describe fully the strengths and opportunities in your plan and the external threats and weaknesses.

- An outline of the risk management process that will be introduced may also be included in an appendix.

continued

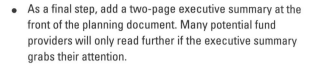

- As a final step, add a two-page executive summary at the front of the planning document. Many potential fund providers will only read further if the executive summary grabs their attention.

- Take professional advice on writing your business plan if you have never written one yourself before.

- If you do write it yourself, seek an experienced second opinion about whether your plan is sound and what improvements you should make.

- Check the final document thoroughly for typing or grammatical errors or anything else that will undermine its professionalism and might cause the reader to lose confidence in the management team.

Kevin R Smith is Managing Director of AWS Structured Finance Ltd, international financial consultants, and can be contacted on 01892 667 891 or e-mail kevin.r.smith@awsconsult.co.uk. He is a partner of Aspen Waite Accountants and a Corporate Associate at Beer & Partners, Europe's largest business angel network.

ASPEN WAITE
CHARTERED ACCOUNTANTS

"MORE THAN JUST ACCOUNTANTS"

We are experts in proactively helping to start up and grow businesses.

We can help in all stages of the business process:

Business Plans	Raising Finance
Tax Planning	Business & Financial Planning
Proactive Advice	Full Range of Services

Offices throughout the South & South West
Visit our website at **www.aspenwaite.co.uk**

INITIAL CONSULTATION FREE OF CHARGE –
PHONE FOR A FRIENDLY CHAT
01278 445151

advertisement feature

Chapter Four
Funding Alternatives

KEVIN R SMITH

When considering the options and funding alternatives available to assist with the establishment of a new business, it is all too easy for the owners or management to think that funding comes only in the form of equity or debt, and that debt can only be in the form of a term loan or an overdraft.

This perception is often caused by the unimaginative approach of many banks, and sadly many of their small business advisers don't seem to know very much more than the businesses they are meant to be advising. Therefore, it is important that anyone considering how to set up their own business has a working knowledge of the many different funding alternatives and the wide range of potential funders that may be available.

If an informed approach is made, there is a whole range of different products available from banks and other more specialized providers of funding. What is the perfect solution for one company may not work at all for a very similar company, and structuring the most efficient, cost-effective financing package can make all the difference between the success and failure of the company. This is particularly true for new and growing businesses; the wrong financing package can, at best, hamper growth.

In recent years obtaining debt funding from banks has become even more of a challenge, although the availability of equity finance has not been impacted so severely.

The following may be numbered among potential funding alternatives.

Proprietors' or founder shareholders' capital

Any business of any size requires capital, and it is unrealistic for any entrepreneurs to expect others to provide funding for their new venture if they are not prepared to do so themselves. Proprietors' capital is important not just from a pure balance sheet perspective, but also because it demonstrates to others that the founders believe strongly in their own chance of success and are prepared to 'put their money where their mouth is'.

In overall funding terms, the percentage of proprietors' capital does not always need to be very large, but other funders will want to be certain that there is a real financial incentive for the owners/managers to ensure the success of the business.

This type of capital is sourced primarily from the founders of the company (either reinvested savings or financed by personal borrowing), but often includes friends, relatives and associates who have faith in the entrepreneur's ability to grow the business.

As anybody who has set up a new business will testify, much time and expense is involved in the early stages, and it is often difficult to reflect this fully in the opening balance sheet. Unfortunately, very few funders give full credit for this 'investment', but often disregard it and focus purely on the cash contribution. Many a new business has failed to get off the ground due to lack of sufficient proprietors' capital.

We shall look at other sources of equity and venture capital later in this chapter.

Term loans and overdrafts

All banks offer senior debt, and in practice many branches only offer senior debt finance. This is debt that is backed by some form of security (often a first fixed and floating charge on the assets of the company) and ranks before almost every other creditor. Banks' standard-term loans and working capital or overdraft facilities invariably fall into this category.

This senior debt is normally provided by way of either a term loan and/or a working capital or overdraft facility, depending upon the needs of the company. For a new business the funder will probably require the proprietors'/directors' personal guarantees as well as physical security on any assets of the company. Again, these guarantees are designed to ensure that the founders of the company have a tangible incentive to ensure the success of the business.

The type of facility will depend upon what the funding is to be used for. Term loans are provided for the purchase of specific assets (such as property, office fixtures and computers) with a medium to long-term life. The term of the loan will reflect the type of asset, its value and expected life. Interest may be charged on either a fixed or floating basis, and repayments will typically be made on a monthly or quarterly basis, although semi-annual payments may be possible.

Normal trading fluctuations are best funded by way of an overdraft facility where the level of borrowing (and thus interest paid) varies on a daily basis. This ensures that borrowing costs are kept down, and the bank exposure is also limited. The bank will constantly monitor the level of an overdraft and expect it to fluctuate, with the account going into credit periodically. If this does not happen and a 'hard core' of borrowing is identified, the bank will often wish to separate this out into a short-term loan and structure a repayment schedule to reduce it to zero. One very important aspect for the borrower to remember is that overdraft facilities are 'on demand', which means that the bank can demand instant repayment at any time.

With most bank lending, the borrower will be liable to pay not just its own costs but also those of the bank. Interest margins will vary depending upon the perceived risk, but are typically around 3 per cent above base rate for an SME with a track record, or 4 per cent for a start-up company. Larger loans may be linked to LIBOR (London Interbank Offer Rate) rather than base rate. LIBOR fluctuates on a daily basis and varies depending upon the term, but is broadly similar to base rate.

Competition between banks is fairly fierce, and this may be shown in the level of service offered, reduced charges (at least in the first few years) or lower margins. It certainly pays to compare the terms offered by a number of potential funders. Unfortunately, this level of competition does not often lead to greater flexibility or to one bank being prepared to provide facilities where another will not. As for any business service, though, it does pay to shop around.

Over the last few years banks have virtually stopped all lending that is not very well secured on tangible assets, making it even more difficult for SMEs to raise funding.

Asset-based finance

Leasing is the most common form of asset-based finance. The major feature of asset finance is that it looks primarily to the value of the asset as security, rather than to the strength of the balance sheet. This can be particularly useful for start-ups and smaller companies with only limited balance sheets, and for companies that operate in asset-intensive sectors. Leases can be either on balance sheet (finance leases) or off balance sheet (operating leases), and depending on the equipment being leased, 100 per cent of the cost can be financed.

Leasing is most effective on assets with an easily assessed market value such as cars or computer equipment, but can be used in a wide variety of circumstances. It can also be useful simply as an alternative or additional source of funding to the main bank borrowing. Depending upon a company's tax and VAT position, certain leasing structures may also be more advantageous than bank loans. With the phenomenon of negative equity in the case of motor cars as well as real estate, leasing is now a safer form of finance for car purchase.

All the banks have their own in-house leasing companies, but leasing facilities can also be obtained from specialist leasing firms.

Factoring or invoice discounting is another form of asset finance, as the lender looks towards the quality of the trade debtors and outstanding invoices as security, rather than the balance sheet. Again, this can be useful for smaller companies, especially during periods of rapid growth, as the facility advances a percentage of outstanding invoices and as such is more flexible. The funding is also available more quickly than a bank overdraft facility, which looks back in time rather than forward and is far more related to the strength of the balance sheet.

Many start-up and early stage companies are restricted in their growth by lack of working capital, and factoring can often be the solution, although it is important for any company to guard against over-trading or growing too rapidly. Factoring facilities can be more expensive than bank debt, but as well as allowing the business more room to grow, they can provide some cover against bad debts, and reduce administrative time and costs.

However, in line with all lending post 'credit crunch' lenders have become more cautious and relative costs have increased.

Government schemes and grants

The area of government grants is complex and confusing, given the number of different schemes, the complicated nature of most of them, and the fact that what is available and on what basis changes constantly.

In simple terms, grants are normally associated with areas that are deemed to need assistance, whether that is due to geographic location, industry sector or other criteria. The country is divided into areas, with the majority not eligible for regional grants. The more deprived areas are split into tiers, with the biggest and most wide-ranging grants available in the most disadvantaged areas. These grants can include investment and employment incentives as well as support in areas such as staff training.

Similarly, most sectors of the economy do not qualify, but certain economic activities such as the recycling of waste do. The grants available are often similar but assessed on different criteria. Details of these grants are available through the government directly (for contact details see Appendix 2).

However, by far the most important government scheme for individuals considering setting up their own business is the Enterprise Finance Guarantee (previously called the Small Firms Loan Guarantee Scheme). This scheme guarantees loans made to small firms by commercial banks and certain other financial institutions where the firm lacks available security and/or a track record. In applying for a guarantee, the lender must satisfy itself that the commercial viability of the company is such that the lender would have made the loan but for the lack of security. If an Enterprise Finance Guarantee is made available, the bank is not allowed to take personal assets or guarantees as additional security, but may require a charge over whatever assets or security the company has available.

The guarantee covers 75 per cent of the loan made by the bank for amounts of between £1,000 and £1 million for qualifying companies with a turnover of less than £25 million. Not only does this scheme unlock bank lending that would otherwise not be available to young companies, it also reduces the cost of such borrowing. Information on the Enterprise Finance Guarantee is available through the commercial banks that operate the scheme. This scheme is due to end on 31 March 2011 but may be extended.

Small unsecured loans of up to £5,000 are available to young entrepreneurs to start up a business under the Prince's Youth Trust. The applicant must be under 30 years of age and is usually required to show that funding has been refused by commercial lenders.

Formal and informal venture capital

Before we look at different sources of equity, it is important to underline the fact that there are many different types, because many people establishing a business will often be reluctant to part with equity. As well as 'normal' equity there can be different classes of shares with different voting rights; for example, preference shares, which rank ahead of 'normal' equity in the payment of dividends, and many other variations on this theme.

It is also worth remembering that ownership of shares in a company and control of the company can easily be separated by using a shareholders' agreement, so that ownership of the majority of shares does not necessarily translate into control. This structure is often used when equity is injected by a venture capital firm that only seeks to own a minority stake, but needs to be able to exercise control in order to limit the risks on its investment.

External equity or venture capital can come from a range of different sources, some more formal than others. Many small firms are set up using equity provided by the founders and their friends, relatives and associates. These sources are often easier to access in many ways than more formal providers, but generally provide only relatively small amounts of money.

Raising small (ie less than £1 million) amounts of equity is often more difficult than raising larger amounts. Many of the equity funds and providers of venture capital take the view that the level of work involved is similar irrespective of the amount actually invested, and that it is not economic for them to invest less than £1 million.

The most common source of funding for start-ups and lower levels of funding is 'business angels'. These are typically wealthy individuals who have run businesses of their own and are looking to invest their own money. As well as their financial investment they often bring relevant experience. Business angels invest from as little as £20,000 but more commonly £100,000 plus. A number of networks exist, and through these, individual investors can club together to form a syndicate to invest larger amounts, the largest and most successful of which is Beer & Partners, with over 2,000 registered, active investors. Given the personal involvement, the investment decision is often taken partly with the heart as well as the mind, and investors normally stick to industry sectors in which they have experience. In practice, this makes the search for the right investor more difficult, but with the benefit that the investor once found can often display more flexibility and vision than a more professional investor. One caveat in dealing with business angels may be that they are more likely to change their minds after verbal commitment.

Individual investors can obtain considerable tax relief on investments of up to £150,000 if the investment qualifies under the Enterprise Investment Scheme. As well as tax relief on the initial investment, no capital gains tax is payable if the investment is held for at least five years.

Perhaps the best-known source of equity is the investment funds and venture capital funds run by City institutions. Investors in these funds are banks, insurance companies, pension funds and the like, and the funds invest in a portfolio of companies. Each fund will normally have a focus on certain sectors and on certain stages of a company's development, as well as other criteria such as minimum and maximum levels of investment. It is worth pointing out that very few venture capital funds are really interested in investing in start-up businesses, irrespective of what their marketing material might claim. Probably the most common level of investment is between £1 million and £5 million. Most funds look for an annual return on their investment in the region of 25 per cent to 30 per cent (this level of return includes both projected dividend income and forecast capital appreciation). The majority of investment funds are members of the British Venture Capital Association.

Alternative capital structures

The actual financial structure of a business will depend on many factors, and while getting the structure right is of paramount importance to the business both at start-up and in the future, there is no certain rule for what that structure should be, as the optimum will vary from one business to the next.

Equity will be more expensive than debt, but has the benefit for a start-up that it does not normally have the same cash requirement (interest on debt needs to be paid irrespective of profitability; dividends do not) and it is available without the need for additional security. Too little equity will prevent the company from accessing loan funding, and make the company far more vulnerable to a downturn in trading and other financial shocks.

By using a little more imagination and identifying the strengths of the growing business's financial structure, an entrepreneur can construct a financing package that is both more flexible and more cost-effective than traditional funding. Finding the right funder (or indeed combination of funders) may not be easy, but it will always be worth the effort.

Kevin R Smith is Managing Director of AWS Structured Finance Ltd, international financial consultants, and can be contacted on 01892 667 891 or e-mail kevin.r.smith@awsconsult.co.uk He is a partner of Aspen Waite Accountants and a Corporate Associate at Beer & Partners, Europe's largest business angel network.

Chapter Five
Raising Capital

KEVIN R SMITH

Having completed your business plan and subjected it to independent review as described in Chapter 3, you are now prepared to embark on the search for whatever capital you need to set up your business and run it for the first few years. This chapter aims to guide you through that process.

Taking professional advice

The biggest problem that affects people wishing to establish a business is the limited amount of financial resources available to them. Raising funding is much easier said than done. It is important that all aspects of establishing a business are properly understood, and the business case must be presented professionally when trying to raise funding.

One way in which some entrepreneurs look to save money is to avoid the use of outside experts and paying for professional assistance. Unfortunately this can all too often be a false economy. Professional assistance can make the difference between success and failure in raising funding or in the business itself.

What professional advice is needed will clearly depend upon the areas of expertise of the management, the type of business and a range of other issues, but there are a number of core areas that must be covered such as accounting and legal issues.

Financial advice is often needed to build up the detailed financial forecasts and to ensure that they are accurate and realistic, that all the issues have been properly considered and that the assumptions are realistic. Mistakes are most commonly to be found in areas such as tax/VAT. Missing out costs or not timing cash flows properly can totally undermine the economic viability of a business case, and at the very least does not instil confidence in the business or management as a whole.

In addition to the general areas of professional advice, there are a number of specific areas on which funders will ultimately require a professional opinion. These include matters such as intellectual property rights, copyright, certain employment and tax-related issues, asset and property values, environmental impact and other areas requiring specialist knowledge.

Independent professional advice or corroboration of parts of the business plan will greatly increase its impact and demonstrate that a thorough approach has been undertaken in its preparation. For all these reasons, careful expenditure on advisers should reap dividends.

What the banks offer

If your financing requirements are modest, say less than £25,000, in normal times it is likely that your own bank or another high street bank will be able to accommodate you. In any case, if you are looking for a substantially larger sum involving equity investment there will probably be a debt finance requirement too, and you and your financial adviser will need to open discussions with a high street bank at an early stage in your negotiations.

It is useful to explore how much of your funding needs can be secured by loans and an overdraft. But it is important that the various funding requirements are funded in the most appropriate way.

Current account

Whatever your funding requirements, your business will need a current bank account to deal simply with day-to-day transactions such as floats, cash takings, expenses, paying suppliers and petty cash.

Subject to status, an overdraft facility is usually available to help you address any short-term cash flow issues. Most high street banks currently offer free current account banking for up to 18 months until your business is up and running.

Business loans

They will also consider favourably the grant of a loan to kick-start your business when you buy new equipment, move into new premises, take on more staff to meet demand or incur other heavy expenditure related to the development of the business.

For small businesses, most banks offer a loan package; the following examples from Barclays Bank are typical:

- Barclayloan for Business
  - For loans between £1,000 and £25,000.
  - Optional up-front capital and interest repayment holiday for the first six months after the loan is received. (Interest accruing during this period will be included within subsequent repayments.)
  - Loan duration of up to 10 years. (When the loan is being used to purchase an asset, the term of the loan cannot exceed the life of the asset acquired.)
  - No early prepayment fee.
  - Interest calculated on a daily basis.
- Flexible Business Loan
  - For sums from £25,001.
  - Repayment periods from 1 to 20 years.
  - Optional repayment holiday of up to 24 months at the outset of the loan (interest is debited to the current account).
  - Choice of fixed or variable interest rates.
- Flexible Commercial Mortgage
  - Any repayment period from 1 to 25 years.
  - Up to 80 per cent of the valuation or property purchase price.
  - Optimal repayment holiday of up to 24 months at the beginning of the mortgage period (interest is debited to the current account).
  - Choice of fixed or variable interest rates, with the option to change during the mortgage term.

A number of sales financing packages are also generally available from the banks, such as factoring and confidential invoice discounting, which enable businesses to release funds that are tied up in their sales ledgers.

Identifying external equity sources

As we have seen in Chapter 4, there are a number of different sources of equity available, ranging from high-net-worth individuals to multi-billion-pound investment companies. While not all of these potential sources of equity are members of an association, the majority tend to be. Identifying individual sources of equity funds can be a slow and painful process, but this can be made much easier by identifying the associations first.

Probably the largest such organization is the British Venture Capital Association (BVCA), with more than 430 member firms that include most of the biggest and best-known investment funds in the UK. The details of all the members of BVCA can be obtained through the BVCA although there is now a charge for this (see Appendix 2). All investment funds provide an outline of the type of investment that they consider, which will depend on stage, sector, size of investment and similar details, but this should be viewed more as marketing material than as something that can be relied upon. Relatively few investment funds advertise that they invest in start-ups, and experience shows that many fewer will be interested in doing so when contacted.

Once possible sources of funding have been identified, there is no substitute for making direct contact in order to discuss whether your requirements fit with the funders' present requirements. In order not to waste too much of your or their time, it is generally preferable to have an initial conversation and then, if a funder is interested in principle, send a written executive summary. If the funder remains interested, it is then necessary to exchange a confidentiality agreement and, once this is returned, to send the full business plan and arrange a meeting.

There are a number of large associations of business angels (ie high-net-worth individual investors) around the country, the largest and most successful of which is Beer & Partners, with over 2,000 registered, active investors. Many of the business angel networks provide a service that allows the company looking for funding to prepare a brief presentation, which is then circulated to the association members by way of a regular newsletter. Alternatively they may hold investment fairs where companies are invited to meet with potential investors. The whole procedure with business angels is rather less formal than with investment funds, and as the decision is often made partly with the heart, the process is rather more hit and miss. Investments sourced from this route can be as low as £25,000 upwards.

Like most aspects of starting a business, identifying external equity sources can take much more time and effort than may at first be appreciated. Once potential sources have been identified, the next steps also tend to drag on, and the whole process can take many months, so it is best to accept this and to allow for it at the outset, rather than hope that matters will progress very quickly.

As with any other 'quote', it is best to obtain more than one initial offer in order to ensure that the best possible deal is obtained. A decision will need to be made as to which offer looks most suitable, prior to spending any time or incurring any costs.

First-round finance

First-round finance, as the name would suggest, is the first tranche of investment into a new company. As with many definitions, though, it can mean different things to different people. Does the capital put in by the founders and their friends and families count as first-round funding or not? Here we will look at first-round funding as the first time a company has sought to attract external equity in order to establish a new business.

Of all the times that a company will look to raise outside investment over its life, none will prove to be more difficult than first-round funding. This is because there are very few sources of such funding and a lot of demand for the limited supply. The reason that so few investors are prepared to invest in start-ups is that the risks are much higher and new companies have no real track record. From the investors' viewpoint, of course, when they get it right the rewards can also be much higher, but this is needed to offset those that do not succeed.

In addition to the difficulties of raising first-round finance, raising small amounts (ie less than £1 million) of equity is often more difficult than raising larger amounts. As noted in Chapter 4 many of the equity funds and providers of venture capital take the view that the level of work involved is similar irrespective of the amount actually invested, and as such it is not economic for them to invest less than £1 million.

The most common source of funding for start-ups and lower levels of funding is 'business angels', who will typically invest amounts of between £25,000 to £1m. (See page 53 for more information on these.) However, perhaps the best-known sources of equity are the investment funds and venture capital funds run by city institutions (see page 53).

From 1983 to 2007, over £35 billion was invested by the UK private equity industry in around 20,500 companies in Britain. However, for the 400-plus member companies of the British Venture Capital Association, over 50 per cent of investments are for expansion of existing companies (ie second and third-round financing) and the next largest type of investment is for acquisitions, management buyouts and the like, leaving only a very small amount for first-round financing.

In the last few years the global credit crisis has meant that many investors have been much more cautious, and obtaining funding has therefore been much more difficult although, rather bizarrely, equity has not been impacted to the same degree as obtaining bank debt. Although 2009 was very difficult, in 2010 the situation started to return to a more normal state.

Preparing for due diligence

Once a potential investor has been found, any investment decision will be subject to due diligence. Due diligence is the process that covers all aspects of the funder gaining confidence by checking out what they have been told about the company, the marketplace, legal titles, ownership of assets and so on. Investment funds will have a well-practised, comprehensive procedure for making these enquiries, but business angels are likely to be rather less formal.

The due diligence procedure will often include external accountants and lawyers as well as other specialists able to provide an unbiased, detailed report. The better prepared the management team is for this process, the quicker and easier it will be. If the management establish a 'data room' of all the required documentation and information that will be required for due diligence then this process can be completed more quickly. It is worth noting that while the due diligence process will be run by the potential funder, and all experts will be appointed by, and report to, the funder, the costs will be borne by the company requiring the investment. (Payment will be made from the investment proceeds, and can quite easily amount to a considerable amount.)

Negotiation and closing

There is an almost infinite number of different variations on how the equity can be structured and, as such, plenty of scope for negotiation. As with any negotiations, there needs to be a degree of flexibility on both sides and a desire to find the middle ground.

It is important for the SME to work with trusted advisers to assist with the negotiations, as the investor will have much more experience in such matters, and it is easy for the SME to fail to push for the best deal simply through lack of knowledge.

The structure of the deal and the negotiations will shape the future cooperation of the parties, and can also lead to a massive difference in the value the founders get for selling a stake in their business. As such it is extremely important.

The final closing meeting will almost inevitably involve more people, take longer and be more fraught with last-minute issues than is often imagined. Not only will the SME and the investor be present, but so too will accountants, lawyers and other advisers from both sides, as well as any other funders (such as banks) that are involved. Once all the documentation has finally been signed, the management team will be free to concentrate on growing the business until the next stage of funding is required.

Kevin R Smith is Managing Director of AWS Structured Finance Ltd, international financial consultants, and can be contacted on 01892 667 891 or e-mail kevin.r.smith@awsconsult.co.uk He is a partner of Aspen Waite Accountants and a Corporate Associate at Beer & Partners, Europe's largest business angel network

Chapter Six
Think Again or
Full Steam Ahead

At this stage, you have either secured the funding that you need to carry out your business plan or you have been turned down by the banks and other sources that you and your advisers approached. If you have been successful, you are at the point of no return – should you accept the best funding offer you have negotiated and form your business, or are you having second thoughts? We will discuss that final decision-making process in later parts of this chapter. But let's review first the reasons for refusal and your alternatives if you have been unsuccessful.

Analysing reasons for refusal

It is important to understand why you have been turned down. Here are some possible reasons:

- Your business plan failed to convince or there were serious flaws in it. If the flaws were exposed in the course of early discussions, you will have had the opportunity to revise the business plan before your next approach. Perhaps the sources you approached simply disliked the field of business in which you wanted to engage because they judged it to have a poor record, to be risky in the short term or to be unattractive in the long term.

- You failed to convince personally as an entrepreneur who could develop and run a business successfully. You may have sensed that from face-to-face discussion. If you had an adviser present, ask him or her for a frank assessment of the impression you made.

- You asked for more funding than the business plan could support, or the lending institutions were not prepared to advance a loan unsecured or against the collateral you offered.

- If you applied to a bank, perhaps its current lending guidelines were too strict or did not allow for funding new business start-ups. Many of the retail banks no longer allow local managers any leeway against the computer-controlled decision criteria of Head Office. If that was the case you were wasting your time and a good adviser could have been expected to steer you away from such institutions.

Whatever the reasons for refusal, you need to know what they were. If you were introduced by a financial adviser, he/she should be able to find out the real reason subsequently. In any case, do not shrink from asking.

What to do next

If the experience of being turned down repeatedly has not deterred you from trying to start your own business, you have several ways of continuing to pursue your ambition.

Back to the drawing board

Develop a different concept that avoids the pitfalls in your original idea that have been revealed, and go through the whole process again, starting with the funding sources that seemed receptive previously.

You will probably find that very difficult. But, if your previous concept was as an online retailer of, say, women's fashion clothing, you might have another product type you could substitute that would be judged more viable. Alternatively, if your preferred field of activity is in business-to-business services (B2B) you could consider offering, say, online preparation of tax returns for SMEs instead of business insurance broking.

Do it cheaper

Review you business plan once more and see if you can reduce the scale of operations or cut out costs so that you can start from a smaller base and either fund it yourself or raise the necessary finance from family and friends.

This approach will probably mean cutting your personal expenditure to the minimum and living on a shoestring. It will certainly mean running your business from home, even if that was not your original intention. Of course, you need to discuss the implications fully with your family and be sure that they will support you and accept any temporary constraints on their lifestyle.

If you decide to take this route, there are two pieces of advice that you should take on board:

- If you intend to borrow money from family or friends, or take them in as 'sleeping partners', be sure to put your arrangements in writing, just as you would with an external source of finance. All too often family feuds or broken friendships are the result of failing to ensure that there is a common understanding of the terms on which money is advanced. 'Pay it back when you can' is a recipe for future dissent. Your 'angels' may think that they have a beneficial interest in the business and not that they financed you temporarily.

- Maintain the discipline of a business plan that you revisit at regular intervals, as well as the basic systems and procedures detailed in Part Two of this book.

Carry on planning

If you are in employment, you may be able to 'moonlight' by researching your business concept more thoroughly and, perhaps, test marketing it in your spare time. There are many people who took the first steps to developing a profitable, sustainable business in this way. A friend of mine who is now a leading business book publisher started out almost 40 years ago by editing and publishing his first annual reference directory, still a bestseller, on the kitchen table.

If you do not have a permanent job, you may have to take on part-time casual work, probably low paid, using what skills you have and doing the same thing in your downtime. They say that 'Nobody ever died of hard work' and you may surprise yourself to find just how many hours a day, seven days a week, you can work for extended periods.

The alternative that this book does not even consider is that you just give up on the idea of starting your own business. If that is your decision, you won't want to read further and have probably wasted the price of this book.

Full steam ahead?

So, you have the funding and are all set to start. Your mood may be one of euphoria, but before making an irrevocable commitment, take this last chance to have second thoughts.

Review the accepted business plan yet again with your insider's critical eye and confirm that you really believe in it yourself. In particular, focus on the cash flow projections and the SWOT analysis. In relation to the latter, consider again any external threats that you might not be able to manage and that could make your business development unsustainable.

External threats and weaknesses

External threats and weaknesses come in all shapes and sizes. The following are some of the more common:

- market size and rate of growth;
- environmental change;
- registration and/or qualification barriers;
- pending legislation or regulation;
- technology developments;
- intellectual property;
- major accident and occupational health and safety risks.

Each of these might have a severe impact on your ability to get your business started or to sustain it as you seek to grow over the coming years. It is easiest to discuss each type of factor in terms of practical examples.

Market size and rate of growth

The research you carry out to answer the question 'Who will want to buy the product or service I plan to sell?' should also provide you with insight into the future outlook for the market you seek to enter. Desk research will establish the size of the market nationally, regionally and locally, and its historical rate of growth.

If your product or service is intended for a sub-market of a larger market in which there are alternatives, you should research the wider market as well. For example, if you are planning to open a keep-fit centre, the market you are addressing is not just the established market for keep-fit centres but the broader leisure market of alternative sports and exercise, including home users of keep-fit equipment. Evidence that the rate of growth in the use of fitness centres nationally exceeds the growth in sales of exercise equipment to home users would strengthen your view of starting up. The converse would be a deterrent.

You should also investigate the characteristics of the local market where you are planning to set up your business in comparison with the national market. For example, if you were planning to open a fitness centre and you find out that the local authority has a forward plan to build 10,000 new starter homes, while a new telephone call centre is about to open bringing 1,500 new jobs to the area, then you might uprate the opportunity.

Alternatively, if you find that the local population is ageing, a new fitness centre opened last year and the largest local employer is in liquidation, you would probably look elsewhere. As noted previously, competitor activity is also a key aspect of the investigation.

Environmental change

This kind of external factor can be the effect of a natural phenomenon or a human-induced change to local conditions. Its occurrence may be unexpected and the effect may be temporary or permanent. For example, if you had invested in holiday cottages in Cornwall in 2000, your business would have suffered in 2001 as a result of the foot-and-mouth crisis but benefited in 2002 from the terrorist destruction of the World Trade Center in New York, which deterred British holidaymakers from flying abroad (both short-term effects). Equally, the effect of soaring oil prices and air fares has financially penalized those flying and has provided a longer-term stimulus to holidaying in the UK. On the other hand, the noticeable change in the British climate where summers prior to 2010 have been wetter and shorter may be a long-term phenomenon that may have an increasing effect in reducing the demand for UK holidays. Other obvious examples of environmental change of the human-induced variety are road bypass schemes that disrupt the pattern of local trade, or airport construction that has an impact on residential property values.

Registration and/or qualification barriers

In spite of what politicians tell us about the reduction or abolition of red tape, most of us are aware that businesses of all kinds, small or large, are increasingly subject to regulation. (Just ask farmers what they think of the increased burden of paperwork generated by completing returns and maintaining records to satisfy government requirements.)

Some of these measures are introduced to protect the consumer or to raise standards of practice and accountability. Although regulation on these grounds is generally beneficial, it does impose barriers for new entrants into a number of business activities. Suppose, for example, that after 25 years working for a national pensions, life assurance and mortgage provider you are planning to set up in business as a financial consultant. Today you are required to register with the Financial Services Authority (FSA), which involves satisfying the FSA of your competence. Although your work experience may be more than sufficient, you may need to acquire an additional qualification, which will delay your business start-up.

There are other occupations that are less demanding in terms of qualification, but in practice you may find it very difficult to get started in your own business without taking out membership of an accepted trade association in that field. Trade association membership is what elevates a construction worker or amateur carpenter into a skilled building trades practitioner. Membership of some trade associations requires qualification through recognized training programmes. Thus, a building society will not recognize the work carried out by an electrician or to roof timbers to remedy infestation or rot unless the contracting individual or firm is a member of one of the recognized trade associations.

Management consultancy is a field into which many experienced businesspeople are drawn, either as sole traders or in partnership, and remains unregulated, although the Institute of Management Consultancy (IMC) is a well-established body with professional standards and entry qualifications. This is not altogether surprising since many managers coming out of industry set up their consultancies on the back of assignments from established contacts including, quite often, their previous employers. However, unless they operate in a very specialized field, the credentials of IMC membership may prove increasingly important in growing their consultancy business. Fortunately, it is possible to gain IMC membership while practising as a management consultant, since admission qualifications are awarded more on the quality of work and experience, including past employment as an internal consultant or project manager, than on academic achievement.

An alternative way to surmount qualification barriers is to join forces in a partnership or limited company with an associate who already has the necessary qualification to satisfy registration requirements and provide the firm's credentials (eg an estate agency with one or more RICS members).

Pending legislation or regulation

Part of the threat of pending legislation is the long period of uncertainty that it generally causes. Election manifestos, government inquiries, White Papers, Autumn Statements and budget speeches all give hints of forthcoming legislation, but uncertainty remains until a Bill is laid before Parliament and becomes law. Pending legislation may therefore be a deterrent to starting a business before the legislative playing field has been redefined. A case in point is the field of life assurance and pensions, where in recent years much stricter regulation has been introduced in respect of both the content of pension schemes and life assurance policies, and marketing and sales. Setting up in this business as a consultant or broker seems even more hazardous in 2011. On the other hand, some established brokers and advisers in this field have become discredited due to the multiplying number of victims of underfunded pension schemes and endowment policies or of calamitous investment decisions, so that there may be opportunities for new firms to enter the market, offering a new generation of more user-friendly products. In this instance, entry timing could be all important.

More mundane examples of changes in regulations are local planning consents that impose (or remove) restrictions on the location of specific types of business.

Technology developments

The effects of developments in technology are often uncertain and can be seriously misread. The latter half of the 1990s and the first decade of the current century produced two examples with unforeseen consequences. The internet bubble was fuelled by marketing assumptions as to how the internet could be exploited commercially and how consumers would react, which proved to be mistaken. Except for a few well-defined products and services (eg books and online banking) the internet has not proved to be the infallible growth channel to market on which a whole generation of e-economy start-ups were based. The logistical problems and costs of physical delivery to fulfil customer orders are often wholly underestimated, and many of the brightest stars crashed or went into non-growth orbit. However, the internet has proved itself as a highly cost-effective medium for the delivery of information, and 'old economy' companies have learnt to use the new capability effectively in their global business operations. Today, almost all businesses of any significance have their own websites on which their capabilities are identified.

The staggered introduction of digital TV over the next three or four years is the second case in point.

Major developments in technology could have a similar impact on your business start-up if you have misread market trends, but the e-business hype is long over (except for the current publishing obsession with e-books), and sources of finance rely once again on the traditional balance sheet and profit and loss account parameters rather than trendy paradigm shifts.

Nevertheless, the potential advantages of e-commerce for small businesses are considerable, including:

- increased exposure in export markets where conventional marketing costs too much;
- secure payments in international trading;
- the facility to cultivate niche markets cheaply;
- the opportunity to arrange remote transactions through secure e-commerce packages;
- ready price comparison of alternative supply sources and procurement from the cheapest source;
- the immediate settlement of invoices through the introduction of straight-through processing (STP) in bank transactions.

However, small businesses need an improved infrastructure that allows them to use continuous, broadband internet facilities to develop their international markets and trade securely 24 hours a day, seven days a week. For a time, the monopolistic hold by BT on broadband access to local areas placed many UK rurally based companies at a disadvantage to their better-served foreign competitors. Other technological problems include the varying ability of traditional small firms to create and maintain their websites or introduce more sophisticated IT platforms.

Intellectual property

One by-product of the IT and internet revolutions has been that companies have learnt to value their intangible intellectual property rights (IPR) more highly than before. Outside the publishing industry, the focus previously had been on patentable designs, technical drawings, processes and products; documentation that is protected by copyright; and brands, corporate logos and marketing aids protected by trademark registration. Computer software and systems are now treated as a further category of product eligible for copyright protection.

In setting up your own business you will be aware that you must not employ these kinds of tangible IPR without a licence from the owner. You must also be careful not to infringe the IPR of other businesses, particularly a former employer, in know-how or 'knowledge assets', that they have articulated and packaged into hard copy, disk, CD ROM or electronic format for delivery as in-house training or to customers, suppliers or other third parties, perhaps under licence. Knowledge assets may also take the form of management systems, training programmes, marketing and customer relations techniques.

However, other people's knowledge assets are not necessarily a barrier to entry. There is no copyright in intellectual concepts, only in the form in which they are expressed and published. Therefore, there is no reason why you should not use the same marketing techniques or sales pitch as your former employer or competitors, provided that you avoid their branding and the use of the same promotional literature, graphics, slogans or catchphrases, and wording in your printed material. The test here is whether anyone examining your product or service might believe that it was your competitor's offering; if so, you are vulnerable to a claim of 'passing off'. Conversely, you should pay attention to the protection of your IPR by making your product or service offering as distinctive and unique in its presentation as you can.

Major accident and occupational health and safety risks

With heightened public awareness of the unexpected disasters that can hit any business, many with environmental implications or staff endangering, it is important to show potential investors that you are addressing and will manage such risks effectively. A good way to do this is to adopt the approach recommended by DNV Consulting, international specialists in the field and advisers to high risk industries, and to go through the risk management process, identified by the DNV acronym IEDIM, as follows:

Risk Management Process

I   Identify Loss Exposure: What could go wrong?

E   Evaluate the Risks: So what?

D   Develop a Plan: What do we do now?

I   Implement the Plan: Let's do it!

M Monitor and Review: Is it working?

(Source: DNV Consulting, www.dnv.com)

Your emphasis of course is on contingency planning and disaster recovery.

Go for it

If further scrutiny does not throw up uncertainties that you had not previously appreciated, then there is nothing to hold you back from completing your funding agreement, aside from some sudden lapse in self-confidence. Given that you have been through an arduous and self-critical process, there is no logic in further hesitation. Take a deep breath, sign on the dotted line, and good luck.

Checklist

- If your attempts to raise finance have failed, find out and analyse why you were turned down. You or your adviser should not shrink from asking.

- Alternatives for continuing:

  - Develop a different concept that avoids the pitfalls of your original plan.

  - Do it cheaper; plan to cut cost and/or start up on a smaller scale.

  - If you take money from family or friends, be sure to have a written agreement.

  - If you have a job, carry on planning and test market in your spare time.

  - If you are unemployed, take casual work, while trying to start up in your downtime.

- If you have received an offer of funding, make a final review of your business plan and confirm that you still believe in it:
  - Pay particular attention to cash flow projections and your SWOT analysis.
  - Consider external threats and weaknesses and be sure that you can manage them.
- If further scrutiny has not damaged your confidence, take a deep breath and get started.

Part Two
Essentials for the Small Business

Chapter Seven
Website Marketing and E-commerce

We are all engaged to varying degrees in the use of the information and computer technology that has impacted daily life. High-speed connection via broadband to the internet has helped to develop responsive communications and channels to market for even the smallest business. Internet marketing is an essential (and cheap) tool for any B2B business and for marketing products and services direct to consumers. You may already have included the use of website marketing and, perhaps, e-commerce in your business planning. For that reason, I have listed this chapter as the first among the essential operations for starting up a small business.

Readers may not need much instruction on the selection of hardware or software for the basic functions of their businesses. For most applications, laptops are bigger and more powerful than ever and their capabilities match those of desktop PCs for normal business use. For those few who are fortunate enough to be able to separate work from leisure time and use their business PCs only in their offices, desktop computers retain the advantage of being a cheaper initial investment.

There are also the ubiquitous Blackberry and other hand-held Smart/Windows telephone devices so that businesspeople are now able to 'take their offices' with them when they travel or go on holiday without carrying a separate laptop or notebook and, thanks to wireless connections, remain in electronic contact with customers, suppliers, their business base and their bank accounts while they are away.

Basic IT functions

Microsoft continues to dominate the office applications market, in spite of the anti-monopoly lawsuits from which it is constantly under attack. However, many people, especially in the creative industries, prefer to use Mac products, and compatibility is no longer a significant issue because Microsoft (MS) Office (and similar programs that will open the same files) are available for a range of different operating systems, not just for MS Windows.

Although the basic Windows technology has become generally available, other software providers will find it difficult to match the constantly developing Microsoft product range. MS Works is an abbreviated version of MS Office, the standard business software package that contains all the core elements you are likely to need when starting up your business. It is included as a part of the systems and software package in the purchase price of some PCs, laptops as well as desktops. It can also be purchased separately if your PC came with a lesser software package and many manufacturers (such as Dell and Hewlett Packard) will offer you a special deal when you buy a computer on MS Office or Works.

The usefulness of MS Office resides in its components, of which the following is a summary:

- 'Excel' and/or 'Access' can be used to build databases of client and customer information, useful for mailings and so forth (see the section below on the proactive use of e-mails).

- Excel may be used to process basic business accounting administration, including financial accounting statements such as profit and loss accounts.

- 'Outlook' is part of MS Office and is useful for organizing e-mail, spell-checking and other tasks. It's a 'client' rather than a 'provider', so that it can be asked to download your e-mail from any web-based service you choose (particularly useful when travelling).

- Outlook's calendar functions with alarms and reminders can be put to good use in keeping the business (and you) organized.

● Basic web pages can be made using Word.

'Open Office' is an alternative to MS Office that will open all the same kinds of files and is available absolutely free. However, there is no technical support and that could be a serious downside.

Beyond the basic MS Office, there are a multitude of specialist business software solutions including:

● Office Project Professional;

● Office Visio Professional;

● Office Web Apps;

● Office Live Meeting;

● Office Live Small Business;

● Office Live Workspace;

● Online Services;

● Windows.

None of these come free; you may want to examine some of them carefully and to decide which are useful or essential for your business, and which are just too expensive.

Accounting and business management software

MS Office Accounting was discontinued from November 2009 but there are a number of specialist business packages that provide accounting software. The better packages of accounting software, such as Sage, include a basic form of contact management in an integrated package with financials, order processing, invoicing and inventory control, and are user-installable. Provided that you are at least computer semi-literate, you won't need to attend a training course. You should expect to pay up to £1,000 for a single-user system.

As your business grows you can add on more sophisticated modular software to manage the nominal, sales and purchase ledgers, as well as cash-book, stock and order processing. Project costing and manufacturing modules are also available. Focus on the sharp end of your business such as order processing, customer relations management and credit control. You will be able to manage your debtor-ageing schedule on computer and to generate monthly statements and reminder letters. At an early stage, you will want to involve your accountant in reviewing your computerized accounting, if only to check that the information provided and held on file is adequate for audit purposes.

Once you have acquired the software, you will be able to computerize your business plan projections, plot the actual results against forecast and generate accurate updated cash flow forecasts quickly. You will also be able to manipulate the computerized spreadsheets for 'what if' scenarios, giving you a valuable decision-making tool for improving the business.

Setting up e-mail facilities and building your website

The elementary first step in using e-mails proactively is to choose a domain name for the business with a hosting provider. You should use a domain name that will give the business a professional image, and you should choose a reliable server (ISP) that provides you with global internet connectivity. Avoid the free e-mail services, which are really only suitable for personal use, and choose one of the independent service providers (ISPs) with proven reliability and a decent technical support service that will ensure that the e-mails you send are properly spell-checked, delivered promptly and archived.

However, even at the outset, you should really be considering your e-mail set-up in the context of creating a website for your business. Most people starting up would rather have a 'name@businessname. co.uk' identity than 'name@someoneelsesbusinessname.co.uk' address for communication with customers, suppliers and all other business contacts. This is much more affordable than it used to be and there is a vast range of different service providers available to assist you.

Criteria for choosing a domain/hosting provider

The following are some of the considerations that you should bear in mind:

- The difference between domestic and business broadband services are: upload speed, band, webspace and web domains. (If you elect to host your own website at home on your own PC, how many of your customers will be able to access it before it crashes, and how long will it take you to restore service?)

- Whether to use services that provide servers, webspace, web domains and so on (can you host your own website – ie by providing a fixed IP address – or will the service need to include hosting?)

- Security of business and customer data from intrusion, hacking and loss. (NB – under the Data Protection Act you are required by law to keep your customers' data secure.)

- Registration of your domain (.com/.co.uk/.org) may be part of the package or a separate cost.

- Whether you want to update and maintain your site yourself or whether you need someone to manage the site for you. How often you will need to update is relevant. (Many business owners run into difficulty when they are unable to get hold of the people under contract to design or manage their websites.)

- How many e-mail addresses you will need (eg one for each employee).

Costs vary very significantly depending on the type of service that is chosen and how much maintenance is involved. The following cautionary notes may help you in your decision making about ISPs:

- ISPs provide both domestic and business services. A domestic broadband service might be sufficient for an early-stage business, but you need to think ahead so that you are adequately resourced to manage expansion.

- A domestic service will give you a particular download speed, but will not support, or even address, the upload speed essential for the operation of a website with any degree of public access.

- A domestic ISP service may include webspace but is unlikely to accommodate a static IP address, or a professional sounding URL (uniform resource locator) for your business, and the e-mail addresses provided by the ISP and any web-based e-mail address will not look professional.

- There are many companies that will rent you space on their servers, providing both maintenance and security, which can be used to host your website only, your e-mail and your data, but it is essential that the service be both reliable and secure (ie both regularly and safely backed up).

- Alternatively, you can run your business entirely on your own computer(s), but then it is your responsibility alone to prevent your website being hacked, your customers spammed and both their and your financial details being stolen, and to ensure that your data is regularly and reliably backed up. In that event you will probably need a business broadband connection together with static IP address, registered domain and so on.

Taking all these factors into consideration, it is clear that the selection process is quite complex and you may feel that you need expert help. Visiting www.[and].co.uk might be a good starting point to find suggestions for a reliable, value-for-money business web (including domain name) and e-mail provider. You will find that they have several different packages for business. Other websites like www. uk.tophosts.com allow visitors to compare the services and prices of the most popular providers in order to arrive at an informed decision.

Doing it yourself

In terms of basic design, one of the best options open to those setting up a business with a limited budget is that of putting together in MS Word the basic web pages (text, links and images on several pages). Alternatively, you can use the software or templates that many web hosting services provide. A good example is www.1and1.co.uk whose templates can be used to create a website very quickly and without prior knowledge. Note that GCSE IT students today learn to put together basic websites as a part of the curriculum; therefore, if you have teenage offspring you may not have to look further to enlist help – no doubt much cheaper than commissioning a web manager!

Remember your objective

Your aim is to set up a professional and very serviceable website for your business that will act as a valuable marketing tool and enhance the company image. For that, you do not need to invest heavily.

If the products or services you supply are for a local market only, your website requirements may be relatively modest. Potential customers are as likely to locate you through the Yellow Pages or the local newspaper; however, there may be information about service, quality or pricing that you can convey more effectively on your website than by any other means. The minimum requirement will be for a well-designed and attractive home page that gives your business, however small, a professional image. There are other businesses where a website is fundamental to the business concept (eg online sales of stationery products) or without which the business could not operate effectively.

If your business is complex, you will need a more sophisticated, but user-friendly website with multi-functionality on which you can store and present updatable detailed information, logically segmented and indexed, to which visitors can readily drill down.

There are many excellent websites where very complex data is carefully arranged, catalogued and easily called up after logging on. Some government department websites, for example, are very well constructed; visit the Financial Services Authority website at www.fsa.gov.uk, which is hardly glamorous but particularly easy to find your way around and with very useful links to other government information sources. Conversely, the websites of some international accountancy firms and major banks are over-complicated and difficult to navigate.

Effective e-mailing

As a channel of communication, e-mail has introduced us to a new world of instant dialogue with the people who supply and advise us or who are potential or existing customers. E-mail dialogue is often quicker and more effective as a means of getting things done than the telephone and has made the humble fax seem like steam radio. However, it is not a substitute for fax in some respects. Whereas the fax is generally accepted as a legally valid way of placing or confirming an order or submitting a quotation or invoice, an e-mail may not be accepted in some contexts as sufficient proof of commitment.

E-mailing without tears

E-mail dialogue has been described as 'ping-pong' communication, and has certainly brought informality to personal communications. However, like all ball games, e-mail communication requires discipline. It is important to communicate clearly without literary flourishes. Conversely, excessive informality may be just as much, if not more of an issue, and can often cause offence. Again, your correspondent may not have your sense of humour and your cherished witticism may be mistaken for flippancy. E-mails are not retractable, so never send one when you're angry or promise what you cannot or do not intend to carry out.

E-mails as a marketing and sales tool

Aside from daily business communication, e-mails can be used proactively as an effective marketing and sales tool, either alone or in conjunction with your website, if you decide to build one. You can generate mailshots on your PC; then, using the customer database that you have created on MS Excel or Access and the MS Office 'mail merge' software, you can e-mail personalized messages to the prepared address lists swiftly and efficiently. Your message is more likely to reach the targeted reader if you embed the mailshot in the e-mail itself rather than as an attachment. Many business people have programmed their PCs to reject attachments automatically except from pre-listed sources as a defence against spam, viruses and other internet intrusions, or are simply too busy to open attachments if an e-mail fails to capture their attention.

Although e-mail marketing can be low cost, measurable, fast and highly effective, there are other barriers to overcome as well as spam filters. There are legal issues arising from the Data Protection Act; the ethical collection of data demands that addressees are given the opportunity to opt out of having their details recorded in your database or receiving circulars via e-mails or otherwise from you. You need to avoid becoming a spam-mailer yourself!

Prerequisites for effective, frequent e-mail marketing include having a technical infrastructure capable of handling large numbers of messages, the ability to track the performance of campaigns, and knowing what will be the full cost of the service to you. EAB, based at St Albans, Hertfordshire, offers services in e-marketing as well as website design, internet and IT solutions for businesses of all sizes. It may be worth visiting their website at www.eab.co.uk.

You can also use e-mails on a one-to-one basis, to make your quotations and convert them to orders on your PC, while updating your accounting data.

Use of social media

Today's fashionable, social online media are another widespread channel to market. For more information on how social media, apps and the like may be used, refer to Kogan Page's quick start guides on Google AdWords, Podcasting, Social Media Marketing and other facilities to be found at www.koganpage.com.

Business on your website

There are basically three ways in which you can use your website commercially:

- As already discussed, you can display information about your products or services and stimulate visitors to call, mail or fax you with orders.
- You can have an interactive website on which you actually sell products or services by taking and confirming orders with credit or debit card payment.

- You can receive cash transfers electronically into your business bank account.

The second function involves setting up a secure payment system that will safeguard both you and your customers' credit and debit cards and bank accounts. One service that others have found reliable is PayPal.

Together these functions embody e-commerce in its fullest sense, but the primary task is to attract visitors to your website. This is achieved by linking your site with the major search engines, such as Google, AltaVista and Yahoo!, which give details of sites that fit the criteria by the search words given.

Use of internet search engines

Google is probably the most comprehensive search engine for locating business services both in the UK and internationally, and offers a wide range of tools and services, some free and some more like paid-for advertising. Choose, within your budget, what will ensure that your website is well-represented and easy for potential customers to locate. Visit www.google.co.uk/services to see how businesses can even have their outlets or head office marked on Google Maps to lead customers to the door. Some information about your visitors and how they arrived at your website can also be recovered from Google.

Skill is required in drafting the brief description that accompanies your website address: you need to know which are the 'buzz words' that will place your site near the beginning of the search engine category list and attract attention best, prompting surfers to log on to your site. Multiple entries on the same search engines may actually be counterproductive; customers may disregard them all as junk and not bother to search any.

Once you start to receive responses from visitors to your website, you can begin building your own mailing list, which you can e-mail regularly with details of your new products or services, and sale offers. When you include a text link to your website in the e-mails you send, respondents can click directly through to visit your catalogues and other information without causing them the inconvenience of logging on to your website separately. As this activity starts to grow while you are in business, you will have to start providing customer service support and, perhaps, think about adding to the website the functional architecture that will enable you to count visitors and customers as they order and make payment.

Harnessing eBay

One service that eBay offers to small and medium-sized enterprises is the opportunity to set up their own trading sites under the eBay umbrella. As of August 2010, around 25,000 people had launched some kind of business on eBay since the start of the current recession, of which 127 are forecast to reach turnovers of £1 million or more for 2010 compared with 66 businesses for 2009. Of the 127, seven only started selling goods on eBay in 2010 and 11 are achieving increases in turnover at the rate of 300 per cent annually (*Guardian*, 21 August 2010). As Jody Ford, eBay's director for SME comments 'the low cost of entry and access to many millions of online shoppers means that it is possible to enjoy rapid success in e-commerce.'

The eBay success stories appear to be for vendors of goods. Whether this particular channel to market can be harnessed for those selling services is uncertain. However, the growing importance of online shopping was also highlighted in August by the agreement of MasterCard to acquire the fraud prevention and electronic payment services of the UK DataCash Group for £333 million.

Affiliate and affinity marketing

You can broaden and deepen your website marketing by forming alliances with the websites of compatible businesses. If your products are complementary to those of another business with an up-and-running website you can negotiate reciprocal links (images as well as text) between your websites so that visitors to one can read an introduction to the other and click on at will. The two websites are then said to be affiliates. These arrangements tend to work better with services rather than products, where there may be a confusion of brand identities. Marketing product ranges that are not in competition through linked websites may simply dilute the brand image of both if customers perceive no added value in the connection.

Cross-linking websites works most effectively where there is a genuine affinity between the two ranges of products or services. For example, a website offering damp-proofing services would have a clear affinity to another offering pest control services or to a third offering double-glazing installation in the same geographical locations.

Some very large enterprises have intranet websites that can be visited only by their internal staff and business associates or extranet websites that are accessible only by clients or customers. If you are running a specialist travel agency for exotic holidays, it might be very beneficial for your website to be linked to the intranet of a global management consultancy or accountancy firm. Similarly, if your firm offers insurance services for high-net-worth individuals, a cross-link with the extranet of the private banking division of a major bank would be very useful.

Other commerce tools and services

Many people who run their own businesses set up an eBay 'shop', which can be basic or personalized to a certain extent. This medium of commerce generates a vast amount of traffic and provides market reach and easy transactions. Key advantages of an eBay shop are:

- *Rating system*: buyers and sellers rate and comment on each other in each transaction so that it is possible to build up a good profile, with testimonials from satisfied customers.

- *eBay terms and conditions*: established business practices on refunds, etc. provide a degree of security.

Checklist

- Even the smallest business can benefit from the responsive communications and channels to market that the internet provides.

- With laptops having similar capabilities to desktop personal computers and wireless connections or Smart/Windows telephones, you can take your office with you when you travel.

- Microsoft Office is the global standard software; Microsoft Works is an abbreviated version included in the purchase price of some computers that gives you all you are likely to need when starting up your business.

- The better packages of accounting and business management software are user-installable. Expect to pay up to four figures for a single-user system.

- Consider seriously the option of setting up your own website and e-mailing facilities in combination.

- Mailshots by e-mail containing your sales message with your website address embedded are a more effective marketing and sales tool than simply referring prospects to a website or an attachment.

- The simplest websites can be bought off the peg very cheaply, but you will have to spend more to create a well-designed and attractive website.

- Take care with your entries on internet search engines and examine the Google alternatives.

- Evaluate carefully the option of a website that provides fully-fledged e-commerce functionality that is integrated with your sales ledger and inventory management system.

- Decide whether you want to use your website just to display information about your products or services or to make sales by taking and confirming orders and receiving payment by debit and credit card or cash payments electronically. Invest accordingly.

- You can broaden and deepen your website marketing by forming alliances with the websites of compatible businesses.

- Consider setting up your own eBay shop.

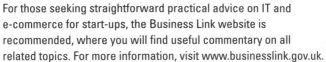

continued

For those seeking straightforward practical advice on IT and e-commerce for start-ups, the Business Link website is recommended, where you will find useful commentary on all related topics. For more information, visit www.businesslink.gov.uk.

Chapter Eight
Cash Management

The number one reason for start-up businesses failing is poor cash management. Thus, good management is essential to enable you to achieve the business growth for which you have planned. The only way to manage the often conflicting forces of growth and weak cash flow is through carefully implemented controls. This chapter will help guide you through the financial and management accounting options to achieve good control and, hopefully, create sufficient cash to grow your business successfully.

Refining your cash flow forecast

The cash flow forecast that was a key element of your business planning is the starting point. Now you are in business, review it again and add more detailed income and cost categories as necessary to ensure that you can monitor your forward cash position, daily if you wish.

For tighter control you may wish to extend the columns on your forecast to show weekly data for, say, the next three months. The timing of direct debits, standing orders and bank charges may be critical to your planned debtor chasing and payments to trade creditors.

Cash control

Two sets of people are interested in how you manage your cash – your bank and your backers (both potential and existing). The latter group will be analysing your accounts with some standardized ratios, so that they can compare your business with the others they may invest in or lend to. Clearly, it is in your best interests to make sure that your business has cash ratios that will be satisfactory to these people. There are a variety of ways in which you can arrange your business to help you achieve this; these are referred to in Chapter 16 on asset management. At this stage, however, it is useful to know what the ratios are, and more critically to gain a good understanding of how they operate.

The most frequently used, and therefore important, statistic is the current ratio. This compares your current assets against your current liabilities to give a figure that shows how many times the former will cover the latter.

Current ratio = current assets/current liabilities.

The figure is expressed as a ratio, such as 2.6:1. This example means that your current assets are 2.6 times greater than your current liabilities. What does this mean? Not a lot by itself. There is no overall ideal figure you should be trying to achieve. Each industry and sector within an industry will have different sets of ratios. The more risky your business is, the more susceptible to market changes, the greater the first figure should be. In an ideal world where you have little risk and you can project with certainty what is going to happen in the future business cycle, the nearer 1:1 you get the more efficient use of capital you are achieving. Thus we arrive at the first dilemma: your backers want you to get the highest possible return with 'their' cash, but without exposing them to an unacceptable level of risk. This is an almost impossible task to achieve consistently to everyone's satisfaction, as different people (and therefore different backers) have different levels of risk aversion.

Your level of risk acceptance is the key here. The first question you must ask yourself when considering your financial controls is what level of risk you are prepared to accept. Given that you are willing to set up on your own in the first place, you are probably not totally risk averse. But does that mean that you were happy to remortgage your house to fund the business? If it all goes wrong, you may lose not only your business but your house as well. Many banks seem to think that this is an acceptable thing to ask someone to do. It may secure their loan, but does it mean they are attracting suitably cautious borrowers?

Having worked out what level of risk is broadly acceptable to you and your backers, you can now look at how to achieve a level of exposure that fits. There are three main elements to managing your cash:

- *Credit control*: overseeing the flows of cash out of and cash into the business.
- *Stock control*: how much cash you have tied up in stock at any one time.
- *Cash management*: what you do with any spare cash or indebtedness that you have.

Credit control

Credit control is the management of both your debtors – those who owe you money – and your creditors – those you owe money to. The best situation is where you have only cash sales but all your purchases are on long payment terms. In this way you may well be able to sell all your purchases for cash before you have had to pay for them yourself. This is not such an unrealistic situation as you may believe. A bakery, for instance, will buy in all its flour, butter and other ingredients from a trade supplier who most likely will give it 30 days' payment terms. If the business is managed well, it can have sold all the ingredients as bread, cakes, buns and sausage rolls for cash well before the 30 days are up. This even allows the business time to gain interest on a cash surplus until it has to pay the supplier.

The opposite situation, where all supplies are purchased with cash but sales have to be given on account, is not unusual; it arises most often with start-up businesses until they have a trading record of, at least, six months' prompt payment. If you are selling business-to-business you will most likely have to offer credit terms to your customers. Your competitors will be doing so, which means you will have to as well. These are extra burdens on any start-up business, but there is no way around it other than ensuring that you have sufficient cash to cover any shortfall.

The most frequent situation is where you have a mixture of trade customers and suppliers on account. There are specific ratios to calculate your exposure to creditors and debtors in any one period, which can be used for comparative purposes. However, at this stage what is important is to have a clear picture of the 'age' of your debtors and their amounts, and a similar view of your creditors. If you know how much is due in and how reliable the debtors are (or are not), and you know how much you have to pay out and how long you have to do so, and that the latter is not more onerous than the former, you will be all right. The trick is how do you do this? The ratios referred to above will give a figure that is useful for benchmarking with others in your industry (if you can find their figures) or against your prior performance; however, the most useful information will be gathered from producing an 'aged debtors schedule' (as in Table 8.1) and an 'aged creditors schedule'. This information should be easily found in your sales and purchase day books, which are discussed further in Chapter 11.

TABLE 8.1 Aged debtors schedule

Customer	Current	30 days	60 days	Older
Mitchell's & Co Ltd		195.20		
Moen & Sons	80.25			
Pollocks		36.50		
J Reuvid				68.68
D Smith			340.85	
Suarez Bros	176.45			
U-Twist plc			277.43	
Whittakers Ltd	594.77			
Total	851.47	231.70	618.28	68.68

If you start experiencing problems with your credit control, it will be necessary to analyse your debtor and creditor schedules to see where you can improve the flows:

- Do you have any persistently late payers (late payers are more likely to be a problem than bad debtors)?

- If so, you may be able to persuade them to shorten their payment period. You may even have some customers who are happy to pay cash.

- For clients where you are on a retainer, you might consider advancing your invoice dates to the first instead of the last day of the month.

It is also worthwhile going through your creditors to see if any will give you better terms.

If you understand your two schedules well, this element of cash management will be relatively straightforward provided that you act decisively and keep your debtors under constant review.

Stock control

Depending on the type of business you operate, the role of stock control will vary in importance. If you are a service provider, such as a software programmer, you are unlikely to have much stock to control. However, any manufacturer or producer and any retailer will have more to consider.

Manufacturers will have three types of stock: raw materials, work in progress and finished products. Every piece of stock you have sitting in your store or warehouse represents tied-up cash. Clearly you need to have stock to sell and raw materials to make your product, but to make your use of working capital (the money required to keep the business running on a daily basis) as efficient as possible, you should minimize the amount of stock without prejudicing your trade.

This is not as simple as it seems. The amount of stock you buy will depend on various factors beyond how much you can afford to buy at one time. Buying in bulk will often be substantially cheaper than buying items in small quantities, because of bulk discounts or because transport costs are high.

Some items may be rare or difficult to source. If you are an antiques dealer, then whether or not you buy an item will have more to do with its value than your immediate cash flow: if you spot a real bargain you will make sure you find the funds to purchase it rather than pass it up. Conversely, if you are a clothing retailer, you will not want to be left holding last season's stock if fashions are constantly changing.

The factors that affect your stock levels are very varied. You are the best judge of what level of risk you can take with your stock to avoid running out, but be aware that apart from certain peculiar items that gain value with age (vintage wine, for example), most stock is losing you money if the alternative use for its value was cash earning interest in the bank. In technical terms, this is the 'opportunity cost' of holding stock.

In today's tough times, it may be better to forego bulk discounts and buy in stock-minimum quantities. Slow-moving and obsolete stock should be jobbed out at cost or lower than cost if necessary. Both actions will affect margins adversely but improve your all-important cash flows.

Pure cash management

This final element of the cash management control system focuses on either the spare cash you have in the business or your borrowing methods. If your business generates large amounts of surplus cash, even for short periods of time only, then you will be wise to gain some benefit from it. Your normal business account is unlikely to pay you interest on any positive balance, so you should get a business savings account into which you can transfer any temporarily surplus cash, so that you earn interest on it. Even when the bank rate is at its lowest, there are deals to be had, particularly with smaller building societies where your money is still safe.

In the more likely event that your small business is a net cash borrower, you should keep an eye on whether your lender is offering you the best rate available. In practice, this will not be at all easy. Your options for borrowing funds as a small business are limited, and often require a sustained relationship with your bank before it will allow you the flexibility to have an extended overdraft. You will probably be wasting your time and doing your business more harm than good by trying to change your lender at every tweak of its interest rate. That said, if you feel you are materially worse off with your bank than with another lender, it is certainly in your interests to point this out to your bank manager or adviser. Lenders have a limited degree of latitude, and while they advertise that they will always look after your interests, in practice they are unlikely to be as protective of them as you are. If you do not ask for a better rate, then it is unlikely that you will get one. One possibility is that your local bank manager offers to consolidate all or part of your overdraft into a personal loan carrying a lower rate of interest.

Budgeting and cash flow forecasts

The sections above on cash management, together with cost analysis, pricing and estimating, which are the subject of Chapter 9, form the core information that will help you to create your budget or cash flow forecast. Essentially, your budget will tell you whether your plans allow you enough working capital actually to run the business, and if so how much you will have to play with. The 'how much you have to play with' element will show you what is available to use for marketing, product development, training and so on.

The budgeting process is often one of iteration, where you can try out different 'what if' levels of investment in your budget model and see the different outcomes. An obvious example of this is considering whether to increase the advertising budget. Does the estimated increase in sales revenue suggest this to be money well spent or not?

For obvious reasons, developing your budget on a computer spreadsheet or specialist software allows you more flexibility and complexity in trying out these different scenarios. Some time invested before you start the business (when you are likely to have more time in any case) in building up as sophisticated and accurate a cash flow model as you can will be time well spent. Your backers and the bank will require cash flow forecasts as a first step before being able to consider whether they will help you or not (see Chapters 3 and 5).

Table 8.2 shows a cash flow forecast for a business that delivers table-ready meals; it consists of the projected costs and revenues for taking on a new sales manager. At first glance it appears to be a baffling array of figures; however, with the aid of the explanatory notes, it becomes more comprehensible. The final figure of increased profit of £33,510 seems well worth the investment. However, it would not take an investor very long to wonder whether the model was fully costed. The manager's national insurance and pension contributions (if relevant) have not been included. Neither are there any figures to approximate his telephone and travel costs (a salesperson who never calls or visits anyone will not be very effective), or any estimates for extra sales and publicity materials.

Thus we see that poorly constructed budgets can be dangerously misleading. It is always desirable to have a third party go over your figures to see if you have overlooked any costs. Another hazard with these models is that they are inevitably built on a series of assumptions. In Table 8.2, the projected increases in sales figures are based on current experience and then reduced on the basis of caution – this is wise. With an entirely new business you may not have 'current experience' to project from, so your assumptions will be based on observations and guesswork. This may be reasonably accurate (or not) for your first week's or month's projections, but a small error can be compounded into a significant one by the twelfth month. It is therefore best to always err on the side of caution with your assumptions – the entrepreneur's natural optimism needs careful controlling at this stage.

TABLE 8.2 A cash flow forecast of incremental profit from the addition of a new sales manager

New Sales Manager Cost		1	2	3	4	5	6	7	8	9	10	11	12	Year	Cumulative
Cost of Manager (6)	£8,500	£708.33	£708.33	£708.33	£708.33	£708.33	£708.33	£708.33	£708.33	£708.33	£708.33	£708.33	£708.33	£8,500.00	
Commission	8.00%	£37.31	£82.98	£133.24	£215.37	£287.78	£340.60	£430.74	£501.28	£555.97	£626.52	£673.55	£740.16	£4,625.49	£13,125.49
Sales to offices															Cumulative GP
Extra Orders/mnth (1)	£35.00	5	12	20	35	45	55	70	85	90	135	115	125	125	Year
Av Order Size (2)															
Ex-VAT	£29.82	£149.10	£357.84	£596.40	£1,043.70	£1,341.90	£1,640.10	£2,087.40	£2,534.70	£2,683.80	£3,131.10	£3,429.30	£3,727.50	£22,722.84	
GP (3)	83.00%	£123.75	£297.01	£495.01	£866.27	£1,113.78	£1,361.28	£1,732.54	£2,103.80	£2,227.55	£2,598.81	£2,846.32	£3,093.83	£18,859.96	£18,859.96
Private sales															
Extra Orders/mth		15	40	60	100	135	160	200	230	260	290	310	340	340	
Av Order Size	£17.00														
Ex-VAT	£14.48	£217.26	£579.36	£869.04	£1,448.40	£1,955.34	£2,317.44	£2,896.80	£3,331.32	£3,765.84	£4,200.36	£4,490.04	£4,924.56	£30,995.76	
GP	83.00%	£180.33	£480.87	£721.30	£1,202.17	£1,622.93	£1,923.48	£2,404.34	£2,765.00	£3,125.65	£3,496.30	£3,726.73	£4,087.38	£25,726.48	£44,586.44
Wholesale sales (4)															
Extra Orders/mth (5)	25.00	4	4	8	8	12	12	16	16	20	20	20	24	24	
Av Order Size	£25.00	£100.00	£100.00	£200.00	£200.00	£300.00	£300.00	£400.00	£400.00	£500.00	£500.00	£500.00	£600.00	£4,100.00	
Ex-VAT	50.00%	£50.00	£50.00	£100.00	£100.00	£150.00	£150.00	£200.00	£200.00	£250.00	£250.00	£250.00	£300.00	£2,050.00	£46,636.44

'Extra Sales GP' less 'Manager Costs' **£33,510.95**

(1) These figures represent the extra number of orders the sales manager is projected to add to sales in each month. The numbers are cumulative. That is month 2's figure includes month 1's figure, and month 3's includes both months 1 and 2's figures and so on. By month 12, we expect to see 125 extra office orders a month, as against month 0. This equates to approximately 6 orders per day (5.68), presuming a 22 working day month.

(2) Average order size is projected on the basis of each office order being for 4 people at just under £9/hd. We currently provide orders to three offices on an irregular basis, and this is a conservative figure on current experience. An average order size of £50 would be closer to our current office order size.

(3) The average gross profit (cost less ingredients) of our own made products is 83%. If the orders were to include a higher than normal proportion of wine/soft drinks/ice-cream, etc (which we sell at a GP of 50%) then the average will clearly fall.

(4) Currently we have one wholesale outlet which orders from us daily, at an average order size of £25+. However, this company orders from us every working day. Thus if we were to find another such company the monthly extra orders would be 22 rather than 4. However, on a cautionary basis I have projected that new wholesale orders would only be for the likes of small delis, etc, which could expect to take 8 to 10 pies per week.

(5) Wholesale food carries no VAT.

(6) The manager position would in fact be a split between four hours of sales work through the afternoon, and four hours plus in the evening for five days a week, thus making an eight-hour day, 40-hour week. This job would replace the current evening manager position which is currently paid approx £6.5K pa. Thus the new position only requires £8.5K extra revenues, although the salary would in fact be £15K pa.

Variance analysis and monthly accounts

Once you have created your budget it is important that you compare it against actual monthly results. This is good practice as it will inform you that you either are or are not meeting your targets. This will have important implications for your spending ability within the business, and you must take action accordingly. It is also important for you to discover why the budget and the actual results have diverged. This process, variance analysis, can be made as sophisticated or as straightforward as you desire. More simply, you can approach variance analysis as working out where your budget and actual results diverged and then finding a good reason for it.

Do not be disheartened by the fact that your budget figures were not entirely accurate; after all, they will have been based on estimates only. It is possible that the figures do not match because of simple errors in your calculations of either the forecasts or the actual figures – it may be worth checking this quickly. It is also possible that the real figures have changed because of a single one-off occurrence that has affected sales or costs but that could not realistically have been factored in to the budget, such as the effect on sales of an increase in the rate of VAT, or a flood in the stock room. This would not necessarily imply that the budget forecasts were unreliable. The most likely reason, however, is that your assumptions were inaccurate somewhere, and it is essential that you discover where so that you do not make the same mistake in the next recast budget.

The most important task when studying the variances is to reset the accounts so that you are measuring like with like. It is easy to think that all your estimates are wrong when in fact only one line has upset the process. So you must identify which are the core variables that have not met expectations and then reset your budget accordingly. To help you identify where the changes are, see Figure 8.1.

FIGURE 8.1 Variance analysis

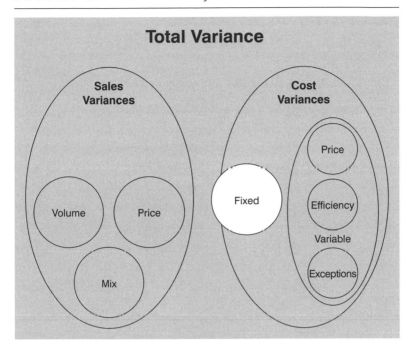

Total Variance

Sales Variances

Cost Variances

Volume

Price

Mix

Fixed

Price

Efficiency

Variable

Exceptions

Checklist

- Review your cash flow forecast frequently. Consider adding additional cost items to clarify, and extra columns to show weekly as well as monthly projections for closer control.

- Do you know the ratios currently used in your type of business to measure and/or benchmark cash management performance?

- Do you have a system that clearly shows your debtors and creditors and ages them?

- How accurately do you know your stock value and optimum levels? Can you reduce the levels without affecting your efficiency?

- Do you have a business savings account? Are you aware of how much you spend on debt interest and could gain in savings interest? Can you do anything to improve this?

continued

- Budgeting is an active management tool – do you use it properly?

- Do you compare your budgets against actual monthly results?

- Do you analyse where the variances have come from and alter forward projections accordingly?

Chapter Nine
Pricing and Costing

Cost analysis

A pound saved is a pound earned, they say; but look at how much a 1 per cent cost saving earns in an increased percentage of profit at the bottom line (see Table 9.1.) Where cash control analyses your use of cash, cost control analysis focuses on whether or not you are getting the best deal for your purchases. In reality most entrepreneurs will be very aware of their costs. While visualizing cash flows is not an intuitive skill (we have to order our information carefully to be able to build a picture of it), we all have a built-in mechanism that alerts us to whether we are getting a good deal or not or, at the very least, gives us the urge to get the best deal available.

TABLE 9.1 Cost savings

A 1 per cent saving in costs, in this example, returns a 10 per cent increase in profit.

	Before		After 1 per cent cost saving		Extra performance	
	£	per cent	£	per cent	£	per cent
Sales	10,000	100	10,000	100	–	–
Costs	9,000	90	8,900	89	–100	–1
Profit	1,000	10	1,100	11	+100	+10

Goods and services differ in quality, ease of acquisition and specifications, as well as price. The only way to ensure you are not paying over the odds is to keep yourself well informed. Read the trade press, search the internet, talk to everyone you can in the same industry, from your suppliers to your competitors to the delivery drivers. Do not forget that your own staff or colleagues may know snippets of information that you do not have.

Do not be afraid to talk to your competitors, unless you are selling exactly the same goods to exactly the same people in exactly the same way; there will be enough differences between your businesses to give you each space to make a profit. They will be encountering the same problems as you and will be as eager to hear your thoughts as you will be to learn theirs. In this way, you will build up a good knowledge of your purchasing options and should be able to benchmark your model against others.

Beyond this information-gathering method of cost control you should occasionally analyse your costs more methodically. Theoretically, you can construct a break-even chart after breaking down your costs into fixed and variable.

Break-even analysis and marginal pricing

The break-even point for a product or service is the amount of units that must be sold in order to stop making a loss on the product and start making a profit. The first step is to distinguish between 'direct costs' and 'fixed costs'. Broadly speaking, direct or variable costs are those that vary according to the volume produced or offered for sale. In a manufacturing context, they consist of labour, materials, packaging and transportation/delivery. Labour costs are sometimes regarded as fixed because permanent employees cannot be dismissed immediately without incurring further cost. You don't have that problem if you are only employing labour and staff on a casual part-time basis.

Fixed costs, on the other hand, are those that do not vary according to the activity level of your business. They include rent, council tax, utilities, salaried staff, insurance, telephone and your broadband server. If you have more than one product line, you will have to allocate fixed costs between them, typically according to volume.

Let's take a simple example as Figure 9.1.

FIGURE 9.1 Break-even calculation

Your company sells a product for £25 a unit. It has the following 'cost structure':

- variable costs £5 per unit;

- fixed costs £1,000.

In this case, if the company sells nothing at all it loses £1,000. The situation is improved by £20 for every unit the company sells. Therefore, fixed costs are completely covered when 50 units are sold. Effectively, every unit makes a 'contribution' of £20 per unit. Break-even is the point at which fixed costs are equal to the contribution from sales. The formula for calculating the break-even point is simply:

in this example:

$$\frac{\text{fixed costs}}{\text{contribution per unit}}$$

$$\frac{1,000}{20} = 50$$

If the company produces and sells 45 items, it will make a loss of £100. If it produces and sells 55, it will make a profit of £100.

The same simple formula can be applied to help you to decide whether it is more profitable to stop producing a particular product which might appear to be unprofitable, as illustrated in Figure 9.2

This approach will give you a useful understanding of the mechanics of your business, but it is difficult to do this accurately for a range of products with different costs and prices.

The same arithmetic can be applied to pricing your products or services. Contribution or marginal pricing that adds turnover without generating gross profit can add to the bottom line by covering a proportion of fixed cost. However, contribution pricing is dangerous if the result is that sales of the marginally priced product or service take sales away from the products that show a gross profit. See what happens in the example above if the sales of

FIGURE 9.2   Continuing vs closing an unprofitable product line

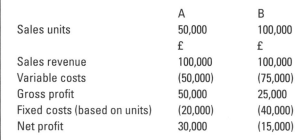

Your company markets two products, product A and product B. It shows the following result:

	A	B
Sales units	50,000	100,000
	£	£
Sales revenue	100,000	100,000
Variable costs	(50,000)	(75,000)
Gross profit	50,000	25,000
Fixed costs (based on units)	(20,000)	(40,000)
Net profit	30,000	(15,000)

At first sight, Product B is unprofitable. It only makes a gross profit of £25,000 on 100,000 units. Fixed costs are allocated on the basis of units (at £0.40 per unit), so for Product B are £40,000, resulting in a loss of £15,000. However, if we remove product B altogether and sell only product A in the same quantity the company will make a loss of £10,000 because all the fixed costs are now attributable to Product A . This is £25,000 worse than the combined result including product B. The reason for this is that the gross profit of product B contributes £25,000 to fixed cost, which would be lost.

Product A are reduced to 30,000 units and the sales of Product B are increased to 120,000 units. With a reallocation of fixed costs by volume, Product B now breaks even but Product B generates a loss of £5,000.

The cost allocation approach

An alternative approach is to work your way through the purchases and wages day books (see Chapter 11) and evaluate each cost individually, considering whether it gives you the best value available. This way you can create a costing system where you identify each element of your business as a cost object (a particular item that incurs costs) or a cost centre (a particular function that generates costs).

When you examine each cost object you will see that it may incur costs purely associated with it, such as raw materials, labour, specific machinery and running costs. The object will also have indirect costs, which are those that support the creation of the object, such as premises (where the cost is rent) or insurance. Allocating the direct costs is fairly straightforward. Allocating (or apportioning) the indirect costs is more difficult, requiring your own subjective judgement. Another method of cost allocation is to work out how much total percentage revenue each product makes, and allocate the indirect costs accordingly. However, this can be misleading, and more sophisticated methods can be used to give more accurate analysis. (For further information on the complexities of cost allocation, see *Accounting and Finance for Managers*, Kogan Page.)

Pricing and estimating

Having gained a full understanding of your costs, you will need to decide on your pricing strategy. There are a variety of approaches to doing this but, as with so much else in running your own business, there is no magic formula. The simplest methods are cost-plus and cost-times (See Table 9.2).

However, these methods do not take account of the market. Your customers do not base their purchase decision on whether or not you cover your costs. Customers choose to purchase on value for money and price comparison. Therefore, while you clearly have to be able to charge more than your direct costs at least, you also have to keep your prices at a competitive and attractive level for the market. The prices of many everyday goods and services are well known to the market, and thus your room to alter pricing is very limited; there is an accepted going rate, which you can undercut but not exceed. If your goods or services are unique or exceptional, then your room to alter prices is much greater. Economic theory provides a range of rules and equations to discover your 'price elasticity', which you may be interested to learn more about to build up a good working understanding of your business (see *Practical Financial Management*, Kogan Page, 8th edition, 2011). However, this is by no means absolutely necessary, as you will probably have a fair idea what price level your business can sustain.

To choose your pricing policy successfully you must know what your sales will be. This is clearly not information that is available before you start to sell. As such you have to estimate what level of sales you expect to achieve. Let's take a simple example of a plumber. He (we'll assume in this case it is a man) knows that his overheads for any given week are the repayments on his vehicle and its running costs, his professional indemnity insurance, his advert in the local paper and what he pays his bookkeeper. This totals £100 per week. He expects to have three jobs a day and work five days a week. That is 15 jobs a week. In pricing Scenario 1, if he charges himself out at £20 per call out and the first hour, plus £15 per hour thereafter, and each job lasts two hours on average, he can expect £35 per job, or £525 per week. He then deducts his £100 for costs, leaving him with £425 profit for the week. If he has incorrectly estimated his number of jobs or the length of time they take, then his profit looks very different (see Table 9.2). In Scenario 2, if he only averages two jobs per day of two hours each, then his week's takings fall to £350. In Scenario 3, if he still has three jobs a day but only of one hour each, then his takings will have fallen still further, to only £300, leaving him with only £200 after his overheads. In this case he would have to increase his call-out charge to £35 to return to his original takings figure, as in Scenario 4.

However, the market may not support a 75 per cent increase in call-out charges, in which case his total number of jobs may fall yet again. Of course, the plumber will also charge out the materials used in each job, and there is a limited opportunity for a profit here.

We see in this example that even where there are few variables that may affect your revenues, the impact of incorrect estimates is large and the effect on your prices therefore critical. Where you are a retailer with many items on sale and need to attract a sizeable number of customers to cover your overheads, the implications of your estimates become even more important.

TABLE 9.2 Plumber example

Scenario	1	2	3	4
No of jobs per day	3	2	3	3
Cost per call out	£20.00	£20.00	£20.00	£35.00
Extra hours	£15	£15	£0	£0
Takings per day	£105.00	£70.00	£60.00	£105.00
Takings per week	£525.00	£350.00	£300.00	£525.00
Costs per week	100	100	100	100
Profit per week	£425.00	£250.00	£200.00	£425.00

Below are a few more thoughts to be borne in mind when finalizing your pricing.

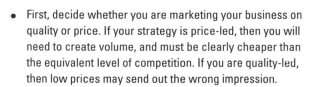

Checklist

- First, decide whether you are marketing your business on quality or price. If your strategy is price-led, then you will need to create volume, and must be clearly cheaper than the equivalent level of competition. If you are quality-led, then low prices may send out the wrong impression.

- If you are a new business and do not know your correct price level, it is easier to start high and then lower your prices than to start too low and then discover that you need to raise them.

- If you believe that your goods or services are of a high quality, do not be afraid of pricing them accordingly.

- Make sure you have fully costed all your product or service inputs before finalizing your price.

- Do you have any goods or services that you can advertise as 'loss-leaders' to attract customers to your business?

Chapter Ten
Sales and Customer Relations

Conducting sales is the pivotal moment of the business process. However, it can turn out to be incidental after all the toil and preparation that has been involved to get you to that point. As stressed throughout this guide, your likelihood of achieving a good performance in any area of business management is greatly enhanced by thinking through the process, setting your objectives and creating a plan to realize them. It is no different with sales.

In fact, building a plan is probably more important for sales than in any other area. This is not because it is a particularly complex task but because the plan will help keep you focused and committed.

Rejection, persistence and the small business factor

There are several key factors that drive the success of any sales strategy or salesperson. Foremost among them is the importance of all those involved in the act of selling being aware that they are being 'paid to be rejected'. That is the salesperson's function. The continuation of this thought is that until the salesperson has been rejected, he or she is not actually doing any selling, just offering. It is the ability to manage the rejection, turn it to advantage and be thick-skinned enough to persist after a string of rejections that marks out the good salesperson from the poor one.

Being rejected is a wearisome business, and the fear of being rejected often a considerable barrier to overcome. If the salesperson cannot view the possibility of rejection in a positive manner, then it will be very difficult for him or her to make another sales attempt, and the fear of further rejection will make the person awkward and reticent – the very factors that attract rejection. In sales, like nowhere else, success breeds success and failure begets failure.

If rejection is the salesperson's function, then persistence is his or her watchword. A salesperson who does not make another sales call cannot hope to get another sale. The statistics are well documented, that the more persistent the salesperson, the more successful he or she will be. The well-worn Pareto Rule or 80:20 ratio works well here: 80 per cent of your sales will come from 20 per cent of your customers. Furthermore, 80 per cent of your sales will come from 20 per cent of your salespeople.

This is where the small business factor comes in. If you are Unilever, then these 80:20 statistics will apply. You can afford a mass of below-average customers if you have a hard core of excellent ones. Similarly, you can cope with fewer able sales personnel if you have an elite team that are excellent. If you are a small business, then there is absolutely no room for this underperformance. You must use all your management skills to achieve the highest return possible from your sales. (Of course, Unilever do this as well and with larger resources – but their margins for error are more generous.)

Building a strategy and the sales process

Your sales strategy and your marketing strategy are inevitably closely connected, and will frequently be part of the same document. The sales strategy will be based on the same set of objectives and data from which your marketing strategy was built. The key to your sales strategy is keeping it simple. If it is too complex, then it may well become entangled and unfocused. Presuming that you have correctly identified your target market, sales success is largely based on hard work and persistence. If your strategy is simple, then following it up, consistently and persistently, will be straightforward.

If it is complex, then you are likely to lose clarity as to whom you should be following up with.

So identify your objectives. What are the key markets and timescales you are going to pursue? Set realistic targets for numbers of prospects to contact and the level of sales increase to be achieved.

You should have already identified from historical data what are likely to be your best-selling lines, who buys them and how the market's development may alter this in the months ahead. Given that you have focused your marketing in this direction, you should already have 'softened up' the reception you can hope to get when the sales force begins. For the purposes of the strategy your sales force may comprise a team of trained sales personnel or it may be just yourself. This does not alter the structure of the strategy.

You have already identified your customer profile, so targeting a list of 'prospects' should be relatively simple. Match your potential prospects as closely as possible to the ideal profile. Having assembled a prospects list, you must work out how best to attract each one. Will they all respond to similar benefits, or are some cost-led and others function-led, while others are perhaps more time or service-led? With most prospects this knowledge will only come from speaking to them; so it is now necessary to make actual contact. The earlier you do this the better – there is no advantage to be gained by prevaricating.

Arrange a meeting if at all possible; buyers will think you less opportunistic if you can plan ahead and give them some time. The arrangement can be made by letter, which is slow and impersonal; e-mail (if you can get their address), which can be more personal but also can be interpreted as lazy; or preferably by telephone. This establishes a voice contact; you can gauge reaction immediately, and if you are confident, it is most likely to gain you a meeting. The rejection will also come more swiftly, if it is going to come. Consider this as being a positive thing as you no longer need to spend time wondering.

The rejection is a sales opportunity. If it is handled correctly, very few customers will say 'no' to your parting question, 'Do you mind if I contact you again in X months?' Attached to your 'prospect list' should be a 'prospects sheet' where you note how many times you have tried to make contact, when you finally do make contact, what the reaction was, and what action is to be taken in the future. From this you will be able to determine whether there is a pattern to the sales approach. Does time of call, type of customer, or some other factor make a difference to the sales result? What are the most common reasons for rejection? Do you have a good response to these reasons? Can they be improved?

The sales plan will therefore comprise a list of objectives, a timescale, targets, and then prospects and notes on what features of your particular product or service may be attractive to them. It will also contain past 'prospect sheets' with the analysed sales data.

Motivating and rewarding the sales team

As we have noted, selling can be psychologically draining. Without some form of incentive, salespeople can quickly lose that vital edge that makes them successful. As soon as the hunger to close a sale disappears, the chances of a successful conclusion fall significantly. It is therefore critical to keep the sales team motivated and well rewarded.

Your initial task is to discover what motivates the sales force. If you do not offer sufficiently attractive rewards they will not act as good incentives. The motivational rewards do not have to be in the form of cash. It may well be that time off, travel vouchers, car parking spaces or meals out are more welcome. Offer a list of alternatives to your salespeople and let them gauge what they would like. It is often a good idea to offer different levels of reward so that there is an incentive for coming second or third, or showing certain levels of improvement, as well as for being the best.

The timescale for any motivational scheme should be clear, both at the beginning and at the end. This creates a sense of excitement and energy at both points, as the participants try to gain a good start or improve their finish. If you sense a flagging of interest during the scheme, you can re-engender enthusiasm by showing how each one is doing and offering some additional sales material to stimulate the drive.

The measurement of success must be based on easily quantifiable data that is not open to manipulation. The scheme is intended to increase total sales, so you are looking for all participants to maximize their sales. As such, percentage rates of improvement are probably better than gross sales as a measurement unit. In this way everyone starts on a relatively even basis. It is up to you to choose the best unit to suit your business, but an open discussion with the sales force before the scheme begins will give them an opportunity to put forward their views and allow them some 'ownership' of it.

Finally, it is worth making a bit of a splash about the handing out of awards. For example, if it is a regular monthly scheme you do not want to hire a room and invite guests, but it may be worth gathering everyone together to announce the distribution, or at the very least putting the results up in a staff area and so letting the month's winners get some recognition.

The risk with motivational programmes is that those who do not 'win' are disincentivized and feel themselves to be 'losers'. Clearly this is not desirable, so you must structure the scheme so that people are not made to feel stigmatized. The easiest way to do this is to ensure that there is not a small minority that gets nothing, with the majority being rewarded.

Customer service

Once you have made the sale, the next most important task is to retain the customer. There is an overwhelming argument for trying to improve your customer retention, but the principal factor is that it costs five times as much to attract a new customer as to retain an existing one. Research at Harvard Business School tells us that reducing customer defections can improve your bottom line by 25–85 per cent. The theory of how to do this is simple: make customers continue to feel cherished. The practice is often a lot harder.

Improving customer service is the major way to improve your customer retention. The more tangible factors of product price and quality, presuming they are not a long way out of line with the rest of the market, are significantly less important in retaining your customers. If the product has broken but the problem was solved quickly and without fuss, then you are likely to retain the customer. It the product breaks and the solution is drawn out and ineffective, you will surely lose the customer.

Your opportunity to offer excellent customer service comes in two phases. The first is at the point of sale. Whether your business is selling a product or a service, the efficiency with which potential customers are seen to have their various options explained, and the level of empathy and understanding for their particular needs, will be significant factors in whether they use your services or not. This clearly goes beyond the basic, but by no means always present, level of customer service that requires the salesperson to be polite, knowledgeable and enthusiastic.

If your product or service requires some degree of after-sales service, then your opportunity to offer a positive, attractive level of customer care is made easier, but the risk of failure is higher. If there is no such after-sales need, then it is very simple to let your customers disappear forever.

First, let us look at the after-sales service element. This may be because your product requires installation, periodic servicing, or more probably delivery, spare parts, refills or other consumables, or a repair. In a small business the level of customer care is assumed to be higher anyway. The cynic would say that this is because there are fewer opportunities to pass the buck. More positively, it is because the chances of the staff knowing how to deal with the problem are higher, because staff in small businesses tend to cover a variety of roles. What this analysis tells us, however, is that knowledge of the business structure and how it deals with customer problems is the first task in creating a successful service environment.

If you can create a system that deals efficiently with customer enquiries and problems, and ensure that all personnel who come into contact with customers understand the system, then you are well on your way to achieving good customer care. The system should have certain key elements:

- All enquiries should be directed to a single central point, whether that is an individual or a dedicated telephone line.

- The responsible person should be as senior as the potential time involved allows. That is, if you expect only occasional enquiries or complaints, then the owner or senior manager can deal with them. If you expect a constant stream of enquiries (hopefully not complaints), then the duty manager or equivalent may be the best qualified to deal with them.

- Promptness in all actions is always appreciated, from answering telephone calls and returning messages to providing answers and repairing faults.

- If a delay is unavoidable, then make sure the customer is notified and the reasons for the delay explained.

- Ensure that customers always know who is dealing with their enquiry and that they are provided with contact details for that person.

- Always accept responsibility when it is your fault. Passing the buck impresses no one and will not solve the problem.

- Give realistic and honest information about costs, timescales and reasons for problems.

To summarize the above, it is always advisable to keep the customer as informed as possible, and to deal honestly. Mistakes occur and, generally, customers accept that they will happen. What they will not accept is not being told what is going on, not being told the truth, and responsibility not being taken for errors.

Should your product or service not present the opportunity to have continued contact with customers, you may still be able to keep them in mind of you. If you can get their names and addresses, then occasional mail outs to inform them of your latest products or sales will be an invaluable resource.

Telesales and call centres

By far the most powerful tool in direct marketing and customer service is the telephone. While the internet has revolutionized parts of this sector and has very powerful applications in gathering usage information, it does not allow person-to-person familiarity between the business and the customer. This arm's length interaction is why the internet is great for promoting information about your products or services, as it allows a customer to make enquiries without being actively sold to. However, as we noted above, a salesperson is not really 'selling' until he or she has been told 'no'. The telephone allows you to get past this initial rejection point. It is probably for this reason that telesales have gained a bad impression in the world at large; so much so that the word is little used nowadays and the function is referred to by its location instead – call centres.

It would be a pity if the power and benefits of the telephone were to be ignored because of the poor image that telesales has conjured up over the years. Successful and non-intrusive use of telesales can be achieved and utilized within a small business environment to good effect. Indeed the very fact that you are a small business will make the negative aspects of telesales less significant. An enthusiastic and knowledgeable caller will be more appealing and convincing than a script-reading employee of a vast call centre.

Although we are all very familiar with using the telephone, using it successfully for sales and customer care functions is a skill that needs to be practised as much as any other in the sales repertoire.

Telephone sales work best in the business-to-business market. They will also produce the largest return on effort and time expended with existing or known customers. Cold calling is much harder work, your reception will be more variable, and your success rate will be lower – but at the end of the day these are the calls that provide your extra margin of profit. Cold calling for retail sales is the most difficult area of telesales, and for the small business is probably not a high priority. It requires the accumulation of a large number of leads or prospects, which can be expensive, and demands a significant allocation of time and even more skill to produce results.

Not all businesses can benefit equally from telesales. Intangible services, such as insurance or advertising space, do not require any physical inspection before purchase and so lend themselves ideally to telesales. But you should not limit your view of telesales to this kind of operation. Businesses with physical products can benefit from contacting their customers by telephone to strengthen their relationship.

Focusing on business-to-business telesales to existing customers need not be a hard-sell tactic. You can use the call to:

- Arrange a face-to-face meeting, which assures you of actually seeing someone when you arrive. This shows planning and organization, which reassures customers, and allows them to have their say when you arrive, which empowers them.

- Discuss any new products or services you have available that may be of interest, thus re-establishing your presence in customers' minds, and creating the opportunity to discover any areas on which you might be able to capitalize.

- Enquire whether customers need to reorder, so prompting them to do so.

- Let them know of any special offers you currently have available.

When making telephone calls to customers it is important to create a positive image of yourself to them. This can only be done by the sound and delivery of the voice and what you say. From this perspective, that is a lot less to work on than if you go to meet the customer in person, when your clothes, mannerisms – and even the car you arrive in – will all add to their impression of you.

It is a plain fact that conversations where neither correspondent can see the other one are more likely to be misinterpreted. It is therefore hugely important to ensure that your speech is clear, so ensure you do not speak too fast or incoherently. Make sure you are sounding animated about your subject, even if it is to arrange a meeting; so banish the monotone and try to sound as natural and relaxed as you can. If you make sure you are smiling when you speak it actually changes the way you sound. Try it.

Having mastered how you sound, it is equally important to manage what you say. Out goes jargon and waffle. Keep all relevant information easily accessible so you can answer queries quickly and accurately, and make your points straightforwardly and succinctly.

It will not be possible to acquire an expert telesales technique overnight; it requires practice and training.

If you wish to carry out a concerted telesales campaign it may be worth outsourcing the work to a call centre to help you out. They will have already made the considerable investment in equipment and technology, will have trained staff and will have access to large volumes of prospect lists should you want them.

Checklist

- Have you accepted that in order to sell you will encounter frequent rejection?

- Do you know how to motivate yourself and your sales staff to ensure they persist in going for the next prospect?

- Have you thought through your sales strategy from core objectives to the marketing details?

- How up to date is your customer profile? Has it changed? Can the product be changed to better meet your existing market?

- Do you have a clear and well-understood customer complaints procedure?

- Do you know what your competitors' customer service is like? Are you better than them?

- Do you and the rest of the sales team have good telephone skills? Is it worth investing in training to improve this?

Chapter Eleven
Bookkeeping and Administration

The basics

Bookkeeping is one of the banes of the entrepreneur's existence but, as every successful businessperson knows, it is ignored at the business's peril. It is a rare person who sets up his or her own business, with all the hard work and risks that it requires, who also actually has an appetite for the careful and meticulous recording of all the transactions the business makes.

Your tax, your VAT payments and your creditworthiness are assessed on the basis of your bookkeeping figures, and it may seem that all this toil is just for them. But it is worth bearing in mind that while you may think that the hours spent keeping your books up to date is work done for the benefit of HM Revenue & Customs so they can take their share of your profit and VAT, a more positive reason for keeping good accounts is as a management information tool. The standardized manner in which a bookkeeping system operates allows you to monitor your progress, assess your areas of strength and weakness in a measurable financial manner, and gives you a range of figures by which you can benchmark yourself against your competitors or the industry averages. These are vital statistics indeed, and while you may be irritated by the compilation of them, you should be hungry for the results and their implications. In those dark hours late at night when you are having to 'do the books', try to remember that, here anyway, while the bookkeeping journey may be tedious the destination is well worthwhile.

Before we examine the hows and whys of bookkeeping and administrative systems, it may be useful to remind ourselves of what bookkeeping is. Essentially the bookkeeper creates a system that will track every single transaction of the business: all the outgoings – the payments – and all the incomings – the receipts. At first glance this should be very straightforward, but as we shall see, the range and timings of transactions can vary greatly (pre-payments, payments on account, pro-forma invoices, credit and discounts, etc) and this instantly makes the tracking of the flow of funds much more complicated.

There are a variety of ways in which the tracking of these flows can be monitored and all will have their advantages and disadvantages. When choosing a system for your business you should endeavour to keep it as simple as possible, but retain the ability to allow the system to grow in sophistication in line with your business. While there is no point in creating a system that can happily accommodate 100 people on the payroll when there is just you working for the business, equally there is no advantage in using a system that will not allow you to add a couple of staff when the moment arrives.

All systems should have the capability to record daily takings and split them into different categories, analyse receipts and payments to your bank accounts, record and analyse miscellaneous expenditure, manage your VAT and wages bills, and draw all these figures together to give you a monthly set of accounts and a business overview. The system should also form a method for filing all the invoices and receipts. Your first real decision will be whether to use a manual (whether paper or spreadsheet-based) or commercially produced software system. If your business is a beautifully simple one (which all should aim to be if they can), such as a cook who sells his own services, or a translator who sells her freelance services to only a handful of clients, with no premises, no staff and minimal overheads, then you may well be able to manage with a manual paper-based system. By increasing the complexity of the business you increase the complexity of the system required to monitor it. If you expect to have employees (even occasional casual labour), premises with all their heating, lighting and insurance costs (whether this is your bedroom or serviced offices), and a range of suppliers and customers, then your system is already a lot more complex than the previous example. A manual system is still perfectly possible for tracking this level of business, but one of the many computer-based systems may be more cost-effective. Be aware that the software packages often also offer useful advice lines, at a price.

Although we have suggested that a commercial software system may be a more flexible and easier option, it is still well worth spending a little time understanding how a manual system operates. This will give you a feel for the figures that either system produces, and therefore put you in a better position to comprehend the options that may be suggested to you. The remainder of this chapter will show you how a manual system works, and will also point out where the computer-based system will differ.

Single-entry bookkeeping

At its most basic, you should create a single-entry cash book. Take a columned sheet and record every piece of money received (gross receipts) and every cost (payments or disbursements). The periodic totals (whether daily, weekly or monthly) should then be totalled for both receipts and payments; then you have started to create a rudimentary system that shows your cash flow.

Table 11.1 shows such a cash book, with the four left-hand columns showing the receipts and the four right-hand columns the payments, with the periodic totals at the bottom of the page. This enables the reader to better understand the cash flows in terms of both time and amount. A further level of sophistication can be achieved if the 'details' column is broken down further into subcategories, such as for the payments analysis: office expenses, travel, marketing, rent and electricity and so on. If each of these is given its own column in the ledger, then a breakdown of where the costs are coming from can easily be seen. While all this can be done on paper, clearly the use of a computer spreadsheet will allow more space and therefore detail to be noted.

TABLE 11.1 Single-entry bookkeeping example

Receipts				Payments			
Date	Name	Details	Amount (£)	Date	Name	Details	Amount (£)
1 May	Balance brought forward		540.00				
4 May	Mckays Ltd	Sales	232.33	4 May	Newmans & Co	Stock purchase	478.54
6 May	Jade Bros	Sales	88.50				
				8 May	Oldmans & Co	Stock purchase	98.65
				12 May	Tricity plc	Electricity charges	113.20
14 May	Smith & Co	Refund on returned stock	153.66				
17 May	Jade Bros	Sales	190.45				
				18 May	U-rent Ltd	Tool hire	66.66
20 May	Frasers	Sales	397.55		Roamaround Mobile phones plc		72.56
31 May	Monthly total		1602.49	31 May	Monthly total		829.61
1 June	Balance brought forward		772.88				

Bank reconciliation

The above system is single-entry bookkeeping and has no self-contained mechanism within its structure to enable you to check whether you have made any mistakes or not. The only proof of whether the books have been kept properly is if your end of month cash total matches that on your bank statement.

However, this is quite likely not to be the case, as the vagaries of the banking system and your customers' own banking habits will inevitably mean some cheques do not clear quickly, credit card transactions go awry and invoices raised do not get paid. For this reason, you must make a bank reconciliation where you check off against each month's bank statement the cheques you have written against those that have cleared, and also those you have paid in that have cleared. As time-consuming and tedious as this checking process may be, it is crucial if you are to retain any control over your cash. Once you start losing sight of which payments and which receipts have actually been cashed, you will also lose sight of your real cash position.

Double-entry bookkeeping

If what you read below is too mind-achingly complicated, tedious or both, then after discussion with your accountant it may be simpler to stick to single entry and let the accountant transfer your simple records to double-entry software to prepare the accounts. This clearly will not work for every business, and it will take your accountant longer to prepare the accounts and therefore be more costly, but it may be better than countless hours spent getting the double-entry system wrong and then having to have your accountant sort it out. Do not despair over the bookkeeping.

Double-entry is more complex but, it is a more effective bookkeeping system. This is the system that all accountants and professional bookkeepers use. It balances every flow of cash with an equal value of goods or service. Thus if you have a telephone expense of £100 you have a balancing cash credit of £100.

Immediately we have encountered the bookkeeping jargon problem of credits and debits. All is not what it seems at first with these expressions. Think of the bank as a third party between you and your suppliers and customers. The credit and debit expressions apply to your relationship with the bank. You sell some widgets and give the proceeds to the bank. The bank now owes you that money, so it is a debit. You buy something with money in your bank account. The bank pays out the money, you now have credit with the bank, so it is a credit.

While these descriptions are often confusing to interpret, the following always holds true: debits go in the left-hand column and credits always on the right. A useful rule to keep you straight is to consider all transactions as 'from–to'. Return to the telephone expense example above. The money to pay the bill comes 'from' cash and goes 'to' the telephone. 'From' is credit, so credit the cash account; 'to' is debit, so debit the telephone account.

In order to record both the entries for every transaction you need to have a 'set of books'. These will take the form of 'day books' or 'journals' and ledgers.

Day books or journals

Day books or journals are where every transaction is entered in date order. In most businesses you will have separate journals for the different types of transactions you encounter. You will have a general journal that will record all transactions in date order, and also area-specific journals that will include a cash book, sales book (for non-cash sales, ie those on account or credit) and purchases. Every book must have at least five columns: date, account, reference, debit and credit. You can have more columns to give greater detail should you wish. It is a good idea to separate your VAT amounts, if applicable, when they are first entered in the day books (see Table 11.2).

Each purchase entry should have an additional internal reference, not so much for the accounting part of the bookkeeping, as from the filing and administration aspect. All your payments are likely to have an associated invoice with a number; however, you should create a new reference for each transaction that identifies where and

TABLE 11.2 Day books

Sales Day Book

Date	Detail	Inv #	Total	VAT	Net Sales	Amt Pd	Date Pd	Chq/cash
02/03	G Goddard	223	44.66	6.65	38.01	44.66	06/04	Chq
02/03	D Fisher	224	145.76	21.71	124.05	145.76	01/04	Chq
05/03	S Pate	225	111.33	16.58	94.75	111.33	03/04	Chq
07/03	K McLeod	226	287.55	42.83	244.72	287.55	13/04	Chq
			589.30	87.77	501.53	589.30		

Purchases Day Book

Date	Detail	External ref#	Internal ref#	Total	VAT	Stock	Power	Telephone	Motor exps	Date Pd
04/05	Newmans	3325	5/1	478.54	71.27	407.27				02/06
08/05	Oldmans	4137	5/2	98.65	14.69	83.96				02/06
12/05	Tricity	2013	5/3	113.20	16.86		96.34			02/06
22/05	Roamaround	1536	5/4	72.56	10.81			61.75		15/06
23/05	Frank's Wheels	2042	5/5	310.00	46.17				263.83	15/06
				1072.95	159.80	491.23	96.34	61.75	263.83	

when it was filed for your purposes. Both the debit and credit side of the entry will carry the reference. This enables you to check your entries against the original paperwork should you need to later.

The day books will build up a mass of transactions that will enable you to analyse your cash position accurately and also gain a picture of how the cash flows operate within the business generally. However, the amount of information on any page will obscure any detailed analysis of who you are paying and who is paying you. To gain this information the information gathered in the journals needs to be re-presented as a ledger.

Ledgers

Ledgers are the same information we have noted in the journals but listed differently. You copy the entries from the journals but into account-specific ledgers, so all the telephone entries go into a telephone ledger and all the widget sales into a widget ledger. Thus you can get a picture of exactly how much you spend on different areas of the business and how your sales of different products are performing.

The copying of the different entries from the journals to the ledgers is called 'posting'. As with journals, there will be a general or 'nominal ledger' and specific ledgers for each of the major accounts.

These two are clearly quite similar. The purchases day book records all supplies for goods and services bought on credit terms. Analyse each invoice according to the type of expense and remember that when payment of the invoice is recorded in the cash book, the total amount must be entered in the 'creditors' column.

Computerized accounts

As should be clear by now, bookkeeping involves careful filing and data entry. Double-entry bookkeeping provides a safer and more detailed analysis of the current state of your business's affairs, but it involves far more entries and cross-referencing. It is precisely this time-consuming data management that computers can eradicate. If your business accounts are at all complex, it would be wise to consider using such software. Discuss with your accountant what is available and would best suit both your needs and your accountant's.

Other administrative issues

Invoicing and credit control

Invoicing is clearly a critical part of the bookkeeping paperwork. It is the source of all your sales and credit information, and has the advantage of being quick and simple to do. If you manage your invoices efficiently you should always be able to construct the debit side of your day books and ledgers correctly. Not only will your invoices record information on your sales, they will also record your VAT and your debtors.

Your invoices should give the following information: your business name, address and telephone number, and perhaps a web page or e-mail address as well. Also include your VAT registration number (if you have one) and, if you are a limited company, your company registration number. This can all be printed on the invoice. Each separate invoice will have a reference number unique to it, and the purchaser's name and address. You may also need to note down a delivery address if this is different from the invoicing address. Finally the invoice will need the date (of sale, if different from delivery) and the items purchased, with their net price, the total including VAT, and the VAT payable (see Figure 11.1). In today's world of direct transfer from bank to bank, you may wish to include your bank details as well (sort code and account number) in the 'Remittance Advice' section of your invoice stationery.

Each invoice ought to have a minimum of two but possibly three copies: one for the customer, one for the cash or sales day book, and a third for the customer ledger. If you are using a computerized system you will only need to print out the customer copy and one copy for yourself. If your hard drive is large enough to record all your sales without occasionally having to clear it out, you may not have to produce any hard copy for yourself, so long as you make sure you back up all your files regularly.

FIGURE 11.1 Sample invoice

Invoice

Bauhaus Ltd
The Quadrangle
30 Newcombe St
London, NW3 8QT

VAT # 709 5632 65

Customer #	80271
VAT #	

Invoice #	765523
Bill Date	12/08/10
Page	1 of 1

Fosters Products Ltd
76 The Square
Ascot
Berkshire, AS6 4RN

Your Ref.:

Detailed Information

Charge Description	Qty	Unit Price	Discount	Net	VAT Rate	VAT
A4 Copier paper	6	2.50		15.00	17.5%	2.63
Coloured Files	10	1.99		19.90	17.5%	3.48
Totals				34.90		6.11

Summary Information

Due Date	13/09/10

Total (Ex-VAT)	£34.90
Total VAT	£6.11
Grand Total	£41.01

REMITTANCE ADVICE

Customer #: 80271	Invoice #: 765523	Due Date: 13/09/10	Amount Due: £41.01

Bauhaus Ltd
The Quadrangle
30 Newcombe St
London, NW3 8QT

Please make cheques payable to "Bauhaus Ltd"
Please write your invoice number on the back of
your cheque

All billing enquiries to our Accounts Dept
020-7633-2445.

With this information you can fill in your sales day book (for non-cash sales) and keep track of your customers' payments. You will also manage your VAT accounts from this information. Each month you should total up the different columns in the sales day book and see that the subsidiary columns (if you have split sales into different columns for analysis purposes), plus the VAT, balance your total gross revenue for that period.

At the end of each month you should see which of your customers have not paid their invoices. You should have made clear your standard payment terms – usually 30 days – either on the invoice or in discussion with them. If you have not received payment by this time, then you will need to chase them up. Two golden rules with credit control are: one, do not be embarrassed about chasing debt. It is why you are in business, and the customers must expect to pay for what they have bought. Two, the softly, softly approach will work much better than an aggressive one. Your customers most probably have not paid because they have other priorities; a gentle reminder will put you back near the top of their list. If they have difficulty paying, an aggressive approach is no more and probably less likely to work than a friendly one. If you create a rapport with their accounts department you are in a better position than if they immediately go on the defensive when they hear from you. If they are being wilfully unhelpful the Small Business Service and Small Claims Courts are able to help you – but this should be a last resort. A good timetable to go by for credit chasing is as follows:

- issue of invoice;
- statement of account two to three weeks later;
- a gentle telephone reminder after another two to three weeks to the accounts department (at this point you can try to find out if there is any problem brewing);
- a polite letter indicating that three months have now passed since the invoice was issued, and prompt settlement is now required.

Only after this has failed is it worth considering legal action. But it is worth weighing the amount outstanding against the time, effort and expense of reclaiming it.

If customers habitually pay late (large companies often claim their settlement departments take two to three months to pay out), then you should discuss this with them if it causes you difficulty. If you are worried about any customers, then you should also suspend their credit facilities, with a clear explanation of why you are doing so. Discounts for prompt payments can help to speed the process up, and the lost revenue is often more than made up by reduced credit-chasing expenditure. Just be sure that the discounts are noted in the day books correctly.

Employee-related administration

As soon as you take on staff, even occasional casual labour, you face two separate sets of extra administration. First, there is the legal requirement to pay National Insurance and income tax for them and also offer a stakeholder pension scheme, if you have more than five employees. Second, you will need another set of day books and ledgers to account for all employee-related expenditure.

To deal with the bookkeeping side first, you will need to record all transactions related to your employees. (See Table 11.3.) Primarily, this will be each week or month, with a line against the employee's name showing his or her gross pay, the income tax due on it, the employee's contribution for National Insurance due and thus the net pay for the period. You will also have to note the employer's contribution for National Insurance.

You may also have to enter any other deductions or contributions you have made to the employee's pay. Sick pay, maternity pay, cash advances, discounts on purchases, private health care schemes, pension contributions and so on must all be accounted for.

The cheques, cash or direct transfer from your bank to employees' accounts to pay your staff will all need to be noted in the cash book or petty cash book, as will the National Insurance and PAYE contributions you send to HM Revenue & Customs. These amounts

TABLE 11.3 Wages book

June entry for A Harris, paid fortnightly.

Date	Name	Code	Gross pay	E'ees NI contb.[1]	Tax	Net pay	E'ers NI contb.[2]
07/06	A Harris	461L	811.21	63.32	130.80	617.09	74.72
21/06	A Harris	461L	753.20	57.52	116.72	578.96	67.87
			1564.41	120.84	247.52	1196.05	142.59

1. Employee's National Insurance contribution.
2. Employer's National Insurance contribution.

must all balance your entries for the period in your wages book. As with the other elements of bookkeeping, the ability to keep your records up to date and in order is critical to avoid future problems. If you are using a computerized system for your bookkeeping, then it may be wise to also use a payroll software package to make your life easier, or alternatively to use a local payroll services firm. The latter, as a third party, can also be useful in taking the heat out of any query between employee and employer over pay issues.

Your employees will require payslips with their pay each pay period. These can easily be acquired from office stationers; they will allow you to show their current pay broken down into basic pay, overtime, statutory sick or maternity pay; the total amount; the pay so far this tax year and the deductions outlined above.

The government requires you to keep certain statutory information about your employees. Each employee must have his or her own confidential file containing at least the following:

- full name;
- address;
- date of birth;
- National Insurance number;
- date of starting work;
- salary;
- position held;
- date of leaving (if relevant);
- record of absences;
- record of injuries sustained at work or illnesses (in some occupations as part of health and safety records).

You should also keep all other relevant information such as job applications, references, contract of employment, letter of employment outlining the employee's pay, hours, job title and so on, notes of any disciplinary action or discussions, and similar information.

The Department of Work and Pensions can provide you with a great deal of information relating to your obligations, rights and requirements as an employer. The Small Business Service is also worth contacting for any specific small business changes in practice. Note that it is a legal requirement to keep all your books for six years, even if you have ceased trading, after which they can be destroyed.

In summary, bookkeeping is an essential chore for any business. However, if you approach it as a management information tool that also provides the tax and company registration authorities with the information they want, then perhaps you can persuade yourself of the need for regular application to keep it up to date. There is no doubt that 'little and often' is the best way to maintain any bookkeeping system. The best system for your business is probably best decided in a discussion between you and your accountant. Bear in mind that there is a wide range of computer software that can help save you time – but that you also need to understand how the system works so you will know if the figures do not look right.

Checklist

- Have you decided what you want your administrative system for: VAT records, corporation tax and accounting purposes, invoicing, credit control, other management information-gathering purposes?

- Have you discovered whether you can manage without a computer-based system?

- Have you spoken with your accountant/tax adviser to make sure your systems meet his or her needs as well?

- Do you file invoices immediately they arrive?

- Do your business's invoices clearly state your terms?

- Do you issue invoices promptly on delivery?

- Do you issue statements promptly each month?

- Do you have a credit chasing timetable, and do you follow it?

- Do you know your statutory obligations as an employer?

- Do you keep proper records on all your employees?

Chapter Twelve
Employment and Human Relations

NATHAN DONALDSON, DWF LLP

From the moment that you move on from being a self-employed sole trader and employ your first member of staff, your business becomes subject to employment and discrimination law. The main provisions of employment law apply equally regardless of businesses' size and whether they are private or public companies. Therefore, this chapter begins with a helpful overview of employment laws and regulations before moving on to the practical business involved in engaging staff and other relevant aspects of relations.

Employment law

The law focuses on the rights of employees, and in part workers (parties who are not employees but are also not truly self-employed). Most employment rights commence from the date of employment and additional rights/protections are gained according to length of service.

Generally and increasingly the size of the employer's business is irrelevant. Discrimination and 'whistle blowing' law has made employee administration more complex and potentially more costly, particularly in the recruitment and appointment of workers. Employment regulations change quite frequently, and it is incumbent on you to keep yourself informed and to ensure that your business complies in the recruitment and administration of staff and in the termination of employment. A helpful government website (www. berr.gov.uk) provides guides to employers (and employees) on a wide range of employment issues as well as updates on the implementation of new national and European legislation.

Comprehensive guidance is also given in Barry Cushway's *The Employer's Handbook* (Kogan Page, June 2010).

In view of the scope and complexity of current UK Employment legislation, this chapter on 'Employment and Human Relations' can only set out a summary of the key issues and cannot be a substitute for taking proper legal advice.

Some recent legislation refers to 'workers' rather than 'employees': for example the Working Time Regulations, with the intention that it should also apply to other employment relationships, such as agency workers on assignment. In this chapter we shall use the word 'employee' to refer to all members of staff whom you may engage to work for your business.

Employee rights from date of engagement

- Equal pay.
- National minimum wage.
- Itemized pay statement.
- Statutory sick pay.
- Maximum 48 hours' work per week (except by choice) and 20 days' annual holiday (pro rata for part time employees).
- Non-discrimination on grounds of sex (including gender reassignment and marital status), race, disability, sexual orientation, religious/philosophical belief and age.
- Non-discrimination because of trade union membership or non-membership.
- Non-discrimination for part-time status.
- Non-discrimination for fixed-term workers.
- Ordinary maternity leave.
- Paternity leave and pay.
- Time off work with pay for antenatal care.
- Emergency time off work to care for dependants.

- Time off work with pay for Health and Safety representatives.
- Time off work with or without pay for trade union duties.
- Time off work with pay for employee representatives.
- Non-dismissal or disadvantage because of pregnancy, parental or maternity leave.
- Non-dismissal or disadvantage for asserting legal rights, whistle blowing or taking action on health and safety matters.
- Consultation about proposed collective redundancies.
- Statutory minimum period of notice.
- Application for arrears of pay, holiday pay, notice etc from secretary of state on insolvency of employer.

Employee rights after one month's employment

- Medical suspension pay.
- Guaranteed payments (short-time working).

Employee rights after two months' employment

- Written statement of employment particulars.

Employee rights after 26 weeks' employment

- Statutory maternity pay (SMP).

Employee rights after one year's employment

- The right to bring a standard claim for unfair dismissal.

Employee rights after two years' employment

- Redundancy pay.[1]
- Time off work with pay to look for work or training if under redundancy notice.

- Application for redundancy pay on insolvency of employer from Secretary of State.

Even from these lists of rules and regulations it is clear that the administration of employees becomes a time-consuming element in running your business as it expands. However compliance with the detailed provisions of employment law is not enough. Maintaining best practice in human relations to ensure that your employees are properly motivated, do their best in working for the business and stay with you requires additional attention and your personal input.

Discrimination law

Direct discrimination is usually apparent, and arises where one or more persons are treated differently or less favourably because of their sex (including gender reassignment and marital status), race, disablement, sexual orientation, religious/philosophical belief or age. The most publicized form of discrimination, which is provided for in the Equal Pay Act, is where men and women are not paid the same wage or salary for performing the same work or work of equal value – invariably to the disadvantage of the woman. There have been some recent well-publicized cases against large companies, mostly in the financial services industry, but the legal process for achieving redress is protracted and can in exceptional circumstances involve recourse to the European Court of Justice. Equal pay litigation is less common in small service businesses, where job functions are usually not shared and there is less 'comparability'.

Outside the public sector, Equal Pay Act claims are becoming less common with the recent introduction of the Equal Pay Act Questionnaire procedure that allows employees to ask their employer about the pay details of their colleagues.

However, there are other forms of discrimination to which specific laws apply:

- *Sex discrimination*: Sex Discrimination Acts 1975 and 1986.
- *Race discrimination*: Race Relations Act 1976.
- *Disablement discrimination*: Disability Discrimination Act 1995.

- *Sexual Orientation discrimination*: Sexual Orientation Regulations 2003.

- *Religious/philosophical belief discrimination*: Employment Equality (Religion or Belief) Regulations 2003.

- *Age discrimination*: The Employment Equality (Age) Regulations 2006.

It is often not appreciated that the implications of the various discrimination Acts apply to all aspects of the employment relationship, from recruitment through the employee's employment to termination. The discrimination laws also apply not just to employees but also extend to workers and independent contractors.

Recruitment

You must take care to avoid indirect as well as direct discrimination, starting with the job profile that you develop for recruitment purposes. The following are just a few of the more common examples of indirect discrimination in job specifications:

- specifying a higher level of spoken and written English than the job demands;

- excluding candidates from a location where the ethnic population is high;

- requirements on height and weight that would clearly discriminate against certain ethnic groups or women;

- age and experience requirements for professional positions that effectively rule out women returning to work after bringing up families.

Avoid any questions that might be construed as discriminatory on the grounds that they imply that factors other than ability to do the job may be taken into account, such as, 'Are you planning any children in the near future?', 'Would you want to take long holidays in *your* country?' or 'Will you have to take more time off for hospital visits?'. The only exception to the regulations on recruitment discrimination is when there is a 'genuine occupational qualification' (GOQ).

Sex discrimination GOQs

- Where the essential nature of the job calls for a man (or woman) for reasons of authenticity as an actor, entertainer or for reasons of physiology (including strength or stamina).

- Where considerations of decency or privacy require the job to be held by a man (or woman).

- Due to the fact that it is necessary for the job holder to live in premises provided by the employer, who cannot reasonably provide facilities for both sexes.

- Where the job is in a single-sex establishment for persons requiring special care, supervision or attention.

- Where personal services to individuals provided by the job holder can be provided most effectively by a man (or woman).

- Where the job is one of two to be held by a married couple.

- To provide personal services promoting the welfare or education (or similar services) of persons of the same sex.

- Where the job involves work outside the UK in a country whose laws or customs are such that the job can only be done effectively by a man (or woman).

Transsexual discrimination GOQs

Discrimination is permitted if being a man or being female is a GOQ, for reasons summarized above, provided the employer can show that the treatment is reasonable. Unlike the usual position, the GOQ defence is also available where an employer dismisses a worker.

- Where the jobholder may have to carry out intimate physical searches pursuant to statutory powers.

- Where the work is in a private home, because of social or physical contact with someone living in the home.

- Because it is necessary to live on work premises and it is not reasonable to expect the employer to make alternative arrangements or equip the premises to preserve decency or privacy. Unlike the previous two exceptions, this exception only applies where the employee intends or is in the process of undergoing gender reassignments, and does not apply once a transsexual has completed the gender reassignment.

- Where the work provides vulnerable individuals with personal welfare or other services, and in the reasonable opinion of the employer these could not be provided by a worker undergoing gender reassignment. Again this exception does not apply once the worker has completed the gender reassignment.

Race discrimination GOQs

- Jobs for reasons of authenticity in the performing arts or as an artist's or photographic model, where a person of a specific racial group is required for reasons of authenticity.
- Jobs for reasons of authenticity in restaurants or similar places where a person of a specific racial group is required for reasons of authenticity.
- Where personal services to individuals promoting their welfare can only be provided by a job holder of the same racial group.

Religious or philosophical belief, sexual orientation and age GOQs

Discrimination may be appropriate if there is a genuine and determining occupational requirement and it is proportionate to apply such a requirement. However due to the developing nature of discrimination law, it is important that you take specialist advice before attempting to apply such a requirement.

Disability discrimination

The Disability Discrimination Act 1995 (as amended) (DDA'95) ensures that disabled people gain better access to small businesses, protects disabled workers from discrimination relating to their disability, and places a mandatory obligation to consider 'reasonable adjustments' to the terms and conditions of employment to ensure that the disabled worker is not unduly prejudiced in the workplace compared with an 'able' worker.

The definition of a disabled person (S.1) is a wide and inclusive definition and therefore it may not always be apparent that a person will be considered disabled and therefore protected under the DDA'95. An employer should have reasonable procedures in place to ascertain whether a person has a disability, such as a medical questionnaire on recruitment, referral to Occupational Health where there is habitual or long-term sick leave, and so on.

As an employer you must be sure that your business does not provide less favourable treatment to disabled people in the areas of recruitment, training and promotion or within the overall working environment. You are also under a positive duty to consider reasonable adjustments to terms and conditions of employment as well as to premises to ensure that any disabled employee is not placed at a disadvantage when compared with non-disabled employees. Whenever there is a need to give consideration to reasonable adjustments, it is strongly recommended that you seek specialist advice.

Even before DDA'95, service providers were required by the DDA not to discriminate against disabled customers. Under the extended law they are now legally required to tackle physical features of their premises, such as steps or high counters, that prevent a disabled person from using their services, or to consider how they might provide their services in other ways.

Disability discrimination is an expanding and complex area of employment law. It is therefore important to seek specialist advice when dealing with disabled workers and job applicants.

Other issues involving employment or discrimination law

- *Part-time workers*: any employee who does not work as many hours as your full-time employees is classified as a part-time worker. The general rule is that part-time employees should be treated no less favourably for an unjustified reason than full-time employees; that is, they should receive the same pay and benefits on a pro rata basis.

- *Fixed-term contract workers*: these should not be treated less favourably than permanent contract workers for an unjustified reason.

- *Employment of children*: children under 14 may be employed only on 'light work'; hours of work for children aged 15 and under are legally restricted; you may not employ any child during school hours or for more than two hours on a school day or Sunday. You may not employ any child under 13.

- *Employment of overseas nationals*: all EU nationals have the right to work in the UK. Other nationals will generally need a work permit.

- *Asylum and Immigration Act 1996*: it is a criminal offence to employ persons aged 16 and over without an NI number or alternative evidence of entitlement to work in the UK.

- *Dealing with absence*: produce a policy with clear written guidelines for reporting absences, notification in the event of sickness, frequent lateness, persistent unauthorized absences and pay during absence.

- *Personnel records*: maintain personnel records and a personal file for each employee within the provisions of the Data Protection Act 1998.

- *Mergers and takeovers*: if you are thinking of acquiring the whole or part of another business or if your company is the target of a takeover or merger, be aware of the Transfer of Undertakings (Protection of Employment) Regulations 2006 (TUPE) and its likely impact. Employees generally cannot be dismissed for reasons relating to a relevant transfer or have their terms and conditions of employment varied following such a relevant transfer. Dismissal of an employee for a reason relating to a relevant transfer is automatically unfair.

There are also complex obligations to consult in good time with any staff potentially affected by the transfer before the transfer takes effect.

- *Dealing with grievances*: you are legally obliged to draw up grievance procedures in writing to be made known to all employees. When holding a hearing, allow for the employee to be accompanied by a fellow employee or trade union representative, if desired.

- *Claims to employment tribunals*: when employment is terminated, a written compromise agreement signed by the employee and endorsed by the legal adviser will prevent him or her from making a later claim to an employment tribunal. In the event of a claim, be sure to take professional advice; do not attempt to handle the proceedings in a court or tribunal yourself as this can often be a false economy.

Recruiting staff

Proper recruitment procedures are probably the most commonly overlooked aspects of employment of staff in the UK. The reasons are probably historical, as until October 1998 staff had to be continuously employed by a business for two years before they gained protection for standard unfair dismissal claims. Therefore employers could take greater risk in employing staff as they had a two-year 'loyalty period' during which to assess the suitableness of any individual employees.

However, this loyalty period was reduced to one year in October 1998 and the numbers of 'exceptional statutory claims' that require no minimum period of employment have also increased.

These changes to the legal landscape mean that proper recruitment procedures are more important than ever. If one considers our European counterparts, where the concept of 'loyalty periods' is unknown or applies in much more limited circumstances, such countries have a far greater emphasis on recruitment procedures in avoiding taking on poor employment candidates.

Deciding whether to recruit and defining the job

When starting up your own business you will aim to keep staff recruitment to a minimum, both to avoid incurring fixed overhead expense wherever possible and to avoid some of the administrative burden that the legal requirements entail. Options that may avoid or defer permanent staff engagements include:

- subcontracting certain activities;
- the use of part-time casual workers on a job or function basis, such as double-glazing installations or bookkeeping;
- sales agents paid on a commission basis;
- temporary or agency staff.

However, as your business expands you will probably require permanent staff to help you handle the workload and to develop the business further. Exceptions include those providing personal services as consultants, skilled experts or sole traders, where partnership or joint venture models may be more appropriate to your business expansion.

The first step in deciding what staff to recruit is an objective, critical assessment of your own business needs and capabilities. Self-assessment is always a difficult exercise, and it may be helpful to ask members of your family or business friends to offer their opinions. If you have started your business by working from home, your family will certainly have formed a view of your strengths and weaknesses that they will be pleased to express – although you may not be entirely comfortable with their evaluation! However, the object of the exercise is to identify the personal skills and expertise your business lacks and that a new recruit should have, to complement your strengths.

For example, if you are a good business developer – and in starting your own business you will have demonstrated your entrepreneurial outlook – but are poor at managing your own time and in delivering your service or product to schedule, then you need someone who is strong in those areas to support you in creating the time for you to provide the technical input or expertise that a project needs.

Operating a small business means that all members of staff need to have multi-function capabilities, and will probably have to take responsibility for or carry out tasks that they find tedious or would otherwise prefer not to perform. As the owner of the business, you are not excluded from this requirement, and your staff will expect you to lead by example.

Moreover, there are some functions for which you and you only should retain responsibility: in particular, the control of cash flow as well as human relations. However tiresome and time-consuming you may find the accounting function, and although the basic bookkeeping may be delegated without risk, you must engage yourself in financial planning and control of the cash flow. As we have emphasized already in Chapter 8, more young businesses founder from lack of cash flow, due either to over-trading or to failure to match expenditure revenue, than for any other reason.

There is no legal requirement for a full job description or a person specification, but both are useful for recruitment, managing performance and in determining training needs later. Therefore, you should incorporate all these considerations into the job specification that you draw up before starting to recruit.

The recruitment process

The four main methods of recruiting externally are by:

- word of mouth;
- local or national advertising;
- recruitment agencies;
- selection consultants or executive search firms ('headhunters').

In the early stages of start-up and growth, only the first three are likely to be relevant.

The first method includes the recruitment of staff from among your own acquaintances, possibly from the company you worked for previously or from a customer or supplier of your previous employer. You are trying to build a small team of multi-skilled people who are prepared to put in long hours and much effort, and are dedicated to the success of the business you have set up. Therefore, personal relationship skills will be at a premium, and it is important that all members of the team are able to work interactively and harmoniously. Someone you have worked with before, or whose work is familiar to you and whom you respect, will probably be more attractive than an unknown candidate. Again, someone who is unknown to you but recommended by a business acquaintance whose judgement you trust may be a better bet than an unknown candidate recruited through an advertisement.

If there are no word of mouth candidates or you prefer to advertise, the most suitable media will probably be the employment pages of the local press, or the trade press of the industry or profession in which your business operates. Alternatively, you might choose to advertise through a recruitment agency for a specialist skill set or more senior position, although this will also involve agency fees.

To summarize a good recruitment procedure will involve:

1 Considered wording and placement of an advertisement externally and if applicable internally within the business.

2 Thorough vetting of job applications received and applicants' CVs.

3 Provision of the job description to applicants called to interviews.

4 Comprehensive interviews; when dealing with senior individuals this process should be a minimum of a two-stage interview process.

5 Obtaining of proper references; a minimum of two references should be obtained and these should not be from friends or family of the applicant.

6 Making a conditional initial offer of employment.

Considered wording and placement of an advertisement

Ensure that you advertise the post as widely as possible and to the best tailored market possible for the role you are seeking to fulfil.

Ensure that the advertisement makes clear the ambit of the role and the type of organization the employee would be joining. If such wording is sufficiently well thought out, you will avoid misunderstanding and ideally attract only suitable candidates who will meet the demands of the business.

In designing the advertisement, the basic details to be included are:

- job title;
- location;
- brief description of the key responsibilities and duties;
- qualifications, skills and experience required;
- summary of salary and main benefits;
- how the application should be made and appropriate deadlines.

Advertisements often omit information about salary for various reasons, such as not wishing to alert other staff, uncertainty about the rate for the job, hope that the hiring can be made cheaply, or even genuine flexibility. Generally, it is a mistake not to indicate a salary range; lack of detail usually reduces the number of applicants.

Both in framing your recruitment advertisements and in interviewing, take care not to offend against provisions of the various pieces of discrimination legislation referred to above. This is not always an easy task as some commonly used phrases are now potentially discriminatory; 'enthusiastic and energetic applicant' or 'recently graduated' may for example fall foul of the age discrimination laws.

Thorough vetting of job applications received and applicants' CVs

Again it is important that you assess such details objectively. Issues to look out for would be an excessive number of previous employers for the applicant's age, any unexplained career gaps and that the applicant has appropriate qualifications/experience for the role.

When recruiting you will have to decide whether or not to use a standard application form or alternatively to ask candidates to submit a CV. When setting up your business you are less likely to be hiring senior staff, so an application form is more appropriate and more easily allows for objective vetting. You can design your application form to provide all the basic information you need, so that it can be used as a template for interviews. If you are advertising and expect a large number of responses, a structured application form will make it easier to compare applicants, and the information can be transferred readily to a database. Again avoid requesting information that could be discriminatory, such as date of birth or whether the applicant is married.

Provision of the job description to applicants called to interview

Providing a job description will generally make the interview more constructive and the applicant may be able to relate any existing experience they have to the proposed role. It will also ensure that the applicant is not under any misunderstanding about what the role requires.

Comprehensive interviews

Interviews are the best opportunity for assessing the suitableness of an applicant. It is often commented that interviewers make their minds up about an applicant in the first 60 seconds. This should be resisted as it is too subjective a basis to make a sound and reliable decision. Though 'gut feel' is important it should be supported by objective factors.

An objective structure for the interview should be prepared for all candidates, and thorough notes should be taken of the interview. This will prevent a decision being made prematurely and will also provide a helpful and *objective* measure for comparing various candidates.

The more senior the role that is being filled, the greater number of interview stages that should be included in the interview process. Also it is always helpful to involve others in the selection process, again to prevent subjective influences dominating the selection process.

Interviewing face to face is a skilled activity in which most of us are unlikely to excel without considerable experience. However, when you start to interview selected applicants for jobs in your fledgling business, you will probably have had experience of being interviewed yourself and have a fair idea of the techniques that do and don't work. The following are among the important points to consider when interviewing others:

- Make sure that enough time is set aside for each interview, that the location is suitable, away from outside noise, and that the interview is free from interruptions.

- Read all application forms or CVs and prepare questions in advance of interviews.

- Avoid any questions that might appear to be discriminatory on grounds of sex, race or disability (for example, 'Do you intend to have (more) children in the near future?' may be an important issue for you as you are seeking continuity from the staff you engage, but you must not ask the question).

- Be sure to ask open-ended questions that demand more than a 'Yes' or 'No' answer, such as:

  - What interests you about this job?

  - Describe your present job.

  - Why did you leave your last job?

  - What do you consider to be your main strengths?

  - Looking back over your career, what would you have done differently?

  - What have been the biggest problems in your current (or last) job?

  - What contribution can you make to this company?

  - How many previous employers have you had? Has your progress been up, down or steady? Is this move part of the overall employment pattern?

  - Are you willing to take a large drop in salary? Why? (There could be a perfectly good reason, but it is worth being cautious).

  - Could you telephone your employer for a reference? (Test their reaction to this request).

- Remember that the interviewee should do most of the talking. Listen carefully to the answers, try to read between the lines, and do not hesitate to probe where there is lack of clarity.

- Keep notes and, in the absence of a photograph, write a short pen-portrait of each candidate. You may find it helpful to prepare an assessment form as a scorecard, where the candidate's ability to satisfy the key attributes for the job can be rated on a three or five-point scale.

- At the end of the interview, invite the candidate to ask any questions he or she has about the job or the company, and explain what will happen next and when he/she can expect to hear the outcome.

Be careful that the job specification stays within the growing range of employment protection legislation. Many employment agencies will advise you on the dos and don'ts of these potentially contentious areas before you start interviewing candidates.

Finally you should ensure that selection or non-selection of candidates has not been contrary to the candidates' rights under the various discrimination legislation discussed above.

Obtaining proper references

Ensure that a minimum of two references are obtained from parties that are not friends or family of the applicant.

Hard copy references, addressed 'To whom it may concern', are often agreed as part of an acrimonious termination of employment and so should be more carefully considered and questioned.

Ensure that all references are obtained. Often employers do not chase an errant reference when one favourable reference has been received. If a referee fails to respond to a request, this in itself may be a point of concern. In such circumstances enquire of the employee why such reference has not been forthcoming and request details of an alternative referee.

Ensure that all referees are also contacted by phone to confirm and elaborate the details of the reference. This will prevent issues of fraud regarding the reference, and the referee may be prepared to be more candid about the employee in an 'off the record' telephone discussion.

Making an initial offer of employment conditional

Don't keep the candidates you have interviewed waiting too long for a decision. Once you have made your selection, the first step is to be in touch with the successful candidate, conduct any final negotiation on salary or other terms, and write a job offer.

You may want to consider making the initial offer of employment conditional on:

- provision of satisfactory references;
- a probationary period of employment;
- satisfactory completion of induction procedures;
- medical fitness to work.[2]

Delay writing to other interviewed but unsuccessful candidates until you have a clear acceptance from your preferred choice, but you should then write to each of them, avoiding any detailed explanation of the reasons for rejection. You may be prepared to offer a verbal explanation if you think that will help the candidate in any subsequent application, but be careful not to suggest any reasons that may infer discrimination in your choice.

As a minimum the job offer should contain:

- the title of the job;
- conditions of the offer (see above);
- definition of any probationary period;
- job location;
- details of wage or salary, payment intervals and annual review date;
- any significant benefits;
- hours of work;
- holiday entitlement;
- the starting date;
- to whom the new employee should report;
- further action (eg acceptance procedure, signing and returning a duplicate copy of the offer).

The job offer forms a part of the contract of employment with an employee, so it is important to make sure that the terms of the offer have been accepted. For this reason, it is normal to send the appointee a second copy of the job offer with a statement of acceptance at the end of the copy letter, to be signed and returned to you.

Contracts of employment

You may have noticed from the first section of this chapter on employment law that there is no legal requirement to give an employee a detailed written contract of employment, and many employers do not go further than the minimum legal obligation to provide a written statement of employment particulars after one month's employment. However, you should be aware that the absence of a written contract does not necessarily mean that no contract exists. Terms implied by the parties' conduct or agreed verbally denote a contract, even where there is no written agreement.

The following points have to be covered in the statement, and you must say if you have not covered one or other of them:

- the names of the employer and employee;
- the date when the employment began;
- the date on which the employee's period of continuous employment began (taking into account any period with a previous employer that counts towards that period).

Additionally the statement must also contain particulars (as at a specified date not more than seven days before the statement) of:

- The scale or rate of remuneration or the method of calculating it.
- The intervals at which the remuneration is payable.
- Any terms and conditions relating to hours at work.
- Any terms and conditions relating to:
  - entitlement to holidays (including public holidays) and holiday pay (the particulars being sufficient to enable the

employee to precisely calculate his or her entitlement, including to accrued holiday pay on the termination of employment);

– incapacity for work due to sickness or injury, including any provision for sick pay;

– pensions and pension schemes.

● The notice the employee is required to give and entitled to receive.

● The employee's job title or a brief description of the work he/she is employed to undertake.

● If the employment is not permanent, the period for which it is expected to continue or, if for a fixed term, the date on which it is to end.

● The employee's place of work, or if the employee is required or permitted to work at various locations an indication of that and the address of the employer.

● Any collective agreements that directly affect the termination of employment.

● Where the employee is required to work outside the UK for more than one month, the period for which he or she is to work outside the UK, the currency in which the remuneration will be payable, any additional remuneration payable and any benefits provided by reason of the requirement to work outside the UK and any terms and conditions relating to his/her return to the UK.

An employee with no principal statement could be awarded up to an extra four weeks' gross pay for this failure.

It may be that you do not feel the need for a more extensive written contract, in which case this 'principal statement', as it is commonly called, including the job offer and other additional terms, could be used as primary evidence of the nature of the relationship in the event of court or tribunal proceedings. However, the principal statement does not have contractual force unless it is signed formally as a contract by both parties. The provisions of a document given to an employee, even if receipt is acknowledged, are not conclusive.

Therefore, to remove uncertainty the simplest expedient is to convert the principal statement into a contract of employment by arranging for two copies of the statement to be signed by the employee and yourself as employer.

Updating employment contracts

It is important to update contracts to encompass new legislation and operational changes.

For such reasons it is necessary to include an express contractual clause allowing future amendments to be made to an employee's contract of employment. Amendments to an employee's contract of employment, regardless of contractual provisions, should also be carried out in consultation with the employee concerned as an employer does not have the right to unilaterally change an employee's contract, especially where the change would affect status and/or remuneration.

Termination of employment

The key to terminating employment in a small organization without incurring the risk of employment tribunal claims is to define and put in place a clear set of disciplinary procedures that follow the recommendations of ACAS (Advisory, Conciliation and Arbitration Service). Essentially, the procedures should:

- be in writing;
- comply with ACAS codes of practice (see www.acas.org.uk);
- provide for swift execution;
- indicate the disciplinary actions that might be taken and under whose authority;
- give individuals the right to be informed of the complaint against them and to state their case before decisions are taken;
- ensure that each case is carefully investigated;

- give individuals the right to be accompanied by a work colleague or a representative;
- ensure that no employee is dismissed for a first breach of discipline, unless it is gross misconduct;
- give an explanation to the individual for any penalty imposed;
- provide for the right of appeal.

However small your organization, you would be unwise to short-circuit these requirements, since employment tribunals always take into account whether the ACAS recommendations have been followed.

A distinction is made in law between poor performance/misconduct and gross misconduct. Poor performance and misconduct cover issues such as inability to carry out the primary function of the job, bad timekeeping and attendance, or inappropriate attitudes. For these you cannot dismiss without having implemented a warning procedure, and dismissal requires notice. There are also positive obligations upon an employer to set clear and ascertainable performance targets and to give consideration to training and support as part of the procedure.

Gross misconduct covers issues such as theft or fraud, threats of or actual violence, refusal to obey a reasonable instruction, fighting, causing a severe safety hazard, or breach of confidentiality code. Where gross misconduct has been 'proven' as part of a reasonable disciplinary procedure an employer may dismiss instantly without a warning, and no notice or payment in lieu of notice is required. It is a good idea to have non-exhaustive examples of gross misconduct defined within your disciplinary policy.

Where an employee's employment has been terminated, it is important to appreciate that he or she may be eligible to bring two types of claim before an employment tribunal: contractual and statutory claims.

Contractual claims are typically wrongful dismissal, usually where the employee has been dismissed without reference to or in breach of the terms of the contract of employment. However, they may also include a claim against non-payment of a contractual bonus or commission following a termination of employment.

Statutory claims are those prescribed by the various employment Acts, such as unfair dismissal, working time regulations, public interest disclosure and discrimination claims, to name but a few. As discussed, certain claims such as standard unfair dismissal claims require employees to have at least a year's continuous employment, whereas others, such as discrimination claims, require no minimum service with the employer.

Common unfair reasons for dismissal that are automatically deemed unfair include dismissals related to:

- race, sex, disability, belief, sexual orientation and age discrimination;
- trade union activity or activities as a redundancy or pension representative;
- maternity;
- 'whistle blowing' (Public Interest Disclosure 1998);
- taking action on health and safety grounds;
- anything contrary to the TUPE legislation discussed above;
- a shop worker's or betting worker's refusal to work on a Sunday.

Finally, there is the category of 'constructive dismissal', where no dismissal is carried out by the employer, but employees consider that they cannot continue in employment. It is important to appreciate that constructive dismissal is not a claim in itself, but a way in law of turning a resignation into a dismissal so that the employee is then eligible to bring a dismissal-related claim such as unfair dismissal or wrongful dismissal.

Constructive dismissal claims are notoriously difficult for an employee to successfully bring before an employment tribunal. This is due to the fact that an employee needs to establish four technicalities to turn a resignation into a 'constructive dismissal':

- The employee must show that the employer has breached their contract of employment. The breach may be of a written term of the contract and/or implied term, such as mutual trust and confidence. The breach of contract may be an actual breach or an anticipatory breach.

- The breach of contract must be a fundamental/repudiatory breach of contract. It is not sufficient to show there has been a breach of any term, the breach must be *fundamental/repudiatory*. Thus late payment of salary though a breach of contract, if the delay was short and due to administrative error, would not be a fundamental breach of contract. A fundamental breach is one that is so serious that it goes to the heart of the contract, making it unreasonable to expect the employee to continue working for the employer.

- The employee must resign as a result of such fundamental/ repudiatory breach of contract and not for some other unrelated reasons, such as a desire to change careers, move to better paid employment or personal circumstances. For such reasons the content of an employee's letter of resignation is key evidence in determining the reason for the resignation.

- Finally an employee must resign promptly after the breach, as to unreasonably delay resignation could be viewed as a waiving or acceptance of the breach by the employee.

Grounds for such a claim could involve:

- being downgraded or moved to a lower-status job;
- having a major benefit removed or salary reduction without due reason and consultation;
- being a victim of discrimination;
- being bullied continually.

In the business that you have set up and are running there should be no instances of claims for constructive dismissal. If there are, the fault is likely to be your own, and any occurrence would indicate that your objective of building a well-integrated and mutually supportive team has failed.

It should be noted that to be eligible to commence a constructive dismissal claim, employment tribunals require employees to first attempt to resolve matters through the employer's internal grievance procedures. Due to this requirement, it is going to be even harder for employees to bring successful constructive dismissal claims.

Employee benefits and incentives

It is important to appreciate that benefits to employees are usually provided in one of three ways:

- Statutory entitlements
  Such rights are bestowed on the employee by statute and can rarely be negated or waived by the employer, examples being statutory sick pay and statutory maternity pay.

- Contractual entitlements
  Those rights are conferred in the employee's contract of employment, such as a guaranteed bonus, fixed commission schemes or contractual sick pay.

- Discretionary entitlements
  These are similar to contractual benefits but the employer has the right to vary or withdraw the benefit. Though such benefits are discretionary, an employer is still under a general obligation not to exercise such discretion in varying or withdrawing benefits unreasonably or perversely.

Since you are the owner or part-owner of a young, growing business, the range of benefits you may consider offering your employees is likely to be limited. Where statutory benefits are provided (eg sick pay, maternity leave and holidays) there is no strong case for providing additions to the statutory minimum. Benefits that are granted to only one or two employees are likely to be divisive in a small company with only a handful of employees, unless there is logic for them in attracting key members of staff. For example, relocation expenses or a season ticket loan might be a necessary incentive to recruit someone from outside the area where the company is located.

When considering what if any benefits to offer to staff, it is often helpful to remember that benefits perform one of two underlying functions for an employer.

Performance-related benefits

Performance-related benefits are intended to motivate employees to improve their own or the business's performance. Therefore such benefits are often dependent on the employee or the business meeting certain performance targets. Examples of performance-related benefits are bonuses and commissions.

Retention-related benefits

Retention-related benefits are designed to reduce staff turnover. Staff turnover is costly, as much managerial time is lost in the recruitment processes, there are risks associated with taking on new personnel regarding their performance, and the business loses the training and experience of the outgoing employee. Examples of retention-related benefits are pension schemes that have loyalty periods for retention of the employer's contributions into the scheme, holiday leave entitlement that increases with length of service and medical insurance.

Some benefits, such as childcare facilities, sports and social facilities or subsidized meals, are clearly unavailable to companies that are too small to provide more than a 'no frills' working environment. The major benefits of pension, car and medical insurance all have tax implications for the employee, and are expensive additions to overheads. In particular, the company car allowances have changed irrevocably, with taxation charges on company-car drivers being set against both the car's price and linked carbon dioxide emissions. It is now common for a car allowance to be paid, rather than a car being provided to employees who need the use of a car for the effective performance of their jobs, and cars are used less than formerly as indicators of status.

If the business you have set up is heavily reliant on a small group of trusted employees, each of whom makes an individual contribution to its operations, then it may be a worthwhile expense to provide group membership of a medical insurance scheme. In the event of serious illness or the need for surgery, you will ensure that the employee gains access to quality care and attention quickly and that absence from the job is reduced to a minimum. You might consider adding death-in-service life assurance benefits in recognition for the long hours and dedication you will expect from your staff.

Pensions

Stakeholder pensions

If you have five or more employees, you are obliged to arrange access to a stakeholder pension scheme for all those who earn more than the national insurance lower earnings limit. The law does not require that you set up a scheme, only that you contact a commercial provider and pass the details to your employees. Introducing a scheme involves: choosing one or more registered stakeholder pension schemes; discussing the scheme(s) with qualifying employees; formally choosing a scheme and giving contact details of the provider to your employees; arranging to deduct contributions from the pay of those employees who choose to contribute through you; and sending any employer and employee contributions to the pension scheme provider within the set time limits. Details on stakeholder pension schemes are available from the Pensions Regulator (www.thepensionsregulator.gov.uk).

Incentives

While you are in the early stages of building up your business, you may be unwilling to commit yourself to any form of formal profit sharing scheme whereby the employees are awarded a proportion of net profits, perhaps above a predetermined level or in proportion to salaries. However, cash incentives, although subject to income tax deductions, are probably the most effective form of incentive. Certainly at such stage of a business any benefits should be made discretionary, in case they become financial unsustainable for the business.

The traditional Christmas or year-end bonus has the merit of putting cash into employees' hands at a time of high family expenditure, but has the disadvantage through repetition of becoming a benefit expected 'as of right' and therefore an element of basic remuneration. Regular salary reviews are preferable, since increases may be performance-related and therefore the incentive rewards are directed to those who are contributing most to the business.

Human relations

For smaller companies, 'human relations' may seem no more than a fancy title for day-to-day management of staff, with the staff administration function covering most of the matters referred to in the employment sections of this chapter. As your business grows you may be able to delegate most of this administrative detail but it will be some time before you will want or be able to afford a full-time human relations (HR) manager focused on career development and training, staff communication and assessment, human resource planning and other HR disciplines. Until that time you will retain the responsibility for what, in a bygone age, used to be called 'man management'.

However, there are lessons to be learnt from HR best practice that you can apply with advantage from the earliest phases of your business development:

- *Communication*: make a point of communicating freely with your staff, both informally on a daily basis and through monthly staff meetings. Install a bulletin board. Be sure to keep them informed of major events – the arrival of a big order or the loss of a major customer (the bad news as well as the good). Their livelihood depends on the success of the business and they have the right to know when it is doing well or badly. Of course, you are not going to make an announcement when the bank manager tells you to reduce the overdraft, but you can give them a general indication each month of how the business is doing. Failures and successes in customer relations and past product or service deliveries can be reported too. As in most relationships, the secret to success is keeping the lines of communications open.

- *Training*: you want your staff to improve their skills and competencies to support the growth of the business. It is up to you to identify where they are deficient and where their particular aptitudes lie. Encourage them – and pay for them – to enrol on courses that you select with them and that don't take them away from the day job too much. Day-release schemes and evening classes will be available locally in a multitude of skills. Help them to gain qualifications. Today, distance learning is available in most management disciplines, both through study guides and online. This kind of education is cost-effective, both in minimizing loss of work time and in the use of content and a delivery method that can be used again by other staff members. Reward attainments with increased responsibility or, where appropriate, promotion. For a business, it is a normal process to invest in premises and technology, yet we often neglect investment in what is every business's key asset – people!

- *Performance reviews*: all staff are entitled to an annual review. Use this as an opportunity to assess performance against pre-established objectives. Involve each staff member in procedures for past performance assessment and in setting attainment targets for the following period. Use performance reviews as a basis for the merit element in salary increases.

- *Standards of practice*: however small your organization, it is big enough to adopt best practice standards in business ethics, customer care, supplier and staff relations and corporate governance. Articulate your standards simply in a mission statement and a company code of practice to which all staff are required to conform.

So long as your business remains under your personal management and control, the driving force will reside in your leadership. This means that your behaviour must at all times embody the company's code of practice, and you will be judged by your treatment of and relationships with all who work for you. In many ways the responsibility is awesome, and goes way beyond the exercise of human relations skills. You will be regarded as 'the barometer' of the company's condition; your staff will tolerate some degree of personal idiosyncrasy, but their confidence, enthusiasm, optimism and calmness in crisis will be a reflection of yours.

It would be encouraging to look forward to an easier time when your business has grown, you are supported by a competent management team, and your primary role is to manage them rather than the workforce individually. That time may well come, but your human relations role will be no less demanding. Managing more remotely through departmental heads requires a further set of people skills that may be outside your experience. And your staff will continue to consult the barometer on the wall.

Checklist

- Most employee rights run from the date of engagement. Others accrue with length of service. Be conversant with basic employment law and ensure that you have ready access to a competent employment law adviser for the more complex or atypical situations.

- Employment recruitment is subject to the laws of discrimination regarding sex, race, disability, sexual orientation, religious/ philosophical belief or age. The only exceptions to such rules are the 'genuine occupational qualifications' (GOQs).

- Part-time employees should be treated no less favourably for an unjustified reason than full-time employees. Be aware of special rules governing employment of offenders, children and overseas nationals.

- Fixed-term workers should be treated no less favourably for an unjustified reason than full-time employees.

- Draw up grievance procedures, and guidelines for notification and treatment of absences, to be made known to all employees.

- Ensure that you have written disciplinary procedures that comply with statutory standards and ACAS codes of practice. Such procedures will minimize the risk of successful employment tribunal claims by dismissed employees.

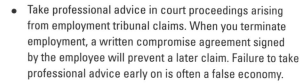

continued

- Take professional advice in court proceedings arising from employment tribunal claims. When you terminate employment, a written compromise agreement signed by the employee will prevent a later claim. Failure to take professional advice early on is often a false economy.

- In the early stages of your business keep staff recruitment to a minimum. When advertising for a position, state basic details including a salary indicator.

- Use a standard application form when you expect a heavy advertisement response. When interviewing, be sure to ask many open-ended questions demanding more than a 'Yes' or 'No' answer.

- A job offer forms part of the contract of employment. Include most of the employment particulars (principal statement) required by law for all employees after one month's service. Require the employee to sign a copy of the job offer. Have the complete principal statement signed formally as a contract by both parties. An additional, more formal contract is not usually necessary. Make an initial offer conditional.

- Keep benefits to a minimum in the early stages (maybe medical and death in service insurance), and consider making any benefits discretionary at first. Limit pension activity to statutory minimum stakeholder pensions.

- Profit-related incentives are preferable to bonuses, which can become taken for granted benefits. Delay option schemes and share ownership plans until your business matures and the future shape of your company becomes clearer.

Notes

1 For a claim of unfair dismissal by reason of redundancy an employee only needs one year's continuous service, though two years' employment is needed to qualify for a statutory redundancy payment.

2 Where the applicant is a disabled person within the meaning of the Disability Discrimination Act 1995, consideration would have to be given to reasonable adjustments to enable the applicant to undertake the role.

LEEDS   LIVERPOOL   LONDON   MANCHESTER   PRESTON

People Management...

Successful business owners often say that people are their company's most important asset; that it is the strength of their workforce that will carry the company through tough times, but will also best exploit the good times. Managing people is a business skill in itself and its importance is growing as a result of the increasing national and European legislation governing employee relations. It is crucial to have specialist legal advice to guide you through the business processes and ensure that developments are delivered in a timely and cost-effective way to your workforce.

DWF LLP is a values led firm. Our People team are experts in all key aspects of human resources issues. With experts in employment, pensions, immigration and employee benefits, we provide clear and commercial advice for your business. We also provide specialist training.

...made easier

www.dwf.co.uk

Professional. Legal. People.

For more information on employment law issues visit our website www.dwf.co.uk or contact **Nathan Donaldson** (author of the chapter on The Legal Ground Rules of HR Management) at nathan.donaldson@dwf.co.uk or call **+44 (0)20 7645 9555.**

DWF LLP is a limited liability partnership registered in England and Wales with registered number OC328794 Ref. 0913a

With over 1,000 titles in printed and digital format, **Kogan Page** offers affordable, sound business advice

www.**koganpage**.com

You are reading one of the thousands of books published by **Kogan Page**. As Europe's leading independent business book publishers **Kogan Page** has always sought to provide up-to-the-minute books that offer practical guidance at affordable prices.

KoganPage

Chapter Thirteen
Conventional
Marketing

There is much confusion about marketing. This stems from two sources. First, the definition of 'marketing' needs to be clarified. And second, the amount of resources a small business should allocate to it needs to be addressed.

The definition issue is simple to deal with. To marketing professionals and academics, marketing can be summed up as 'making what you can sell'. To the public it is more usually thought of as 'selling what you can make'. If you are to run a successful business, the first definition is the better one to be guided by, and so a more holistic approach is necessary, involving what those in the trade refer to as the 'four Ps': product, price, place and promotion. To these the public relations industry adds a fifth 'P': perception.

The amount of resources you can or should allocate to marketing is much more subjective. There is no empirical test to tell you what you must spend in time or money in order to achieve any specific level of return. The marketing industry, in all its many forms from advertising salespeople and trade show organizers to copywriters and PR agents, will make cogent arguments for the necessity of using its services. And being salespeople they will often make you worry that you will be left behind if you do not use them. The bottom line should never be 'Can you afford not to?', but always 'Will the marketing return justify the costs?' No doubt everyone would like to take full-page colour spreads in the weekend supplements backed up by television and billboard campaigns, but clearly that is not an option to those on a limited budget. This chapter will try to indicate some of the options available to those on a small business budget.

More about market research

Your marketing process should begin long before you start trading your new product. This applies as much to Microsoft's latest software as to the new hairdressing salon on the high street. They must both establish whether there is a market demand for a new product and what exactly the demand is for: they must conduct market research. The difference is that Microsoft has rather larger marketing resources than the hairdresser.

Established businesses have a huge advantage over start-up businesses in carrying out market research. They have an enormous exposure to market sentiment and reaction every day through their current business activities. Added to this is their database of past and current customers that they ought to be able to analyse and, should they wish, use to contact for views and opinions. This information can also form the basis for extrapolating their current data to build up likely market information for different geographic areas or market sectors.

The brand-new start-up company is unlikely to have any of these resources readily available to it, and while discussion among like-minded competitors is often a lot more open than you might expect, you will not be handed databases and customer views by your future competition! As such, the prospective entrepreneur must try to build a picture of what the market for the intended product or idea is currently like, and whether there is sufficient demand for the concept with its benefits.

This can be done by collecting either brand-new data direct from the marketplace specifically for your own purposes (primary data) or data already gathered by others that you can shape for your own use (secondary data). Obviously primary data will be more relevant and more current, and you can assess how reliable it will be as you will know how it was collected and collated. (Study Chapter 2 again if you decide to go the field research route for primary data.)

Secondary data may well require you to make some assumptions as to how and where it was gathered and how reliable it is; it may be slightly out of date, and it is also likely to be only partially about the information you require. However, it will be vastly cheaper to acquire. In today's economy there is no shortage of information available.

The trick is to sift the wheat from the chaff. Identifying the correct questions to ask is important. You must think carefully what factors you need to sell your product or service successfully. These will include the profile of your potential customers (age, spending power, where they live, family status, gender), a profile of the market (whether it is growing or shrinking, which sectors of the market are doing best and why, the long-term trend), and some marketing research (what your competitors are doing to sell their products, what is working and what is not).

If you intend to sell locally, then your market research can be done more on a primary than on a secondary basis. You can go out and speak to potential customers; you can observe the competition. The more widespread your potential customer base, the more difficult it will be for you to track customers down and have a useful dialogue with them. If it is very broad, secondary data collection will become more important, and it will be your only option for tracking sector trends.

There is a range of sources of secondary data. Among others:

- Trade magazines and financial press will offer some information but probably unsystematically – that is, it will be pot luck what you find.

- The information you seek will most likely be somewhere on the internet, but sourcing can be difficult, and it is often difficult to assess its reliability and how up to date it is.

- Larger libraries will have a range of market research books that can give you useful information.

- In addition to these sources you may find that your local authority business advice unit will have current information available to you, as will the local Chamber of Commerce and Business Link.

Most of these sources of information will be either free or inexpensive to access. If you still require more information, you can purchase market information from market research and business information companies. The British Market Research Association will be able to provide a list: visit www.bmra.org.uk.

Segmentation and strategy

Having gathered the relevant market information for your concept's sector, your next marketing task is to identify where exactly your product or service fits within the field. The most basic division is whether you want to sell to businesses or consumers. Consumers are more numerous and normally will pay higher prices, but they are more difficult to reach (they do not list themselves as companies in trade directories, magazines or the *Yellow Pages* with contact names and numbers), more fickle (most companies will not change their suppliers just because a new one comes around), and purchase in smaller quantities less regularly.

As a small business you will need to focus on specific segments of the market, as you will be unable to offer all things to all comers. Are you going for high-end users who are willing to pay for quality and/or uniqueness, or are you trying to provide a service locally where none currently exists? What is your 'unique selling proposition', or USP in marketing jargon, which differentiates you from the competition?

With your sector knowledge and your segment identified, you must now design your marketing strategy and thence plan. The information you have gained will indicate what is the best way to reach your potential customers:

- trade magazines;
- local press;
- national press;
- radio;
- bus advertising;

- promotions;
- trade shows;
- leafleting;
- direct mail;
- inserts.

You will have an idea of how generous or frugal your marketing budget can be, so you will have a feel for how much advertising and PR you will be able to afford. The research you have carried out up to this point in identifying your gap in the market, who you should be selling to and what in particular it is they want, will provide a clear indication as to what type of media you should be using.

If your target market is well-paid young individuals who purchase goods for their image and lifestyle associations rather than pure value for money, then your advertising must be in media that project image and lifestyle. While this is obvious from the unpressurized standpoint of writing the business plan, when you are in the thick of trying to get some media exposure you can easily start to lose control of the original plan. Even the smallest business will be approached occasionally by sales departments wanting it to spend its money on promotion in their publications, on their products or at their shows. It is for this reason that it is very important to design a clear marketing strategy that you can refer to and keep as a controlling influence over the media offers that will come your way. Amend and update the strategy as an ongoing project certainly, but in your own time, not because someone else tells you to!

The strategy you build is like a road map: it will show you where you are and where you want to get to. It will also show the preferred route for getting there, and the most comprehensive strategies will also be able to show you how to get back on track if you lose your way or are deflected by events beyond your control. The first task is to set your targets – where you want to go – whether that is to increase sales by 15 per cent or open a new outlet. Then plan a timetable of marketing 'events': these can be any marketing action, such as a press release, placing adverts, leafleting the local area, a trade show or whatever you choose. All will be chosen because they reach out specifically to your target market, and you believe they will bring in more in sales revenue than they cost.

Critical to all these 'events' is the evaluation process that you must go through after each one of them. Especially for a new business where the response to any event is fairly unpredictable, it is vital to know which types work and then work out why. The simplest way to track the success of events is to note down all responses you get from potential customers from the event and how many positive sales it leads to. It is very easy not to ask customers enquiring about your product where they heard about you, but it is also very foolish. Nobody will mind being asked; it gives an impression of a well-organized company and, vitally, it provides you with critical information on which to base future marketing events.

Image

Part of the marketing function is to build your business's and product's image. As a small business you will have very limited resources to commit to this area of marketing. You should be focusing your product trading on a homogeneous sector of the market, and your goal should be to present as coherent an image of your business as possible, across all its aspects. Essentially, all companies do this. If we look at the Ford Motor Company, their Ford branded cars are placed so as to be attractive and affordable to the mass market, but Ford also used to own Jaguar and Aston Martin, executive and super-luxury cars, which it kept very distinct from the Ford name in its marketing, although it was well known that many components were shared between the different cars in the group range.

It is therefore important to consider the impact that every marketing event you undertake will have on your entire range of goods, not just the single item you are promoting. The quality of the material used in your advertising or promotion will underscore the message you want to get across. That your business's reputation takes years to build but can be destroyed in moments is no less true for being a well-worn cliché.

Direct mail

Direct mail is often considered to be the black sheep of the marketing toolbox. However, it is really a victim of its own success. If the response rate to direct mail was not so high, in terms of cost to increased sales, then it would not be as prevalent as it is currently. It is this prevalence that leads to the problem of 'junk mail' piling up behind your door every morning.

The advantage of direct mail to the marketer is that it is very flexible. You can choose your recipients' geographic area, their income level, their leisure preferences and so on. You can also choose how much you wish to spend on any given mailout with great flexibility. The drawbacks are in choosing whom the mailout should be sent to, the expense and the legal implications.

For the start-up business, purchasing a list can be relatively expensive, and also requires a degree of specialist knowledge in selecting your list broker and the criteria by which the particular list is built up. It is worth researching the use of direct marketing carefully if you intend to spend a significant percentage of your marketing budget on it. The British Direct Marketing Association (www.dma. org.uk and 020 7291 3300) can provide much useful information.

If your business is well established you are likely to have built up a database of past customers' details. If your business is not of the type where you collect your customers' details as a matter of course, it is worth considering methods by which you might be able to gather such information through a loyalty card, notification of sales offers or similar schemes. When you have a list of customers you are in a position where not only can you re-contact them, but you may be able to trade your list with other companies in your area. However, there are increasingly strict data protection laws governing notification of customers (at the time of taking their details) if you wish to share their details, in any way, with other bodies. Again the DMA can guide you with this.

The use of e-mail as a direct marketing tool has already been discussed in Chapter 7.

Advertising and PR

It should be so simple to get your message across. You know your product or service inside out, you understand the benefits and you recognize the quality. What is more frustrating is you also know that people will enjoy using your product – all you have to do is persuade them to try it. And that is the problem.

The situation is difficult because all your competitors are trying to gain the consumers' attention as well. There is a lot of 'noise' out there in the marketplace and your job is to make sure you are heard above everyone else. Advertising and PR are your routes to doing this, but be aware that the market in the UK is very sophisticated and it will take a fair amount of expertise to make your business stand out. This chapter is not able to cover the vast range of skills and advice needed to ensure that your advert or press release is eye-catching, but the basic principles are simple enough, although the details are where the difference is made:

- ABC – accuracy, brevity, clarity – make good copy.

- Avoid jargon and formality.

- Never bend the truth (this includes phrases like 'once in a lifetime chance' if it is not); it cheapens the message and damages your reputation.

- Keep it interesting and relevant (if you are writing a press release, open with an idea that will work as a headline).

The ability to write good adverts and press releases is gained more through experience than natural skill. If you have the time to learn about it, then it will be time well spent; if not, it may well pay you to find an expert to help you out. If you have any contacts in the media, they may be able to help draft the copy for you and show you what makes the difference. If this route is not available and you feel your attempts with only a book to help you are uninspiring, then it may be time to seek professional help – the PR agent.

Advertising agencies

You might expect that typical advertising agency fees will be up to 17.5 per cent of your advertising budget. However, agencies can usually negotiate discounts with the media, and these will reduce the cost of insertions by 10 to 15 per cent.

When preparing an advertising budget, make sure that you have calculated the total costs of your campaign. Advertising will not be effective unless it is backed up with brochures, adequate stock levels, trained response staff and the overall ability to deliver the promise of the advertisement. In addition to the cost of the advertising space, the budget should therefore provide for design costs, print preparation, sales literature and fulfilment costs.

As a general guide, consider using an advertising agency if you plan to spend more than £10,000 on advertising, and make sure that the agency you select passes on media-buying discounts to you. Look for an agency that has direct experience of your type of business. An agency that also deals in PR may help to keep your overall promotional costs within budget. Most of your sales advertising can be monitored quite simply by direct means:

- using coded advertisements;
- asking enquirers to quote the code when they respond to your ad;
- using reply coupons;
- using readers' reply sections in trade journals where appropriate;
- always asking new enquirers how they heard about your business.

Advertising that generates a large number of enquiries that do not convert into sales will result in a very high cost per sale. If your conversion ratio is poor, analyse what is going wrong. Perhaps your prices are unsuitable for the target market; check that the employees who are handling the response are sufficiently trained; review your sales literature to make sure that it provides enough information and lives up to the promise of the advertisement (or vice versa).

PR agencies

The problem with PR agencies is that you have to pay them! That in itself is not surprising, but quantifying their success is awkward. Most agencies will be keen to get you on a monthly retainer. If your marketing budget can afford this, then it will probably be worthwhile to sign up to a limited-term contract, as you will then be able to set out exactly what you expect the agency to provide, over what time period, and discuss with it what it hopes to achieve in this period in terms of copy placed or extra sales achieved.

The advantage of PR agencies, beyond their ability to write successful copy, is that they should have a good selection of media contacts through which they can get your message heard. Your business is to produce and sell a successful product; often this will not give you much space to build relationships with the media, and your PR agent is there to overcome this barrier. PR agents' businesses are based on their ability to get their clients' messages into the media, be it the local press, national press, radio or any other medium that works, through an established network of contacts.

In choosing an agent or agency you must therefore make sure of a number of key points:

- The most important is that you trust the agency. This means that you should get hold of references from their existing clients and see what the agency has done for them.

- You should also feel completely comfortable working with the agency. Do you have a rapport? Does it understand your business implicitly? Does it have time for your business? How quickly do staff return your initial calls?

- Beyond your relationship with the agency staff, you need to know how effective they are. What are their copywriting skills like? Not all are as good as each other by any means. What are their media contacts like, especially in the area of the media you are interested in?

- Get a limited-term contract written up that sets out your requirements and budget. Alternatively, you might want to restrict your commitment to a single event, such as the launch of your business.

- Keep a very tight rein on costs – often the retainer fee will be small, while the 'extras' can mount up quickly.

Towards the end of the limited-term contract (you may need six months before any real progress can be judged), evaluate what difference to your profit margins the PR agency has made. If you feel that it is negligible, then discuss this with the agency and, if you are not satisfied, close the account.

Damage limitation

An area often overlooked in small businesses is a damage limitation or crisis management plan. PR agents should be good at helping develop these, but they are essentially straightforward and you should be able to create a plan yourself.

No business wants a crisis, but inevitably these crises will occur from time to time, in varying degrees of severity. If you have taken time to consider what is best to do in various disaster scenarios before they occur, you will be very much better placed to deal with them should the scenario become reality. Not only will the plan give you a clear idea of how to progress, but its very existence should reassure you and give a sense of calm.

Crisis management falls into two parts. The first is how to deal with the practical side of the problem, whether it is power or machine failure that stops production, transport problems that prevent distribution to customers, accident or injury to personnel or – perhaps the most business-critical – a problem with the product that causes illness, injury or significant financial problems to the customer. Your plan will identify each different scenario and then follow it through certain stages: action to stop further damage and action to restore service.

The second element is the communications side. There should be clear procedures to inform your customers what the problem is, how long it will continue, what measures are being taken to rectify it, and what measures are being taken to ensure it does not occur again. With health and safety issues you will also need procedures to notify relatives of injury or, heaven forbid, fatality.

You will also need to have a plan for dealing with the press. From a marketing point of view, this is where the plan comes into its own. The reputation of your business will rely on a single coherent message being put out about the crisis. A single senior person, essentially the owner or chairperson, should be the spokesperson. That individual should unambiguously give out all the known facts, avoid any conjecture, indicate how the problem is being contained, and ensure that any essential safety information is clearly provided. The silver lining to crises is that the media attention can be turned to the business's advantage if it is correctly handled. The eradication of panic and chaotic reaction will go a long way to doing this. It is very clear in retrospect that BP's damage limitation plans (either for the physical disaster or the impact on its image) for the Gulf of Mexico oil spill in 2010 may have left something to be desired.

The internet

We have already discussed website marketing and e-commerce in Chapter 7 in some detail, and there is nothing to add here. Indeed, that is why this chapter is titled 'Conventional Marketing'.

Trade shows and exhibitions

Trade fairs and exhibitions are great opportunities to showcase your business and increase your sales, but like all other parts of the marketing equation you have to know why you are there and what you want to get out of the event. Just turning up and 'being there' will be an unrewarding experience. Therefore you must go through the – now hopefully familiar – routine of asking yourself what your objectives are from being at a trade fair. They might be to launch a new product, heighten your profile in a particular geographic area or increase sales to a specialist sector. Evaluate a realistic target for the exhibition: get 200 new potential customer names, sell £10,000 of product, get a profile in the local press, and so on.

Having identified your specific objectives, you will find it much easier to decide whether or not the trade fair is appropriate. Ask for the media pack from the organizers to see who is going to be there, where they are from and what you can expect them to spend. Time and money invested in an unsuccessful trade show can easily be avoided by a little research at this point.

Once at the exhibition hall, as with other advertising, you must make yourself stand out from the crowd. A little money invested in bright and clear display materials will pay dividends quickly if the alternative is an amateurish look. Probably the most important task is to make sure that your staff are enthusiastic and knowledgeable. An upbeat and animated person on the stand will be more successful than a bored and embarrassed person, regardless of the product or quality of display materials.

The post-exhibition follow-up is vital. Throughout your marketing process, any lead that is not followed up is a lost lead, and therefore money wasted. With trade shows you should plan your follow-up procedure before you go to the show, so that you can get it dealt with swiftly afterwards. This avoids the risk that you delay it too long so that it never happens or happens too late, and also ensures that your follow-up, whether it be an enquiry form or telephone call, gets to the customer before anyone else's.

Finally, ask yourself the questions: what did I get out of it? Did I get value for money? Was the journey really necessary?

Checklist

- Do you 'make what you can sell' or try to 'sell what you can make'?

- How carefully do you collect and analyse your sales data?

- What are the key research objectives you need to answer? Have you carried out any primary research? How objective have you made it?

- What is your ideal customer profile? Does it exist in your area?

- Have you clearly identified your USP? What sort of potential market does this direct you to? Does it exist in your area?

- Have you considered all potential markets in your area? Are you going for the most accessible and/or lucrative? If not, are you happy why this is the case?

- How can you best reach your customers? Do you have any experience with this form of media? Do you know how best to utilize it?

- Are you confident your cost of marketing for any event is less than its minimum likely return? If not, do you know why you are spending money on it?

- Does your product or service lend itself to direct marketing? If not, are you sure there is not an angle you are missing?

- Consider using an advertising agency if you plan to spend more than £10,000 on advertising.

- Have you considered investing in a PR agent? If so, do you have a mutually agreed list of targets and a timetable to achieve them by?

- Be careful to evaluate the benefits of taking space at trade exhibitions before committing to the expense.

Chapter Fourteen
Purchasing Guidelines

More attention is given in most books about managing small businesses to sales and marketing than to purchasing and procurement, and this book is no exception. However, as the reverse side of the commercial coin at the heart of your business operation, the procurement and purchasing function merits similar if not equal attention.

When starting up in business you will probably act as purchasing officer yourself; certainly, you will not want to delegate authority to commit the business financially to an employee until you have established a formal purchasing function within the business. This will mean that you select products and suppliers, negotiate the terms and sign the orders in the early start-up phases. Initially, the task may not seem too onerous; unless your business is in manufacturing or retailing, daily purchasing requirements will be quite modest, related to office consumables, except for the setting-up phase when you will be procuring more expensive capital items – office equipment, furniture and maybe vehicles – and entering into contracts for insurance, telephone and cleaning services, and the supply of utilities.

Even at this stage, it is important that you distinguish between procurement and purchasing activity. Procurement encompasses the setting of specifications that you require products and suppliers to meet, selection of shortlisted suppliers against specifications, and negotiation of purchase and supply terms, from prices and minimum order value to payment and credit terms, and from delivery times to returns procedures. Purchasing is the more mundane activity of placing orders against agreed terms from approved suppliers on a timely basis, progress chasing of undelivered products, rejection and return of sub-specification products, and approval of invoices for payment.

As the business grows you will be able to set purchasing guidelines and to delegate the clerical purchasing duties with confidence, but it will be some time before you will feel able to delegate the decision-making procurement role.

Civil law and the purchase of goods

Civil law lays down quite clearly your rights as a purchaser and seller, which are the same as those of your customers and suppliers. Most activity in business, as well as our personal commercial relationships in the community, is governed by civil law. Aside from employment law, which is covered in some detail in Chapter 12, only two aspects of civil law – contract and tort – will concern you most of the time in running your business.

Contract law

Breach of contract arises when one party to a contract fails to perform the obligations it has undertaken. In the context of purchasing, your supplier is in breach of contract if it fails to supply the product or service you have ordered to specification and within the agreed delivery time. In such circumstances you have a claim against your supplier for the damages or cost that you have incurred through their failure to supply you to your contract, which may include the cost of any claims your customers may have against you for your failure to perform your contracts with them as a result of your supplier's failure. In practice, most claims of this kind are settled between the parties for a lesser sum than the original claim without a court action; neither party will want to incur the costs of litigation, which often represent a substantial proportion of the value of the claim.

Contracts between purchasers and suppliers of goods and services can be verbal or embodied in a formal legal agreement. The latter is more common in the case of contracts to provide services, such as the design and installation of computer software or an outsourcing contract to provide facilities management. In the case of orders placed to provide a tangible product, it is more common for the parties to rely on their standard terms and conditions of purchase and sale, which are typically listed in the small print on the reverse side of offer documents and acceptance forms. The main purpose of small print terms and conditions in a vendor's offer document is to limit the liabilities of the seller and to reject responsibility for consequential loss. We will discuss the issues of what constitutes a contract and standard conditions of buying and selling later in this chapter.

Tort

First, the second element of civil law that may impact your business is the law of tort (French for 'wrong'). Tort actions arise from the commission of any of the following civil wrongs:

- *Conversion*: selling stolen goods, even if purchased innocently.

- *Defamation*: damaging a competitor's, supplier's or former employee's reputation.

- *False imprisonment*: for example, detaining on suspicion of theft a visitor or employee who is later acquitted.

- *Negligence*: failure to repair damaged equipment or buildings and their fittings that results in accidents to staff, customers, suppliers or any other third party.

- *Nuisance*: such as making noise or smells or blocking access to neighbours' premises.

- *Passing off*: maintaining that products were made by someone other than their manufacturer.

- *Trespass*: entering property without authority or invitation.

The form of tort that businesspeople meet most often is negligence. Third-party personal accidents may be covered by an employer's liability insurance, but the policy could be nullified in the event of negligence on the part of an employee. Accidents due to negligence are also likely to give rise to prosecution by the Health and Safety Executive for breach of the laws requiring you to provide safe working conditions.

Contract essentials

There are three necessary elements for a contract to be in force:

- offer of goods or service from the vendor;
- acceptance by the purchaser;
- consideration – a payment of some kind, not necessarily money, in exchange for the goods or service supplied.

A contract may be made on specified terms, such as, typically, delivery within 10 days and payment within 30 days of invoice. In practice the contract exists and is legally enforceable when agreement is reached over what is offered and at what price. Although agreements made verbally are enforceable, it is clearly much easier to prove what was agreed if there is a written, signed document. The only common exceptions to the validity of verbal agreements are land sales in England, Wales and Northern Ireland, which must be in writing, and cases where members of the public place an order or sign an HP or credit sale agreement in their own homes or at their place of work, when there is the legal requirement for a 'cooling off' period in which the customer has a right to cancel the agreement.

There are also implied conditions in all contracts, which do not have to be spelt out, that:

- The seller has the right to sell (ie that the goods are not stolen or already on HP).
- The goods comply with the description (eg if reconditioned, not described as new).
- The goods are of 'suitable quality' and 'fit for purpose' in the way that the customer expected.
- The sample corresponds with bulk.

It is the third of these conditions that tends to be at the core of most disputes between vendors and purchasers, where the meaning of words is ambiguous or uncertain. Legal actions on these grounds are time-consuming and likely to be profitable only for the legal profession.

Terms and conditions of buying and selling

This chapter focuses on your procurement and purchasing activities, but remember that there is a 'do as you would be done by' element in this discussion, since the terms and conditions that you seek to impose on your customers may be the converse of those that your suppliers try to use when selling to you.

With your buyer's hat on, it is important to specify what you want the goods to do as a part of placing the order, and to place an official written order on which your terms of trade are entered (printed, if you use a standard order form). Your standard terms may differ significantly from the standard terms of which the supplier has already advised you on their quotation or order confirmation, and the rule is that the last one wins. Therefore, you should make sure, whenever possible, that you are buying on your terms. The terms on your official order will prevail provided that the seller does not send an order acknowledgement on which its terms are specified.

Remember that even if the supplier's sales rep promised you that a particular condition would not apply in the case of your order, there is probably a disclaimer somewhere in the small print that staff have no authority to agree any variation.

Another area of the supplier's small print to which you should certainly pay attention is the procedure for complaining if the goods are delivered damaged, or in some other way are not what you ordered. Unless you process your complaint as instructed and within the specified time limit, you may still have to pay for defective product.

With your seller's hat on, the following are some of the terms and conditions of sale that you might consider adopting for your business. As a buyer, you may expect to find them among the terms and conditions of a 'reasonable' supplier (another ambiguous term on which lawyers are happy to charge their 'taxi meter' fees in litigation).

Terms and conditions of sale

1 Descriptions shown in brochures, advertisements and by way of samples, are correct at the time of going to press, errors and omissions excepted. They are liable to amendment at any time without notice.

2 Prices will be those ruling at the date of dispatch and exclude VAT, which is due at the current rate in force. We may revise prices without notice. Any invoice query should be made in writing within 10 days of the date of invoice.

3 Quotations and estimates remain current for one month.

4 All accounts are payable in full within 30 days of invoice date.

5 No liability is accepted for delay in dispatch or delivery.

6 Orders for goods may be cancelled only with the written agreement of a director of this company.

7 Carriage may be charged in addition to the quoted price, except for orders over £100, which will be delivered free within 30 miles.

8 Liability cannot be accepted for non-delivery of goods unless written notification is received within seven days of the date of invoice.

9 Shortage of goods or damage must be notified by telephone within 48 hours of delivery, and confirmed within seven days of delivery, or no claim can be accepted. Delivery of obviously damaged goods should be refused.*

10 No liability is accepted for any consequential loss or damage whatsoever.

11 Acceptance of the goods implies acceptance of these conditions, which may not be varied except in writing by a director of this company.

12 Under some circumstances we may cancel the contract without notice or compensation. Such circumstances would include: strikes, lockouts and other forms of industrial action or dispute, fire, flood, drought, weather conditions, war, civil disturbance, act of God or any other cause beyond our control making it impossible for us to fulfil the contract.

13 We reserve our title in goods supplied until they have been paid for in full.

continued

14 Any invoice unpaid in full by the due date shall attract interest charges accrued at base rate plus 5 per cent from the due date.

15 A 'quotation' given is a firm price for the job but subject to these terms and conditions. An 'estimate' is our best estimate of the final cost but may be subject to fluctuation due to the unforeseeable exigencies of the job.

*This condition should mirror your carrier's conditions which you accept, including identification routines and the retention of damaged goods for verification.

Product selection

Purchasing decisions for capital and high-value items are necessarily more critical than for lower-value items of current expenditure. Some guidance on the former is given in Chapter 16 on asset management, and the methods of financing the acquisition of capital equipment and vehicles, both on and off balance sheet, are described in Chapter 4 'Funding alternatives'. Although the choice of make and model of any kind of equipment, whether PC or motor vehicle, is largely subjective, you should consciously apply certain business criteria in the selection process:

- *Fitness for purpose*: don't consider buying equipment that is unnecessarily refined or of a capacity in excess of your business needs (eg your choice of motor car or telephone switchboard). On the other hand, be sure that it will do the job for which you need it. In particular, if you are financing a capital item by leasing or rental, be careful not to commit yourself to equipment of an inferior specification or lower capacity than the business will need, as lease terms may mean it is a year or more before you can replace it.

- *Cash flow*: some equipment manufacturers may offer financing packages that demand lower monthly payments than others, or that can be procured from third-party finance providers. If the product specification and quality are acceptable, this may determine your ultimate choice. However, preferential payment terms may not be sufficient to offset the risks of an inferior guarantee, high servicing costs, or an unreliable product, which can disrupt your business and cause expensive repairs and replacements. The net effect on cash flow, including lost sales, could be severe.

- *Net profit effect*: the higher the net price of the capital equipment, the greater the charge against profit is likely to be – however preferential the financing package. This is a similar consideration to the impact on cash flow with one important difference. Remember that, in addition to running/operating cost, there is the cost of depreciation charges that must be taken against profit if your business is purchasing the asset. If the expansion of your business depends on maintaining healthy financial results, depreciation may be a significant factor.

- *Competitor practice*: if in doubt, check what equipment your most effective competitor uses in its business. Maybe you can gain a product advantage by using improved equipment that will justify the incremental cost. Of course, the argument could go the other way. If you spend less on equipment, you might be able to afford to offer your customers additional service benefits that would be still more appealing.

Purchasing consumables does not generally demand so much deliberation. The critical factors in the decision are, of course:

- price;
- quality;
- reliability of supply;
- delivery time;
- payment terms.

In the early stages of running your business, payment terms may be more important than the last 5 per cent of discount. Cash on delivery for a 10 per cent price advantage is no substitute for 30 days credit when cash flow is critical. In some product areas, like office stationery, direct purchase from national or regional wholesalers can give you all the advantages of good quality, low prices, excellent service and credit; but this is not so in all areas. For example, land-line and mobile telephone services, or professional services, are not such 'no-brainers'.

Purchasing via the web

Using the web to source your consumables will probably waste more of your time than the value it might gain in identifying new sources of supply or keener prices. However, the web will give you useful price comparisons and could produce serious savings on higher-value items. For the main part, you may be able to use the prices of products on the web to elicit matching offers from your local suppliers.

Purchasing professional services

Possibly the most difficult procurement and purchasing activity is the selection and engagement of professional services. This is one function that you will probably wish to reserve to yourself so long as you occupy the chief executive position in your company. You may well share the reluctance many businesspeople have in investing time and money with professional advisers beyond the bare necessities of the annual audit, completion of your tax return or entering into a commercial lease. That reluctance extends to areas like fund-raising, human resource requirements and pension planning.

Practical selection and engagement

Finding a professional adviser through personal introduction is a traditional route, but requires caution. An adviser who is suitable for one business may not be appropriate for your requirements because of differences in outlook, objectives or cultures. Alternatives are a search among local professionals or direct contact through the national directories of the Law Society or Institute of Chartered Accountants. Whatever route you choose, do not be embarrassed to interview and evaluate several firms, having provided each with a brief, as you would in any important procurement area. Aside from technical expertise, experience and the capacity to take on your assignment, satisfy yourself of the compatibility of those who would be working with you before arriving at a decision. Before making a binding commitment, take up references. Any excuse or attempt to avoid giving references should be regarded as a disqualification.

Implementation is as important as any advice that may emerge from the reports of professional firms you engage. Therefore, before making your final choice of advisers, be sure that they will be able to help you to carry out their recommendations with their own staff or by transferring skills to members of your staff.

Be clear about the fee basis and how any additional costs may be triggered. Agree in advance details such as invoicing frequency in writing, together with the exact scope and timing of the work. You should insist that any changes in fees, schedules and phasing are advised promptly and fully justified. Avoid agreeing extensions to the assignment or new tasks until the original assignment is completed to your satisfaction.

Purchasing practice

As we suggested at the beginning of this chapter, you will probably want to delegate the routine part of the purchasing function as the business expands. The best way of doing this securely is to draw up a set of rules for your purchasing officer, which anyone in the firm, including yourself, should observe. The following are among the most important:

- No commitment to a supplier of goods or services may be made without a formal purchase order issued by the purchasing officer.

- Any commitment to purchase outside the expenditure budget requires the express approval of the managing director.

- Quantities purchased will be determined by usage and negotiated terms (for consumables, no more than two or three months' usage at a time).

- Orders may be placed only within limits of authority (any expenditure above authorized expenditure to be sanctioned by the managing director).

- Selection of any new supplier or supplier of capital equipment must be against quotation from alternative suppliers (typically, two alternatives).

- There will be an annual review of every supplier's terms and prices against competition.

- Quality, delivery performance and the incidence of defects of every supplier should be monitored and logged. Equally, you should remain aware of your own firm's performance against agreed payment terms. Even the most reliable supplier's service can become unsatisfactory if it is alienated by your failure to pay promptly.

Checklist

- Understand the distinction between procurement and purchasing. As the business grows, set guidelines and delegate clerical purchasing duties, but retain the decision-making procurement role for some time.

- Aside from employment law, contract law and tort are the only two aspects of civil law that will concern you most of the time in running your business.

- Your supplier is in breach of contract if it fails to supply the product or service you have ordered to specification and within the agreed delivery time. Contracts between purchasers and suppliers can be verbal or embodied in a formal legal agreement. In practice, the parties commonly rely on their standard conditions of purchase and sale.

continued

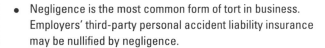

- Negligence is the most common form of tort in business. Employers' third-party personal accident liability insurance may be nullified by negligence.

- The necessary elements for a contract to be in force are: an offer of goods or service; acceptance by the purchaser; consideration (payment) in exchange for the goods or service. Among the implied conditions, 'suitable quality' and 'fitness for use' represent the most common causes for dispute.

- Whenever possible, make sure that you are buying on your terms. The terms on your official order will prevail unless the seller sends an acknowledgement on which its terms are specified. The rule is that the last one wins.

- To ensure that you do not have to pay for defective product, follow the supplier's procedures for complaint, and return goods within specified time limits.

- Select and purchase capital expenditure items by reference to fitness for purpose, the effects on your cash flow and net profit, and competitors' practice.

- Purchasing consumables on the web probably wastes more time than the value gained in keener prices, but web prices may help you to secure matching offers from local suppliers.

- When selecting and engaging professional advisers, pay attention to compatibility as well as technical expertise and experience. Any excuse or attempt to avoid giving references should be treated as a disqualification.

- Before choosing your advisers, make sure that they will help you to carry out their recommendations or transfer skills to members of your staff. Do not agree extensions to the contract until the original assignment is completed to your satisfaction.

- As the business expands, draw up a set of purchasing rules that everyone in your organization, including yourself, must observe.

Chapter Fifteen
Taxation

PAUL WAITE, ASPEN WAITE

Caution

At the time of writing, the June 2010 budget has just taken place and proposed measures based on this are referred to in this chapter. Readers should exercise caution, as changes to proposed legislation may take place during the committee stages of the Finance Bill before it receives royal assent.

Tax planning

Tax planning should form an integral part of the overall plan of every business. In order to plan effectively it is necessary to take advantage of every possibility the law allows for reducing the burden of taxation. Efficiently organizing a business's tax affairs helps to reduce reliance on external finance and to maximize the business's existing resources.

There are two golden rules in tax planning: pay only the minimum amount of tax due, and pay tax on the latest date permissible. Simple as the strategy may sound, carrying it out is one of the most complex challenges in the life of a business, starting even before it comes into existence. The planning begins with the decision as to what kind of organization to create in the first place, in order to realize the best tax position for the owner(s). Basically, the decision is whether to operate as an incorporated or unincorporated business: that is, as a private limited company or as a sole trader/partnership. In certain cases a limited liability partnership combining the tax position of a partnership with the limited liability status of a company may be more appropriate.

Over recent years there have been many changes to the rates of corporate taxation applying to smaller companies, some of which have made incorporation very attractive. With a new Conservative–Liberal Democrat government, it would seem that there is a commitment to encourage companies with lower rates of corporate taxation. On tax grounds alone, there would seem little reason not to operate as a limited company, although the additional legal responsibilities and 'red tape' reduce the attraction for the smallest businesses. Essentially incorporation enables funds to be taken from the business by both salaries (in recognition of work done) and dividends (as a return on the investment); dividends do not attract a National Insurance liability, thus enabling a higher proportion of profit to pass in to the hands of the business owner(s), than is the case with sole traders or partners.

Historically a decision whether or not to incorporate depended largely upon one of two factors: the owners' attitude to risk, and whether or not business profits were such that an unincorporated business would create substantial higher-rate income tax liabilities for the sole trader/partners, particularly when reinvestment in the business might mean that the profits would not be available to the proprietors. Individuals pay tax at a highest rate of 50 per cent. With employees' national insurance, the higher tax rate is in reality 51 per cent (52 per cent from April 2011). The highest rate of company tax is now 28 per cent (reducing by 1 per cent in each of the next four years), although marginal tax rates may be higher than this on part of the taxable profit.

It should be borne in mind that incorporation may not be appropriate for a new business that is expecting to make losses initially. The company's losses may not be set off against the income of the business's owner(s), whilst this is often possible with a sole trader/partnership.

Tax planning is as important when considering the cessation of a business as it is at start-up.

Income tax

Each individual is responsible for tax on his/her own income. Companies pay corporation tax instead of income tax. Income tax is charged broadly on the income of UK residents, whether it arises in the UK or abroad, subject to certain different rules for individuals who are not ordinarily resident or domiciled in the UK, with foreign tax credit relief available if such income has also been taxed abroad.

The tax year runs from 6 April in one year to 5 April in the next. Tax is currently charged on income at the following rates:

- the basic rate of 20 per cent;
- the higher rate of 40 per cent;
- the additional basic rate of 50 per cent.

In some cases where non-savings income is small (less than £8,915), some interest received may be taxable at 10 per cent.

The most common sources of income to be taxed are earnings from employment, and interest from banks or building societies. Tax on employment earnings is collected through the Pay As You Earn (PAYE) scheme, at whichever rate the earnings are taxable. Individuals trading as sole traders or through partnerships also pay income tax on the income derived from their businesses, after deduction of allowable expenses incurred in the running of the business. Interest from banks and building societies is taxed at basic rate and withheld by the banks and building societies. Higher and additional rate taxpayers have to pay the difference between higher or additional rate and basic rate tax on this income through their self-assessment tax return. Non-taxpayers may receive bank and building society interest gross on signing a confirmation of their non-taxable status.

Taxable income may be reduced by certain allowances. The personal allowance and blind person's allowance are deducted from income, and save tax at the individual's highest tax rate where total income is less than £100,000. Personal allowances are withdrawn by £1 for every £2 by which total income exceeds £100,000. Current personal allowance rates are set out at the end of this chapter.

Under self-assessment, half-yearly payments of income tax and Class 4 National Insurance contributions for the self-employed (and others required to complete tax returns) are made on 31 January and 31 July, based on the previous year's figures, with any balancing adjustment shown in the tax return and payable or repayable on the following 31 January.

National insurance contributions

Contributors fall mainly into one of two groups.

Employed earners group

Class 1 contributions paid by both employees and employers account for over 97 per cent of the National Insurance Fund's contribution income. Class 1A employer's contributions are charged on all taxable benefits in kind.

From April 2011 there is to be a 1 per cent increase in rates of Class 1 (both employers and employees) and Class 4 contributions; there will be an increase in the level at which employers start to pay National Insurance so as to prevent the rate increase from becoming a 'tax on jobs' in respect of employees earning less than £20,000 per annum.

Self-employed earners group

A self-employed person pays both Class 2 and Class 4 contributions. Class 2 contributions are payable at a flat weekly rate and entitle the contributor to incapacity benefit, basic retirement pension, widow's benefit and maternity allowance. Class 4 contributions are payable at a fixed percentage on profits chargeable to income tax under Schedule D, Class I or II that fall between specified upper and lower limits. They carry no entitlement to benefits of any kind.

Class 2 contributions

If an individual becomes self-employed, he or she should notify HM Revenue. He or she must also make arrangements to pay Class 2 contributions, unless he or she is not liable to pay. Penalties will arise if notification does not occur by 31 January following the tax year in which self-employment commenced.

Class 4 contributions

Class 4 contributions are collected with income tax through the self-assessment tax return. If someone has more than one self-employment, all the profits are added together when calculating the Class 4 liability. In general, profits are calculated for Class 4 contributions in the same way as for income tax, but certain special rules apply.

Self-employed and employed in the same year

An individual who is both self-employed and an employee will be liable to pay Class 1, 2 and 4 contributions, and if he or she has more than one employment, he or she will be liable to Class 1 contributions in each employment. However, there is a maximum figure above which contributions will be refunded. If you expect that your contributions will exceed the maximum, you should apply to defer payment of Class 4, 2 or 1 contributions (in that order) as appropriate.

Corporation tax

Since 1964, companies have been liable to corporation tax on their 'profits', defined as net income after deduction of allowable business expenses and chargeable gains in each financial year. Corporation tax is charged on profits of 'financial years', which run from 1 April, so the 'financial year 2010' means the year from 1 April 2010.

The profits of a company are calculated by reference to its accounting periods. The reduced rates of corporation tax that apply to 'small' companies are defined by reference to their profits in an accounting period.

Any company that is resident in the UK is liable to pay corporation tax in respect of all its profits, wherever they arise. A non-resident company that carries on a trade in the UK through a branch or agency is liable to corporation tax on the income and gains of the branch or agency. Members of a group of companies are each dealt with independently, but there are a number of special provisions relating to the taxation of such members.

Capital gains tax

Background

Capital gains tax (CGT) commenced in 1965 as a tax on profits arising on the sale of certain assets. It relates to chargeable gains in a 'year of assessment' accruing to individuals, personal representatives and trustees. The year of assessment is the year ending on 5 April.

Previously relief had been given to compensate for inflation and length of ownership (indexation relief and taper relief), but no such reliefs are currently available, except for companies (see below). From 23 June 2010, chargeable gains (net selling price less related costs) are taxed at 18 per cent on the amount in excess of the individual's annual exempt amount to the extent that, when added to income, they are within the taxpayer's basic rate band. Net chargeable gains, when added to income, in excess of the basic rate band are taxed at 28 per cent, as are all net chargeable gains made by trustees and personal representatives of deceased persons. From 23 June 2010 Entrepreneur's Relief gives an effective rate of 10 per cent on the first £5 million of gains from qualifying business disposals in a taxpayer's lifetime (on the first £2 million in respect of gains arising between 6 April 2010 and 22 June 2010 and on the first £1 million, in respect of gains arising in 2009/10).

Individuals' liability to pay tax

Usually a person is liable to pay capital gains tax in respect of chargeable gains made by him or her in a year of assessment. Transfers between spouses/civil partners living together are made on a 'no gain, no loss' basis; this can create opportunities for couples to reduce their overall capital gains.

Companies' liability to pay tax

Capital gains made by companies within the scope of corporation tax are not chargeable to capital gains tax; they are taxed in the same way as their other profits and at the same rate. Indexation relief remains available to companies.

Capital allowances

In preparing their accounts, businesses will make a provision for the depreciation of assets, matching the cost of an asset with the income stream it is able to generate over its useful economic life. This provision is not allowable for tax purposes, but a substitute, known as 'capital allowances' is allowed instead. Capital allowances presently apply in respect of:

- industrial buildings;
- plant and machinery;
- agricultural buildings.

In each case the total allowances are given as a deduction in arriving at the profits to be charged to tax under income tax or corporation tax.

Industrial and agricultural buildings

Industrial buildings allowance (IBA) is given in respect of buildings used for productive manufacturing, processing and some other specified trades; agricultural buildings allowance (ABA) is given in respect of buildings used for agricultural purposes. These allowances are being phased out, so that no such allowances will be available in 2011/12 and subsequent years. The rate for 2009/10 was 2 per cent and that for 2010/11 is 1 per cent. As part of the phasing out of industrial buildings allowance and agricultural buildings allowance, there are no balancing adjustments on disposal of such buildings.

Plant and machinery

Plant and machinery are not defined in law, and the term has been subject to close scrutiny in the courts in a number of cases over the years.

First year allowance and annual investment allowance

Apart from the annual investment allowance giving 100 per cent allowance on expenditure of up to £100,000 per annum, no first year allowances are presently available for general plant and machinery. The annual investment allowance is not available for cars, but may be used for long-life assets and integral features of buildings. It has been proposed in the June 2010 budget that the annual investment allowance will only be available in respect of expenditure of up to £25,000 with effect from April 2012.

Writing-down allowances

Where a general pool of plant and machinery is in existence, the writing-down allowance is calculated as 20 per cent of the value of the pool, having regard to disposals. The writing-down allowance is available in respect of qualifying expenditure in the year in excess of the annual investment allowance. It has been proposed in the June 2010 budget that this allowance will reduce to 18 per cent with effect from April 2012. Certain expenditure (thermal insulation, integral features, cars with emissions of over 160g/km and long-life assets) are allocated to a special-rate pool, where the writing down allowance is 10 per cent. It has been proposed in the June 2010 budget that this allowance will reduce to 8 per cent with effect from April 2012.

Energy-efficient plant and low-emission cars

Certain energy-efficient plant, including low-emission cars, receive a first year allowance of 100 per cent.

Balancing adjustments

Where a pool is in existence there will only be a balancing adjustment either when the business ceases or when the disposal proceeds in any year exceed the written-down value of the pool.

Capital allowances are an essential part of tax planning, and are given regardless of the length of time the asset is owned in an accounting period. Careful consideration should be given to the timing of major expenditure with regard to the annual investment allowance, particularly in view of the proposed reduction of the annual amount in April 2012.

Relief for trading losses

Companies may incur losses in their trades, in the course of letting property, in relation to investment income if expenses exceed the income, and in their capital transactions.

Relief available

Trading losses of companies are calculated in the same way as trading profits. The following alternatives are available for obtaining relief for such losses:

- set-off against current profits from other sources;
- carry-back against earlier profits from all sources;
- carry-forward against future trading profits;
- group relief.

Trade loss carry-back has been extended from the previous one-year entitlement, in respect of losses incurred up to 23 November 2010, to a period of three years with losses being carried back against later years first.

Partnership losses

Relief for partnership trading losses may be claimed by each partner quite independently of the others. Thus, one partner may decide to carry forward his/her share of the loss, another to set it against income of the same tax year, another to carry back against the income of the previous three tax years of being a partner and so on.

The carry-back loss rules for the first four years of a new trade only apply to a new partner, not to the continuing partners. Similar loss reliefs exist for sole traders.

Value added tax (VAT)

Definitions

VAT is a sales tax levied by businesses. All goods and services that are VAT rated are called 'taxable supplies'. VAT must be charged on taxable supplies from the date the business first needs to be registered. The value of these supplies is called 'taxable turnover'.

There are currently three rates of VAT:

- 17.5 per cent – known as 'standard rate supplies', levied on most goods and services;
- 5 per cent – known as 'reduced rate supplies', levied on fuel and power used in the home and by charities;
- 0 per cent – known as 'zero-rated supplies' on which VAT does not need to be charged. Examples include most food, books, newspapers and young children's clothing.

There are also 'exempt supplies', which are business supplies that have no VAT charged on them at the standard or zero rate. Exempt supplies do not form part of the taxable turnover. If the only services supplied are exempt supplies, the business cannot normally be registered for VAT. If the business is registered for VAT and has some exempt supplies, it may not be able to get all of its input tax back. Some examples of exempt supplies are insurance, leasing, letting land and buildings.

It has been proposed in the June 2010 budget that the standard rate of VAT will increase to 20 per cent with effect from 4 January 2011.

VAT compliance

If a business's 'taxable turnover' goes over a certain limit, the business becomes a 'taxable person'. It must then register for VAT. Taxable turnover is the total of all business supplies.

If a business is registered or needs to be registered, VAT must be charged and accounted for whenever there is a supply of any standard or reduced rate supplies. These supplies are called 'outputs', and the tax charged is called 'output tax'. If the customer is registered for VAT and the supplies are for their business, these are called 'inputs' by the customer.

From 1 April 2010 the VAT registration threshold was raised to £70,000. Therefore, registration must take place if, first, at the end of any month the total of taxable supplies made in the past 12 months or less is more than £70,000, or second, at any time the value of taxable supplies is expected to be more than £70,000 in the next 30 days alone. To register for VAT, Form VAT 1 must be completed.

If only zero-rated goods are supplied (but exceed the registration threshold) a business may not have to register for VAT, but must inform HM Revenue & Customs of the liability to be registered and apply to be 'exempt from registration'.

Cash accounting

Provided that turnover is below an annual limit of £1,350,000, a taxable person may, subject to conditions, account for and pay VAT on the basis of cash and other considerations paid and received. The main advantages of the scheme are automatic bad debt relief and the deferral of the time for the payment of VAT where extended credit is given. This scheme would be unsuitable for most retail businesses that receive payment at the point of sale but enjoy credit from suppliers.

Bad debt relief

If a customer fails to pay, VAT may be reclaimed on any debt that is more than six months old and has been written off in the business's accounts, when cash accounting is not in operation.

Annual accounting

With a turnover of less than £1,350,000, it is possible to account for VAT annually, but estimated payments on account have to be made through the year.

Flat-rate scheme

With a turnover of less than £150,000, it is possible to account for VAT through a flat-rate scheme. Under this scheme VAT is accounted for through a fixed percentage of VAT-inclusive sales with no deduction for input tax, except in respect of capital assets costing in excess of £2,000. The flat-rate percentage varies according to the industry sector in which the business operates. Care must be taken before applying to join this scheme as it may not be beneficial where input tax is higher than is normal in the industry sector. However, a number of businesses are able to benefit financially from the flat-rate scheme, in addition to simplifying the procedure for completing the VAT returns.

Tax planning for close company shareholders

All businesses should have a tax strategy, which will involve considering:

- the interaction of income against corporate taxes;
- commercial considerations, such as the need to demonstrate a high level of profit to satisfy the company's lenders;
- availability of cash flow;
- the age and extent of the company's fixed asset base;
- what is likely to happen in the future – tax planning has to be proactive;
- when to time expenditure to best advantage;
- if applicable, how to plan expenditure to avoid the company paying tax at higher marginal rates;
- the most appropriate corporate structure if the owners have more than one business interest;
- the optimal remuneration strategy.

The majority of close companies are small companies, and vice versa. A 'close company' is defined as a company under the control of five or fewer shareholders, or any number of shareholders who are also directors of the company: that is, it is controlled by director shareholders.

As we noted at the beginning of this chapter, UK corporation tax rates are favourable at the moment (and reducing), and if they practise good tax planning, it may be possible for companies to have an effective rate of tax well below the company's rate of 28 per cent (21 per cent for companies with smaller profits).

Remuneration strategy

Personal remuneration options include:

- salary;
- dividends;
- bonuses;
- benefits such as car and private health insurance;
- pension funding;
- maximizing spouses'/civil partners' allowances.

A dividend strategy can be effective, as basic rate taxpayers can receive dividends right up to the higher tax rate starting point, an effective rate of 21 per cent. Dividends also have the advantage of being exempt from National Insurance (both employees' and employers').

From a tax viewpoint, shares should be held equally by a husband and wife unless the wife receives substantial income from an external source. (This also applies to civil partners.) Roughly £44,000 can then be received without paying any income tax or National Insurance – an attractive proposition. However, it is important to ensure that entrepreneur's relief for capital gains tax is not compromised. Companies that are bound by IR35 legislation should not implement such a strategy as, upon investigation, the Inland Revenue will substitute for the dividend, wages taxed under PAYE. If you are in any doubt you should contact your professional adviser.

The downsides to dividends are:

- They do not represent a deduction from profits assessable to corporation tax.

- They do not make a contribution towards earnings necessary to maintain the basic National Insurance record.

- They do not represent earnings for pension funding purposes.

- External parties such as mortgage lenders prefer salaries, regarding them as a more permanent form of income.

- The related tax credit is not repayable to the taxpayer.

- While dividends can be waived, if there is a dividend policy all shareholders will receive the same amount per share. This can be a problem if there are passive shareholders, or there are large imbalances in shareholding.

In most cases it is advisable for the owner-manager to receive a salary. Salaries represent allowable deductions against taxable profits, and while pensions have had a bad press in recent years, everyone should make some provision. Pension funding in excess of £3,600 per annum cannot take place in the absence of a salary, and tax relief is restricted to contributions of up to 100 per cent of annual earnings. Restrictions to tax relief and potential tax charges exist in terms of substantial pension contributions and for those with an income in excess of £130,000.

Bonuses are excellent for planning purposes and can create good management incentives. HM Revenue & Customs allows bonuses to be paid up to nine months after the financial year end, making it possible, certainly in the first year, to get tax relief effectively one year early on normal salary. The principle can be applied to all employees. On a cautionary note, particularly for companies with financial year ends after 5 July, HM Revenue & Customs may challenge a bonus paid within nine months if it falls within a new tax year.

Benefits tend to create a state of well-being but, as discussed in Chapter 12, 'Employment and human relations', they have been highly targeted by HM Revenue & Customs.

The taxation treatment of the car and car fuel benefit is now arguably the most unfair in operation, and if you intend to award yourself the use of a company car, you should research the matter fully with your tax adviser.

Company planning: minimizing corporation tax

Any business with serious aspirations should draw up an annual capital expenditure budget. Interest rates are reasonably attractive at present, so buying assets on finance is a good option. Remember that capital allowances can be claimed for the whole year even if the asset was purchased on the final day of the accounting year, so timing is highly relevant. However, HM Revenue and Customs will disqualify the expenditure in certain cases if the asset was not 'brought into use' by the end of the year.

If applicable, expenditure on research and development attracts favourable tax treatment, potentially receiving more tax relief than has been spent. If profits are high, try to plan other expenditure so that, where possible, it is brought forward into the applicable financial year.

Of course, reality may be rather different and may impose its own agenda. Tax planning should never prevail over other commercial considerations, particularly if cash is a scarce resource. Some regard also has to be given to the likely profit in the next financial year.

Corporate structure

If more than one company is under common control, then the rate levels are divided by the number of such companies. To ascertain whether there is common control, one needs to look at the fewest individuals who can control a company. For tax purposes, control is deemed to be more than 50 per cent of the voting shares. It may well be worth having companies under common control in a conventional group environment, since tax losses can be transferred between companies as can assets. If there is no need for a group environment, subject to the demands of corporate and inheritance taxes you should seriously consider arranging the corporate structure so that each company can be run separately on its own merits.

In considering the optimum corporate structure, regard should also be given to corporate and inheritance taxes.

Tax rates

TABLE 15.1 Tax rates

Main income tax relief	2010/11	2009/10
Allowed at top rate of tax*		
Personal allowance*	£6,475	£6,475
Personal allowance (65–74)*	£9,490	£9,490
Personal allowance (75 and over)*	£9,640	£9,640
Blind person's allowance	£1,890	£1,890
Allowed only at 10 per cent		
Married couple's allowance +*	£6,965	£6,965
Income limit for age-related allowances	£22,900	£22,900

Notes
*Personal allowances in 2010/11 are withdrawn at £1 for every £2 by which total income exceeds £100,000. Age allowances are reduced £1 for every £2 by which income exceeds the income limit, until the age allowance is reduced to the normal allowance. Personal allowance is reduced before married couple's allowance; MCA is reduced to a minimum of £2,670 (2007/08: £2,670).
+Only available if born before 6 April 1935.

Important annual limits

	2010/11	2009/10
Individual savings account annual limit+	£10,200	£7,200
Rent-a-room exemption	£4,250	£4,250
Enterprise Investment Scheme annual limit*	£500,000	£500,000
Venture Capital Trust annual limit**	£200,000	£200,000

Notes
+£10,200 for those aged over 50 from 6 October 2009.
*Relief at 20 per cent.
**Relief at up to 30 per cent.

Income tax rates and bands

	2010/11	2009/10
Starting rate band*	£2,440	£2,440
Basic rate band	£37,400	£37,400
Higher rate band	£37,401–£150,000	Over £37,400
Additional rate	Over £150,000	–

Note
*Starting rate band is within basic rate band and applies to savings income only; if taxable general income exceeds the band , the 10 per cent rate is not available.

Tax rates

Rates differ for General/Savings/Dividends	G	S	D
2010/11			
Starting rate	N/A	10%	10%
Basic rate	20%	20%	10%
Higher rate	40%	40%	32.5%
Additional rate	50%	50%	42.5%
2009/10			
Starting rate	N/A	10%	10%
Basic rate	20%	20%	10%
Higher rate	40%	40%	32.5%

Notes
General income (salary, pension, profit, rent) uses lower rate bands first, then savings (interest), then dividends.
Discretionary trusts: basic rate as above applies to first £1,000 of income, then highest rate.

Car benefit assessment 2010/11

Charge based on a percentage of the initial list price of the car, including accessories, delivery charges and VAT. The percentage depends on the CO_2 emissions rating of the car, and whether the engine runs on petrol or diesel. For 2010/11, the taxable benefit on an electric car with no emissions is nil.

Ratings	Petrol	Diesel
0–75g/km	5%	8%
76–120g/km	10%	13%
121–130g/km	15%	18%
Over 130g/km	+ 1% for each	extra 5g/km
Maximum	35%	35%

Notes

Special rules apply to older cars that do not have a CO_2 rating.

Employee contributions for private use are deducted from the taxable figure.

Company vans are charged at £3,000 if private use is more than home-to-work travel. An additional amount of £500 is charged if fuel is provide free for private use. There is no taxable benefit for an electric van.

Car fuel benefit

The benefit of free fuel for private use in a company car is calculated, using the same percentage as that used for the car benefit, applied to a standard figure of £18,000 (2009/10 – £16,900)

Tax-free mileage allowance (2010/11 and 2009/10)

	Higher rate	Lower rate
All cars	40p	25p
Motorcycles	24p	24p
Bicycles	20p	20p
Business passengers	5p	5p

Note

Higher rate allowed up to 10,000 business miles.

Fuel-only allowances for company cars (From 1 January 2008)

	Petrol	Diesel	LPG
Up to 1,400cc	11p	11p	7p
1,401–2,000cc	14p	11p	8p
Over 2,000cc	20p	14p	12p

Capital gains tax

Annual exempt amount 2010/11 and 2009/10: individuals £10,100, most trusts £5,050.

For disposals up to 22 June 2010, net gains after all reliefs and annual exempt amount are taxed at 18 per cent. From 23 June 2010 the tax rate is 18 per cent for gains that when added to income are within the basic rate band. Any amounts that exceed the unused amount of the basic rate band are chargeable at 28 per cent. Gains qualifying for Entrepreneur's Relief will be taxed at 10 per cent within a lifetime limit of £2 million of gains to 22 June 2010, and of £5 million of gains from 23 June 2010.

Entrepreneur's Relief is available for disposals of sole trade or interest in a partnership trade or shares in a trading company by an employee owning at least 5 per cent of the share capital and with at least 5 per cent of the voting rights.

Corporation tax

Corporation tax on profits – £ per year (unless stated)

Rate	2010/11	2009/10
Main rate	28%	28%
Profits above	£1.5m	£1.5m
Small companies rate	21%	21%
Profits up to	£300K	£300K
Small/large marginal band	£300k–£1.5m	£300K–£1.5m
Fraction (effective rate)	7/400 (29.75%)	7/400 (29.75%)

Note
Rates for future years have been announced, with the main rate coming down by 1 per cent per annum to reach 24 per cent in 2014/15, and the small companies rate coming down to 20 per cent with effect from 1 April 2011.

National Insurance contributions (2010/11)

Class 1 (employees)	Contracted in	Contracted out	
		Salary related	Money purchase
Employee contributions:			
– on earnings between £110.01 and £770 pw	11.0%	9.4%	9.4%
– on earnings between £770.01 and £844 pw	11.0%	11.0%	11.0%
– on earnings above £844 pw	1.0%	1.0%	1.0%
Employer contributions:			
– on earnings between £110.01 and £770 pw	12.8%	9.1%	11.4%
– on earnings above £770 pw	12.8%	12.8%	12.8%

Note
Employer contributions (at 12.8 per cent) are due on most benefits in kind and on tax paid on an employee's behalf under a PAYE settlement agreement.

Class 2 (self-employed)	
Flat-rate per week	£2.40
Small earnings exception; profits per annum	£5,075
Class 3 (voluntary)	
Flat-rate per week	£12.05
Class 4 (self-employed)	
On profits £5,715–£43,875	8.00%
On profits over £43,875	1.00%

Note
Increased rates of National Insurance have been announced for 2011/12, but with an increase in the level at which employers have to make contributions. Targeted reliefs for new employers outside London and the South East are expected to be introduced in September 2010.

Retirement provision

Maximum annual tax efficient gross contributions to age 75	
Individuals	£3,600 or 100 per cent of earnings to £255,000
Employers	£255,000 less employee contributions

Notes

Maximum tax efficient fund on taking benefits in 2010/11: £1.8 million, staying the same until 2015/16.

Only current earnings count for the 100 per cent limit. Most personal contributions are paid net of basic rate tax.

Extra contributions over £20,000 by those with income over £130,00 may suffer a clawback of relief. From 6 April 2011 higher rate tax relief will be restricted for those with an income in excess of £150,000.

Inheritance tax

Charges on or after	Rates (%)	
6 April 2009 (no change for 2010/11)		
0–£325,000	Nil	Nil rate band frozen until 2014/15
Above £325,000	40%	

Notes

Lifetime chargeable transfers at half the death rate, ie 20 per cent, but subject to an additional charge on death within seven years.

Business property relief of 100 per cent for all shareholdings in qualifying unquoted trading companies and for most unincorporated trading businesses; agricultural property relief at 100 per cent for qualifying holdings of agricultural land.

Annual exemption for lifetime gifts: £3,000.

Small gifts: annual amount per donee: £250.

There are also exemptions for gifts in consideration of marriage, varying from £1,000 to £5,000 according to the relationship.

Tapering relief applies to reduce the tax on transfers within seven years of death. The reduction in tax is 20 per cent for survivorship of 3–4 years, 40 per cent for 4–5 years, 60 per cent for 5–6 years, and 80 per cent for 6–7 years.

Value added tax

Standard rate (7/47 of VAT-inclusive price)	17.50%
Registration level from 1 April 2010	£70,000 per annum
Deregistration level from 1 April 2010	£68,000 per annum

Scale charges

The scale charges for private use of business fuel are based on the CO_2 emissions rating of the car. A different charge will apply for each 5 g/km increase between 130 g/km and 230g/km (max). For a three-month period:

120 or less	£120.00 net	£21.00 VAT
121–134	£180.43 net	£31.57 VAT
rising by per 5g/km, approx*	£12.06 net	£2.11 VAT
230 or above	£422.13 net	£73.87 VAT

Note
*Exact figure should be obtained from the published table.

Main capital allowances

Plant and machinery	Allowance %
– annual investment allowance: £100,000*	100
– certain energy efficient plant, including low-emission cars	100
– writing down allowance: general pool	20
– writing down allowance: special rate pool	10

Notes
*£50,000 to 31.3.10 (companies) or 5.4.10 (sole traders and partnerships)
The special rate pool includes long-life assets, integral plant in buildings, thermal insulation and cars with CO2 emissions over 160g/km. The general pool contains other plant and machinery.
The old system of cheap/expensive cars has been abolished.
Industrial building allowances are being phased out: 2 per cent in 2009/10; 1 per cent in 2010/11; nil thereafter.

Chapter Sixteen
Premises and
Business Assets

Your business's assets are worth careful attention for a variety of reasons – all of them important. A business can be valued on a number of criteria: turnover, profit, future growth and assets. If at some point you expect to sell the business, the value of the assets will clearly be part of the equation. In the more immediate term your assets represent your ability to operate – take away any one part of your machinery, your transport, your premises or your personnel and you will be severely compromised. It is therefore critical that all are maintained and retained. Finally, your assets have a current value that has to be paid for. The way in which you choose to do this will mean that you have more or less cash available for other purposes. Your choice of asset financing has implications for your whole business.

Finding the right premises

Your choice of premises is likely to have an effect on your business for a significant period of time. It is therefore wise to make the right decision. As with all asset selection there are two parts to the process. First you must identify your requirements, and second, you then must find the 'best fit' from what is available that meets those requirements. The first part is relatively simple, the second much less so as it requires those elusive business elements, luck and timing, as much as skill and judgement.

Perhaps the first question to ask yourself is 'Do I need premises?' Maybe a mobile phone, laptop computer, website and PO box will be enough. Presuming that you do need premises, you must decide how important location is. If you are a retail or distribution-based business this is likely to be critical. If you are manufacturing something, space may be a higher priority. How much room for growth do you require? What specialist services will you use (eg broadband access, three-phase electricity, suitable storage for chemicals)? What transport access do you need both for customers (public transport facilities, perhaps) and suppliers (eg large lorries/forklifts)? What storage facilities do you need? Only you can know what your business processes require. Work your way through all the different parts of the business and list all their requirements in terms of space, remembering height as well as area, power and services needs, and transport and location requirements.

You will also need to identify your budget for the premises; we discuss the financing options below in more detail. Once you are furnished with all the above information, you are in a good position to start looking for your premises. This is where you are likely to need third-party assistance. Contact either a local chartered surveyor or a commercial estate agent. They should have a good knowledge of the current market and be able to tell you whether your requirement list is achievable and affordable or not. The property market is far from perfect, so you should trawl for as much information as possible. Other sources are the local press, internet property search sites, trade magazines, local authority business-assistance units and other business agencies. You will be well served by driving around and seeing what advertising boards offer. As ever, the more people you talk to, the better informed you will become.

Working from home

An increasing number of people are now working from home. It is no longer seen as an unusual way of working. However, it is a *different* way of working, and if you are thinking of doing it there are a number of issues to consider.

Be aware that there are probably almost as many downside factors to working at home as there are benefits, but the benefits are likely to outweigh the downside factors. The clear benefits of working from home are reduced start-up costs and overheads (which can be critical for your cash flow when setting up a business) and increased flexibility in organizing your working time, including the elimination of any commuting time. There may also be 'lifestyle benefits', such as sufficient time to continue looking after your children or any dependants.

However, the downside factors are numerous. While none of them individually need be an absolute problem, cumulatively you may find them stressful. Most of the problems are related to separating your working and non-working life. However, we should mention there are tax implications of working from home (you can lose some of your principal residence capital gains exemption) and possibly some planning restrictions as well. Space is often the first issue to be noticed. Most people find that they need a dedicated space, whether it be a room or a desk area, that is their 'office'. If you find yourself having to use the same area for non-work activities it may become confusing and then irritating. Your business will inevitably accumulate papers and files that will need to be stored and yet be accessible; you must have space for these as well.

When your office is also your home you will have to consider what to do if you need to have a meeting with a client or colleague. Ushering clients past the pram and over the dog bowl is not very professional. If space is limited this becomes even more of a problem. It may be wise to meet at a hotel or have access to a serviced office or similar short-term facility.

The ability to stop working is often compromised at home. Sooner or later you will leave your office each day and go home. If your office is also your home there is always the temptation to check your e-mails before you go to bed, answer the business telephone at 10 pm or just nip into the office on a Sunday afternoon. Occasionally the opportunity to do this is a real bonus, but it can become routine to the detriment of the rest of your and your family's life.

The final series of problems to consider is less tangible but no less important. Working from home means working alone, usually. At first you may revel in the freedom that this offers. Over time, however, you may begin to feel cut off and isolated. The paradox is that as the internet makes working from home much easier, it can also increase the feeling of isolation. With the vast majority of your communication in the form of brief e-mail messages, you may spend days without actually speaking to anyone! This is a problem that you should manage actively; try to arrange lunchtime meetings with colleagues or other homeworkers. It can revitalize and invigorate you and your work. For more detail on this topic see Kogan Page's publication *Starting a Business from Home* by Colin Barrow.

Buying or leasing property

If your business owns its own property it frees itself from the uncertainties of rent increases, potential lease termination and, if you have an unhelpful landlord, the possibility of poor maintenance, constant interference, an inflexible approach to changing needs of the business and so on. That said, most of these complaints should not arise if you have a good relationship with your landlord and a well-worded lease agreement. What you will definitely acquire with owning your own premises is an increased cash requirement before you even start trading.

Commercial mortgages are difficult if not impossible to obtain for start-up businesses, which have no track record, and you certainly will not get the same attractive rates and high percentage of purchase price loans that residential buyers used to be offered before the credit crunch. Your mortgage repayments may be fixed for a short period, but they are essentially at the mercy of the world capital markets, and where the Bank of England (or possibly the European Central Bank, if the UK ever decides to join the euro during the period of your mortgage term) chooses to set interest rates.

The main reason for purchasing your own business premises will be as an alternative business investment to your start-up business. If you believe the property will increase in value, then it may be worth considering when the present slump in property prices appears to have bottomed out. However, you must make a clear distinction between your property investment and your business one. They are separate businesses. Historically, the return from a successful business will be greater than from successful property investment, although the former's risks are usually higher as well. You may find that it is more tax-efficient for you to own the premises personally and rent it to the business, or to set up a separate company to purchase the business. In this way you remove the mortgage debt from your balance sheet. These issues are best discussed with your tax adviser, having regard to the specifics of your situation.

The most usual way for a business to acquire its premises is through leasehold. In this way you do not need to find any capital to fund your premises; you just ensure that the business creates enough cash to pay the rent. The rent can be fixed for fixed periods of time, with rent reviews that can be subject to impartial third-party arbitration should you think them unreasonable.

The law (Landlord & Tenant Act 1954 and subsequent amendments) operates reasonably strongly in the commercial tenant's favour. You have the right to renew your lease at the end of the term, with a few exceptions: if you have exhibited unreasonable behaviour as a tenant, or the landlord requires the premises for its own purposes or wishes to redevelop them. The tenancy agreement is critical, and will require you to employ a good property lawyer to advise you. The landlord may well try to restrict you as much as possible in terms of landlord obligations and tenant rights. You cannot read the small print of tenancy agreements closely enough. Ensure that you have as much flexibility in the agreement as possible, with break clauses, options on changes of use, minimal maintenance responsibilities for yourself, control over any service charges and, if possible, the right to assign the lease. Avoid, if possible, any provision that obliges you to 'make good' the property to its initial condition when you vacate the premises. Your property adviser should be able to guide you through the minutiae of the agreement and help you to secure reasonable terms.

Finally, before signing any agreement double check that you fully understand how much you have to pay, not only in rent but also the other charges and the deposit, and that you will certainly be able to afford all these costs. Your business will benefit from a good working relationship with your landlord, and ensuring that your rent is paid on time can only help this. In return, it is likely that you will receive a more sympathetic ear if anything goes wrong with the premises in the future.

Local authority issues, planning and business rates

The start-up process of your business will be affected by the approach your local authority has to encouraging and fostering your type of business. Most local authorities have a unit designed to help small businesses. How effective it is will depend on the individual authority. At the very least you should contact your local authority and discuss with the business development or support unit what help they have available for you. This is likely to range from straightforward business advice to financing help. Your premises may be located in an area that attracts special assistance or loans. The local authority should also be able to guide you through any planning issues that you may encounter.

Planning issues can cover a wide range of different problems, and it is wise to contact the planning department at your local council to find out what planning or business registration your business may require. Clearly, you must check that your premises have the relevant planning permission for you to carry out your business there. (See Table 16.1.) Also, many businesses need to register with the local authority, such as those in the catering or building trades. Many of these registrations are mere formalities, but they are also requirements, and in the event of an accident or problem the fact that you have followed the correct procedures always helps your case.

The other role of your local authority is less benevolent; to levy business rates. Business rates are generally paid by the occupier of non-domestic properties. This means the owner-occupier or leaseholder. Some non-domestic properties are exempt from rates, such as agricultural land and buildings. If you think you may be exempt, check with your local valuation office. Your home may be eligible for business rates if you work from there; again you can ask the local valuation office for clarification for your specific circumstances.

TABLE 16.1 Planning use classes

Use Class	Use	Whether change permitted
A1 *Shops*	Sale of goods and cold food, retail warehouses, hairdressers, travel and ticket agencies, post offices, domestic hire shops, funeral directors, dry cleaners	No change of use without permission, except to A1 plus single flat
A2 *Financial and professional services*	Professional (excluding health and medical services) and financial services (banks and building societies); other services appropriate in a shopping area where the services are provided principally to visiting members of the public	Change to A1 permitted only if there is a ground-floor display window
A3 *Food and drink*	Sale of food and drink for consumption on premises, eg in restaurants, pubs, cafes and wine bars; shops for sale of hot food to be taken away	Change to A1 or A2 permitted
Sui generis	Shops selling or displaying motor vehicles for sale	Change to A1 permitted
	Launderettes, taxi businesses, car hire businesses, filling stations, scrapyards	No change of use permitted
B1 *Business*	a Offices other than financial and professional services providing for the visiting members of the public b Research and development c Other industrial processes appropriate in a residential area	Change to B8 (only up to 235 m² of floor space) permitted
B2 *General industrial*	General industry, not within B1	Change to B1 or B8 (only up to 235 m² of floor space)
B8 *Storage or distribution*	Storage or distribution centres	Change to B1 (only up to 235 m² of floor space) permitted

Use Class	Use	Whether change permitted
Sui generis	Work registerable under Alkali etc, Works Regulation Act	No change of use permitted
C1 Hotels	Hotels, boarding and guest houses, provided that care is not provided	No change of use permitted
C2 Residential institutions	Residential accommodation for provision of care (eg old age homes); residential schools and colleges and training centres; hospitals and nursing homes	No change of use permitted
C3 Dwelling houses	Dwelling houses for individuals, families and up to six individuals living as a single household	Subdivision of dwelling houses into two or more dwelling houses not permitted
Sui generis	Hostels	No change of use permitted
D1 Non-residential institutions	Clinics, health centres, crèches, day nurseries, day centres, consulting rooms (not attached to doctor's house); museums, libraries, art galleries, public and exhibition halls; non-residential schools, colleges and other educational centres; public worship or religious instruction	No change of use permitted
D2 Assembly and leisure	Cinemas, dance and concert halls; swimming pools, skating rinks, gymnasiums; other indoor and outdoor sports and leisure uses, bingo halls, casinos	No change of use permitted
Sui generis	Theatres, amusement arcades and centres, fun fairs	No change of use permitted

The bill you pay for your property depends on the rateable value that the valuation office has assigned to it. These values are set every five years; the next valuation will occur in 2015. You can challenge the rateable value for your property if you believe it is unreasonable, but you should take advice from a solicitor or chartered surveyor before pursuing this. The local authority only levies the charge; it is central government that sets the 'multiplier' by which your actual bill is calculated. So if your premises had a rateable value of £1,000 and the multiplier was 43p for every pound of rateable value, your rates bill would be £430 for that year. The multiplier is reset every year, but cannot increase by more than the rate of inflation. You may benefit from transitional or other relief; you can get details on transitional relief from your local authority or valuation office.

Purchase, hire or lease? The options for plant, machinery and vehicles

The purchase of large pieces of hardware, whether of manufacturing machinery, office equipment or vehicles, will be potentially your single largest capital outlay. There are various ways you can finance the use of these capital assets – and with today's sophisticated financial industry vying for your business, it is wise to familiarize yourself with the various options.

Many large pieces of equipment are offered with various financing packages. However, it is wise to check whether these are the best deals available. It may well be that you can do better by paying the vendor the full cash amount and borrowing the money from elsewhere, either your bank or a specialist financing firm. In this way you can ensure that the repayments are structured to take account of your cash flow, by specifying that you want monthly or quarterly payments or, indeed, that you want to pay reduced repayment instalments during quiet trading months.

There are many financing options. It is sensible to know the features and benefits of each so that you know which one is for you in any given set of circumstances. *Contract hire*, for example, is arranged directly with a company that provides both the equipment and the financing. The arrangement will be based on a fixed-term contract of, say, 24 to 60 months, from which a fixed periodic rental will be calculated. At the end of the term the hire company takes back the equipment. The principal financial advantages of this are that:

- You do not need to find a large amount of cash to purchase the equipment at the outset, when you have limited borrowing opportunities.

- You can budget your costs accurately over an extended period.

- The money saved from not having to make an outright purchase can often be used more effectively elsewhere.

- The equipment is 'off-balance sheet', as it is not owned by the company (just rented), which improves the key ratios mentioned at the outset of this chapter.

- As such you do not have to depreciate the assets.

- VAT efficiency – the VAT on your repayments is recoverable.

- Rentals can be offset against corporation tax, as a legitimate expense.

Often contract hire companies will also offer you maintenance and repair contracts, which can provide a reduction in your administrative costs and peace of mind. These contracts should be analysed closely for value, as they are often the area where the hire companies make the bulk of their profit.

Another common method of financing is *finance leasing*. This is similar to contract hire with the same advantages, but has one key difference. At the term outset a future value is calculated for the equipment at the end of the term. This value must be paid at the end of the contract, and is known as the 'balloon payment'. Effectively your company is taking on the risk of either purchasing the equipment for its use, or selling the equipment to someone else at the end of the contract. Because you are taking the risk in agreeing to dispose of the equipment at a fixed price in the future, the finance company will offer you much cheaper monthly payments for the duration of the contract, as it knows you must pay the balloon payment at the end. The advantages with finance leasing are:

- The instalment payments are lower.

- You have the opportunity to purchase known equipment at a low fixed price.

- If you do purchase equipment, your depreciation exposure will be reduced because of its lower price.

- You may be able to sell on the equipment at a higher price than the agreed 'balloon payment', thereby further improving your cash flow (conversely, however, the balloon payment may be greater than the equipment's actual residual value, as is becoming the case in current contracts relating to motor vehicles).

A third option is *lease purchase*. If you know that you want to continue owning the equipment at the end of the contract term, this may be a suitable option. Structurally it is similar to the two finance options already discussed, in that you avoid the initial capital outlay and instead pay in fixed instalments over the contract term. With lease purchase you are deemed, for accounting purposes but not legal ones, to have full ownership of the equipment from day one of the contract; as such, it is less VAT efficient as you must pay all the VAT up front or add it to your instalments. It is therefore more costly than the previous options, but can be a useful tool for non-VAT registered businesses.

Hire purchase is another method of equipment purchase, which allows you to buy equipment or vehicles and pay for them over time in a straightforward way. Typically, you will pay a lump sum down-payment at the outset of the contract and then fixed equal instalments over the rest of the fixed term. You can reclaim the VAT you pay on your instalments and you could also offset any interest payments against taxable profits. At the end of the agreement you take 'title' of the equipment or vehicle and from then on you are the owner. It makes sense to use hire purchase for assets that will have a working life and significant residual value after you have finished paying the instalments.

Companies that already have a significant amount of capital tied up in vehicles and equipment can often set up a *sale and leaseback* contract with a finance company. This allows them to sell their vehicle fleet, for example, to the finance company and so remove the depreciating asset from the balance sheet while gaining a cash injection, and then lease them back with all the advantages of contract hire.

For the sole trader or small partnership there are some newer financing options specifically designed for the car market. These are similar to the options above but available to private individuals. Personal contract purchase is where the future estimated value of the vehicle is deducted from the initial cost, and the remaining amount is spread across the term as instalment payments plus interest. Usually at the end of the term you can either pay the 'balloon payment' and keep the car, or just return it. This allows you access to the same buying power as fleet car companies, as well as the budgeting opportunities of financing deals.

Vehicle taxation

Specific tax rules apply to cars and vans, and they are therefore treated differently from other capital equipment. Because of the lack of clarity in recording private and business usage of vehicles, HMRC have special rates of VAT that allow them to compensate. It is best to speak to your tax adviser to discover exactly what you may and may not reclaim.

Similarly, the tax benefits for company cars have become less generous and more complex in recent years. The government no longer determines company car taxation on mileage and vehicle age, as it claimed this method encouraged more driving in older vehicles, which was not environmentally friendly. Now it bases the tax charge on a percentage of the car's price, graduated according to the level of the car's carbon dioxide (CO_2) emissions. The charge builds up from 15 per cent of the car's price, for cars emitting 165 grams per kilometre (g/km) CO_2, in 1 per cent steps for every additional 5 g/km over 165 g/km. The maximum charge is 35 per cent of the car's price.

Insurance

A classic economic definition of profit is the reward for taking risk. On the basis that you are in business to make a profit, you will therefore be taking a risk. The size and effect of the risks you take should be closely related to the profit you can expect to make. There is no point in taking large risks if you are only going to make small profits. Not all risks are financial; some are physical, some ethical. But in business most risks have a financial element – even the physical and ethical ones. If your employee is injured in the course of his or her work you may well be liable to pay compensation. If your products are discovered to be polluting, then adverse publicity may affect your sales.

Insurance provides a simple way of reducing large downside risks to manageable levels. For most businesses specialist insurance will not be necessary. General insurance can be relatively cheap and is easily obtained to cover most commercial liabilities.

There are a few legal insurance requirements that you must comply with:

- *Employer's liability*: as soon as you employ someone the law requires you to have employer's liability insurance, of a minimum of £10 million.

- *Public liability*: the law requires you to have liability insurance to cover any damages payable arising from bodily injury, illness or damage to property incurred during the course of your work.

- *Product liability*: there is a legal requirement to be able to compensate in the event of your product being defective and so causing injury.

Beyond these statutory insurance requirements, a risk-aware business will probably want to cover itself against a range of other potential risks. Commercial insurance is usually split into three categories: liabilities, property and buildings, and business assets and equipment. The last two are fairly self-explanatory, but your liability insurance can cover a wide range of alternatives.

In addition to the legal liabilities above, you may also want to consider professional indemnity insurance (against damages caused by your giving poor or negligent advice); key staff cover (in a small firm the loss of one key person either temporarily or permanently can cause major disruption to your provision of services); business interruption (damage to plant or supplies can cause your business to temporarily cease production); transit cover (protection for goods in transit); credit insurance (insurance for bad debts); directors' and officers' liability (covers due diligence and fiduciary duty); and computer cover (insures against accidental damage, theft, breakdown, etc).

Insurance should not be a significant proportion of your costs unless you are undertaking a particularly hazardous project. Specialist insurance is available for almost any event imaginable – at a cost. For any trade overseas you will need to consider a further range of risks, from export guarantees (for payments) to political risks and exchange rate risks.

With your basic insurance requirements most commercial insurance companies will be available to offer you a standard package to cover your legal and essential liabilities. For more specialist cover you will need to contact a broker who can arrange cover for you. As with all such business contracts, it will pay to ask friends and business contacts who they recommend for price, efficiency and reliability.

Risk mitigation

Many insurance policies will require you to take some action to mitigate any risk before they will cover you. At its most basic, you will be required to fit good locks on your doors and windows to be eligible for business equipment insurance. For other liabilities you will also find statutory health and safety requirements that must be complied with. The laws covering these requirements are often only evident once a problem has arisen. Your duty as business owner or manager is usually to ensure that all reasonable precautions have been taken to prevent foreseeable accidents or damages, whether this is with office equipment (eg that electric sockets are not overloaded, and that machinery is regularly serviced), food hygiene (that due care has been taken to avoid contamination, etc) or on building sites (that correct safety procedures have been followed) or whatever area of business you operate within.

The principle to adhere to is that you are able to prove that you have followed such procedures, and not just state that you have. This inevitably requires a 'paper trail' where inspections are noted down, instruction on procedures is written down and issued to all relevant personnel, and occasional testing of this knowledge is carried out. There is clearly a fine balance between taking these actions so that they can prove you have fulfilled your 'due diligence' and their obstructing the efficient performance of your business. A friendly discussion with the local authority officer in charge of such issues may help to clarify your particular situation.

Checklist

- Do you need separate premises?
- If not, can you work from home effectively?
- If working from home:
  - Do you need a separate phone line, broadband internet access, etc?
  - Do you need planning permission?
  - Do you know whether there are any capital gains tax implications of working from your home?
  - Have you discussed implications with other householders?
  - Have you considered whether you will feel isolated?
  - Do you have other homeworkers to discuss work issues with?
- If seeking premises:
  - How much space do you need?
  - Does this allow for all your equipment dimensions?
  - Does this allow you room for growth?
  - Do you require any planning permission?
  - Is location important to you and your customers?

continued

- Purchase or lease: remember that purchasing your premises is essentially a separate business proposition.

- Lease contract:
  - Get professional advice.
  - Negotiate your terms: at the outset you have your best chance to get the lease you want.
  - Ask about rent-free periods, break clauses, assignment rights, and rent-review terms.
  - Make sure you understand the fundamentals: what upkeep and charges you are responsible for; who pays the insurance; and what your arbitration rights are.

- Asset financing: familiarize yourself with all the options, such as:
  - contract hire;
  - finance leasing;
  - lease purchase;
  - hire purchase;
  - personal contract purchase.

- Insurance: double check you have all your legal obligations in place:
  - public liability;
  - product liability;
  - employer's liability.

- Think through your other insurance risks:
  - building and plant;
  - stock;
  - professional indemnity;
  - key staff cover;
  - business interruption;
  - credit insurance;
  - transit insurance and so on.

- Risk mitigation: have you thought through a crisis management plan?

Chapter Seventeen
Transportation

Your customers will judge the quality of your products and the physical services your firm provides in terms of their delivery, as well as by their intrinsic value. This is partly a matter of fulfilling orders promptly, delivering to schedule and carrying out service calls on the due date and at the agreed time, and partly the personal service that your staff or your contractor's personnel give at the delivery point. It is not possible to provide prompt delivery or efficient service without quality transportation, and that is the theme of this short chapter.

Contract delivery or own transport

When you start your business, one guiding principle is to keep fixed costs to a minimum, so any investment in vehicles, whether it involves interest and repayment of principal on bank loans or hire purchase, leasing or rental charges, is unwelcome if it can be avoided. If you are supplying goods over a wide area, perhaps nationally, contractor services will offer the most appropriate means of delivery. There are a multitude of courier and parcel services available whose charges are based on the size or weight of the package and distance delivered. If you are able to invoice your customers for delivery charges, it should be possible for you to convert your contractor's tariff into a scale of charges that you can quote on your order form and your customers can check on their invoices received.

Whatever terms you may negotiate with your selected contractor, it will probably apply standard terms and conditions to every consignment regarding acceptance and returns, which limits its liability in the event of late or non-delivery, damage to and the return of goods. You should include these terms in your standard terms and conditions.

Be sure to monitor the quality of your contractor's delivery service rather than wait for customer complaints. The contractor's documentation, which should include a delivery log signed by each customer on receipt of goods, enables you to check delivery times against the promised service. Supplement regular inspection of the contractor's records with periodic surveys to test customer satisfaction. The very act of consulting customers will add to your service image. If the contractor's service performance deteriorates and there is no effective response to requests for improvement, do not hesitate to change your contractor.

If your distribution pattern is concentrated in a limited area, the alternative of own transport may be more attractive, particularly when it will be fully utilized. It may make good sense to run one or more vehicles to serve your home territory where there is a density of local customers, and to employ one or more contract delivery services elsewhere.

There are some kinds of business where contract delivery is not a viable alternative. For example if you are a retailer of television, video and hi-fi equipment, installation is an important part of your total service that your customers will expect to be carried out on the spot when the equipment is delivered; by definition, your business is also likely to have a local clientele. Delivery by a contractor and a follow-up visit by your fitter may be cost-effective for you but will damage customer satisfaction. Similarly, if you offer a central heating and plumbing service your business depends on the use of properly equipped vans with supplies of tools and components so your staff can carry out emergency repair jobs. The customer will have no objection to the separate delivery of major items of equipment, but will expect the engineer on the job to have at hand everything necessary to complete an installation or repair job.

When you start up, you may be a one-person business requiring a single van, but as this kind of service business grows, the number of vans in permanent use will increase in direct proportion to activity and the number of customers. Quite quickly you will become a fleet manager in your own right.

Vehicle procurement strategies

The financing alternatives for vehicle procurement – contract hire, finance leasing and contract purchase – are discussed in Chapter 16. Each option has its attractions for the small business. The relative merits in terms of taxation, depreciation charges and capital allowances are discussed there and do not need to be repeated in this chapter. However, for those with funds available to whom none of these financing schemes appeals greatly, it is worth summarizing the arguments for and against outright purchase.

Advantages of outright purchase

- Access to capital allowances.
- The full benefit of residual value.
- Complete control of the vehicle/fleet.
- VAT recoverable when the vehicle is used exclusively for business purposes.

Vehicles purchased outright are, of course, assets that must be registered in the company's balance sheet. However, the maximum writing-down allowance permitted by HMRC of £3,000 per year per vehicle implies a first-year value of £12,000, based on the maximum rate of depreciation allowed of 25 per cent. Vehicles costing more than £12,000 are treated as individual assets, and a balancing charge is made when the vehicle is sold on – either the remaining depreciation if the selling price is less than the balance sheet written-down value, or a taxable profit if the selling price exceeds the written down value.

Similarly, if the VAT charge when the vehicle was purchased is recovered, VAT must be added to the price when the vehicle is sold on.

Disadvantages of outright purchase

- Possibility that motor vehicle assets, perhaps backed by borrowing on the balance sheet, may adversely affect gearing ratios and return on asset measures of importance.
- Exposure to interest rate fluctuations on borrowings.
- The risk that residual values may not meet expectations.
- The opportunity (for most cars) to recover 50 per cent of VAT on lease charges.
- The inability (for smaller fleets) to benefit from the buying power of the lessor.
- If more than several vehicles are involved, the need for operational, administrative and fleet management expertise.

Fleet management services

A vehicle fleet of more than just a handful of vehicles imposes legal, administrative and managerial burdens, and demands skills to achieve efficiency and effectiveness of operation that your business probably lacks in-house. Outsourcing some or all of these tasks to fleet management specialists may be a cost-effective solution.

In the case of contract hire and contract purchase agreements, fleet management is very likely to be included. Fleet management can also be the subject of a stand-alone contract to cover the management of user-owned or leased vehicles. Under such a contract, the fleet user reimburses the fleet management company for all costs incurred plus a management fee. For user-owned vehicles VAT is recoverable, and the costs of fleet management are a tax-allowable charge against income.

Among the services commonly included in a fleet management contract are:

- sourcing of new vehicles;
- the preparation of vehicles to the operator's specifications (eg car phones, corporate livery, specialist racking for vans);

- registrations with the Driver and Vehicle Licensing Authority (DVLA, Swansea);
- servicing and maintenance;
- breakdown replacement;
- accident repairs;
- insurance claims submission and management;
- fuel services (eg the provision of corporate fuel cards);
- settlement of accounts for running costs;
- maximization of residual values and disposal of used vehicles;
- cost monitoring and control routines, covering vehicle utilization, mileage, fuel economy and risk assessment of the fleet and drivers.

Many fleet management added-value services involve information gathering and analysis by the management company. Before signing up, you should ask the company to demonstrate its successful application of IT to reduce operating costs and simplify administration. Whether the fleet management company you select is independent or linked to a finance house, you should arrange for the contract period for fleet management to coincide with that for the hire contract or lease.

Disposal of vehicles

Fleet management schemes require a disposals policy that is compatible with the assumptions made in the original financing. Whether your fleet has been financed by purchase or a financial lease, a successful outcome will depend on maximizing the residual value when it is sold.

Residual values can be estimated quite accurately for any model of vehicle of given age and mileage by reference to *Glass's Guide*, the motor trade's monthly publication, or by reference to a number of internet websites. However, residual values can be volatile as they depend not just on the supply of used vehicles, but on the extent to which the new market is over-supplied and the discount terms available, which may attract private buyers to new rather than used vehicle purchases.

The original financing is based on estimates of residual value, and the fleet management scheme disposals policy is framed accordingly. If these assumptions prove over-optimistic, it may be necessary to intervene and dispose of a vehicle before its due date, to avoid a greater loss later. Alternatively, it may be beneficial to keep the vehicle in service until maintenance costs become excessive or until it is more fully depreciated.

Alternative disposal routes

If you are a sole trader or a small-fleet operator replacing only a few vehicles at a time, and you seek to purchase replacements outright, negotiating a trade-in against the cost of the replacement may be the most effective course of action. The services of specialist car auctioneers, such as British Car Auctions, are available to operators with larger volumes to dispose of at the same time. Both the trade-in and the auction route carry the advantage that the vehicles are sold 'as seen' and that there is no potential liability towards a subsequent owner.

Extras and accessories

Vehicles can be supplied to almost any factory specification by lessors and hire companies. Of course, factory extras increase the initial vehicle cost and therefore the monthly payments; they also tend to depreciate quickly and may not be reflected in residual values. On the other hand, in the case of used passenger cars, private buyers' demand is usually higher for 'mid-range', if not 'top of the range', models compared with the basic model.

'Extras' fitted to the vehicle, such as car phones, stereos and extra lights, are also likely to affect residual values adversely. Many hire and other financing contracts, where ownership does not pass eventually to the user, impose restrictions on extras or insist that they remain in place when the vehicle is returned. Similarly the respraying of a vehicle and the fitting of advertising decals may be subject to restrictions, and will be taken into account in contract purchase agreements where the user has the right to sell the vehicle back. There may be a financial case, after all, for retaining that anonymous plain white van!

Checklist

- Your customers will judge the quality of your firm by your delivery service, as well as the intrinsic value of your products or services.

- If you are supplying goods over a wide area, perhaps nationally, contractor services will probably offer the most efficient delivery.

- Incorporate in your standard terms and conditions those of your contractor relating to acceptance and delivery that limit their liability.

- Monitor your contractor's service by regular inspection of its delivery records, and carry out periodic customer surveys.

- Run your own vehicle(s) where your distribution pattern is concentrated or the success of your business relies on installation and repair services.

- Review the alternative merits of contract hire, finance leasing and contract purchase, in terms of taxation, depreciation charges and capital allowances, against the advantages and disadvantages of outright purchase.

- For more than a handful of vehicles, consider outsourcing fleet management services to a specialist firm.

- The successful outcome of fleet purchase or a financial lease depends on maximizing residual values on disposal. If residual value estimates prove optimistic, you may need to dispose of a vehicle before its due date to avoid later loss, or to retain it until it is more fully depreciated or maintenance costs become excessive.

- Both the trade-in and auction routes involve selling the vehicles 'as seen' and avoid potential liability towards a subsequent owner.

- Factory extras increase initial vehicle cost and monthly payments to hire companies; they also depreciate quickly and may not add to residual value. Hire and financing contractors may insist that accessories remain in place on return and restrict respraying or fitting of advertising decals.

Part Three
Spreading Your Wings

PART THREE CONTENTS

Chapter Eighteen
When Small Is No Longer Beautiful

If you have a business, you have a problem. It does not matter what size the business is, there will always be issues to deal with. Even if everything is proceeding to plan, you will have to look ahead to prepare the business for future challenges.

This chapter looks at the main elements of 'the next stage' in your business's development. Before we look at the three main obstacles that will need to be dealt with when you try to grow the business, there is a vital question to address. Do you *want* to grow the business? For some, being your own boss, making decisions in a small group without responsibility for many tens of employees, avoiding large amounts of debt and not diluting the ownership of the business may be very attractive. If you are earning a decent amount and no longer struggling to get business from one day to the next, you may already have reached a happy and sustainable level. If so, read the rest of this chapter and enjoy knowing that there are plenty of stresses and strains out there that you will not be putting yourself through!

However, for many entrepreneurs, building the business is 'what it is all about' and perhaps for you 'small' is no longer 'beautiful'. If this is your position, then the same old mantra laid out elsewhere in this guide will be needed again. Identify your objectives, then create a plan and timescale to get there. Unless you know where you want to go, no plan is going to be of any use.

Identifying why you want to grow your business is important, because your answer will impact the manner in which you grow it.

If you are looking to keep the business in the long term and wish to manage a medium-sized business of your own, then keeping 100 per cent control of the ownership may be a high priority. If you are looking to grow the company quickly to a size where it will be attractive to a potential purchaser, then you will have a different set of priorities and timescales.

Having identified why you wish to grow the business, you will create the plan to carry this out. At this stage, you will need to identify whether your growth strategy will be an organic or acquisitive one. Organic growth is when the expansion is created internally, with increases in turnover achieved by extending your current product range, or perhaps widening your sales area. The alternative to this approach is to buy other companies that will give your business greater depth or breadth immediately. Clearly both choices have their pros and cons. Of course, you may combine the two approaches. They are not necessarily incompatible.

Whatever the direction you intend to take your business in, having decided to grow it, you will encounter the same three basic sets of problems. The way you tackle these problems will differ depending on your ultimate objectives, but the problems will be the same: financial problems, predominantly cash flow and secondary funding; process problems, creating systems that work efficiently for larger and more diverse organizations; and personnel problems, the larger the organization, the more people are needed.

Financial problems

Cash flow

As we noted in Part Two, cash flow is the most notorious slayer of small businesses. Some businesses are very cash generative when they work well; pubs, for example, can take a lot of cash upfront and pay their suppliers later. Most businesses are not so lucky. If you are not only trying to pay your current bills but also to expand your advertising, pay for some research into a new product or market, or most probably pay the interest instalments on the new piece of equipment you require to expand production or distribution, then you may find your cash situation very much stretched.

The problem scenario

If you are following the organic growth strategy, managing your cash flow will be critical to your success. It will require you to cost out all your expansion requirements very carefully against a timeline of expected sales increases. You are unlikely to be able to run all your growth projects simultaneously on current cash flow, and this may lead to problems with implementing your strategy. You will need to prioritize which elements are required first. It is not worth spending large sums on an advertising campaign if you do not have the capacity to manufacture or distribute product to meet the increased demand. However, you may not be able to pay for the new equipment if you have not increased sales, which will require extra marketing expenditure – the classic 'chicken and egg' situation.

The solutions

The solutions to your requirement for increased working capital are that you will have to either borrow it or buy it (sell a share of your business in return for the money). The decision as to which course you follow will be dependent on the answer to the question posed above (what you are growing your business for?) and also on the amount of extra cash you require.

If your extra working capital requirements are not vastly greater than your current situation – that is if, say, your monthly expenses are currently £10,000 per month and your new requirements increase this to £15,000 per month and not £40,000 per month – then your bank will probably be able to help you. If the new situation is a multiple of your current situation, that is the £40,000 per month scenario, then your bank may be less obliging, and a number of alternative solutions present themselves.

Whatever your new need, the providers of the extra cash will require to see a fully costed business plan for the project. The more detail and accuracy in your plan, the more weight it will carry. You will probably also need to produce the figures with a number of different sales scenarios. This will show how the repayment amounts can be met with expected sales, and lower than expected sales. If you are selling some of your business to fund the expansion, a set of better-than-expected sales figures will whet the appetite of the investors. In any case you will need a number of the investment evaluation tools described in Chapter 19.

Bank provision

Your bank will be the simplest source for accessing your extra cash needs. It can either loan you a lump sum that you repay in predetermined instalments, or extend your overdraft facility. The lump sum loan will probably be less expensive than the overdraft, but you may find that you do not really need a single large sum to accommodate your cash flow requirements, but rather, occasional short-term funds. In this case, the overdraft facility may well be more cost-effective. You will have to determine which is the best for your particular situation.

If you have managed to establish a good, communicative relationship with your bank manager (increasingly rare in these tough times) or adviser, and have produced a well-constructed business plan, your bank ought to be sympathetic to your plans. If you cannot persuade your bank to either loan you the money or provide an extended overdraft facility, or if you are unhappy with the terms it offers you, you should speak to other banks that favour small businesses. Often a particular bank may have a computer model that, for whatever reason, has a problem with an aspect of your business plan. Another bank's model may be constructed in such a way that your plan is acceptable to it, or its own internal targets may be more open to business lending at that moment. It is always worth asking around, especially if you already have a good business plan to present to the manager. However, at this time of writing more doors are closed than open.

From the other side, it may be that your plan is flawed, and that the bank manager is unhappy with it. If the manager is unwilling to give specific reasons, take it to a Business Link adviser or other consultant for a second opinion. If there is a fatal flaw to your plan, it is much better to discover it before you borrow and spend the money.

Private funding

A survey of British small businesses, made shortly before the 'credit crunch', showed that the majority of funding for both new enterprises and second-round finance came from private sources. That is the owner, his or her family and friends.

The reasons for this are not difficult to discern. Private funders will usually accept more risk, because the business involved and its owners are personally known to the cash providers, whether they are lenders or investors. These people are less likely to have to provide a return; so they will be less picky and less experienced in analysing small businesses. This makes it easier to get money from them. The downside is that you will not necessarily be receiving any expert third-party opinion on your plan; it will not be being benchmarked against other opportunities, so you will not be able to gauge its attractiveness. Finally if you cannot pay back the money you may well be ruining more than just a business relationship, which, when the chips are down, can be doubly damaging.

It is imperative that the terms of the private funding are contracted as carefully as a bank loan would be. Make sure that everybody concerned understands the downside risks, the time the loan is for, and the potential maximum upside return as well. You should get your accountant or solicitor to advise you on the documentation and terms applicable to your situation.

Grants and soft loans

Another source of funding for your business, whether it is at start-up stage or established, is through local authority and central government grants and special funds. It is worth contacting your local authority small business advisory team, Business Link and the local Chamber of Commerce, and also enquiring at your bank whether they know of any such funds that might be available to you. Your local reference library may also be able to provide some useful ideas.

The problem with grants is that they are often very specific (for perfectly valid reasons) as to how, where and when the funds can be used. As such, your plan may not fit with their requirements. Do not alter your plan just to get funds. In the majority of cases you will be required to provide a substantial part of the money yourself in order for the granter to release its percentage of the planned costs. If the plan and the grant fit, you should assess the grant's value, including the bureaucracy often involved in applying for and receiving funds, in just the same way as you would assess the offer of a bank loan.

Outside investors

This source was once the glamorous end of the funding search. When the technology bubble was fizzy with excitement a few years ago, a lot of the froth surrounded the ease with which venture capitalists and business angels showered new business ideas with capital. When the bubble burst, reality gripped the venture capital (VC) industry, and trying to get funds from these providers is today more difficult. Private equity funding for larger, established businesses became more readily available. Today, the private equity market is recovering from an extended period of recession.

The venture capital market Typically, the VC industry is uninterested in any project smaller than £250,000, and most likely £1 million. Venture capitalists are investing other people's money on the basis of their own business judgement and acumen. They will be therefore meticulous in their appraisal of your plan – the 'due diligence' required of them will often take as much time for a £250,000 project as a £1 million one, but their percentage return is clearly much more worthwhile for the latter. The British Venture Capital Association (www.bvca.co.uk) will be able to provide you with more information if you think this is the route for you.

Business angels Business angels are private individuals who invest their own money in businesses. They tend to be much more flexible with the sums they will invest. The problem is finding an angel willing to invest in your business. Angels tend to invest in only a small number of projects, in sectors about which they are already knowledgeable. A good starting point in searching for angels is the National Business Angels Network (www.nban.co.uk).

With both VCs and angels you will be expected to sell a percentage of your company in return for the funding, probably not less than 25 per cent. You should also expect to find the funds provider(s) sitting on your board as company director(s). Clearly their business advice and experience can be a real bonus, but you must be comfortable with the risk that you will disagree on the company's direction. Through its funding, the investor will have enormous leverage over your company. It is important that you are as comfortable with the investors as with their money.

Process problems

The biggest single change to your business model when you find that your business grows is that your ability to control, communicate and change things becomes diluted. When you started your business, perhaps there were three of you in an office or shop. Three years down the line there may be 15 staff in three different locations. If you want to find something out, you cannot just swivel your chair around and ask your two colleagues; you now have to 'speak to the right person'. So from now on everyone has to have a defined role; otherwise no one knows who 'the right person' is or should be.

When there were three of you the risk of someone leaving or being away when you needed them was relatively low; now you do not know everyone's movements or timetables, so you must have a procedure to access their work and files if you need to. When you were all in the same office all deliveries could only come to one place, all stock could only be in one place and all customer information could only be in one place. Not so when you have multiple sites.

In order for you to remain quick, responsive and in control of your business when it grows, you need to create a structure of procedures. It is this necessary imposition of systems and 'processes' that stops your business becoming chaotic, unfocused and inefficient. You grow your business because you wish to enhance the economies of scale: bulk purchasing, more cost-effective advertising, lower per-unit administrative costs and so on. But you will also notice that you lose the small team atmosphere, the camaraderie created by having your backs against the wall, and some of the excitement – unless you actively work to create this culture across the business.

The building of processes to ensure that your business works efficiently and effectively is greatly helped these days by computer technology. The existence of networked computer systems that centrally store customer information, product data, sales data and so forth immediately solves many of your information process problems. Mobile technology (laptops and telephones) also allows you to contact staff easily wherever they may be. The more significant process management decisions will cover multiple applications through the establishment of supply chain management, resource applications and a raft of standardized procedures. As the need for more integrated procedures grows, you will become accustomed to the management jargon that they entail, and appreciate the role of recognized national standards such as ISO 9000 and quality standards like 'six sigma'.

It is this movement away from an informal communications and information structure to a formalized one that most characterizes the development from a small business into a mature medium-sized enterprise.

Personnel problems

The third element of your business's growing pains is the change associated with an increased number of employees. As the business grows, the original management team will find that it is unable to attend to all the day-to-day decisions and the strategic planning that is required. You will inevitably find that all levels of employment are stretched, from the warehouse staff to yourself.

Increasing the number of people employed at the customer service end of the business will bring with it a number of issues. First, you will want to maintain the business's culture and atmosphere and try to keep alive the customer-driven spirit. With a large recruitment drive, it will become increasingly more difficult with each extra employee to find personalities and skills that fit your company. You will also need to keep front-end staff motivated and enhance the team spirit.

Further up the company you will be faced with management issues as well. If you have brought in outside investors, you may find the need for a full-time finance director who can liaise with the investors and manage the assets actively, as well as produce the monthly and quarterly reports that investors demand. The growth of different departments may also mean that specialist skills are required. This creates the dilemma of whether to promote from within or seek people who already have the relevant skills from outside the business. Either approach can create an environment whereby existing employees feel left out or passed over – which can demoralize and cause resentment.

Essentially, you have to look to your growth objectives to determine your method here. If you are looking to grow the company in order to sell it, then you may want to bring in skills quickly to achieve growth as soon as possible. If you are intent on a longer-term organic growth, then promoting and training in-house may be the best way to achieve the cohesive, motivated team spirit. If you intend to grow through acquisition, part of your acquisition strategy may be to buy in companies that already possess the skills you need as well as the customers you want.

Finally, you should have a plan for management succession. This is as much an insurance policy as anything else, if you have no intentions of letting go of the reins for a while. However, you may find when you have nurtured your company from its start-up to a mid-sized company that your particular set of skills are not suited to managing and promoting such a business, but that they lie in the faster, looser, more flexible and creative world of start-ups. If this is the case it may be difficult to let go, but it may be wise to hand over the detailed management to someone with more mid-size company management experience.

With all these growth issues, the earlier they are faced up to, the more easily the transitions will be made. Clearly, you are not going to be seeking out a list of venture capitalists for second-round financing, creating a supply chain management framework and employing a finance director while you are still having to do the deliveries yourself. But when the growth phase starts, it is as well to think through the implications of any new processes and assess them for their suitability to further and wider expansion at a later date. If you can build systems that can grow with the business, you will be avoiding a lot of extra unnecessary upheaval and expenditure further down the line. Growing up is traumatic and stressful – laying a solid foundation will ease the process and enhance value.

Checklist

- Do you really want to grow your business – or are you happy with it performing at its current level?

- Why do you want to grow it? The answer to this will determine how you should grow it.

- Focus on cash flow. Do you want to buy capital (sell shares to raise cash) or borrow it?

- Have you tried your family and friends? Most small businesses get finance privately.

- Your bank is your best chance to borrow money.

- For amounts of £20,000 to £250,000, business angels and local government enterprise funds are your most likely sources.

- For amounts over £250,000, some venture capital funds may help, but in the main they only operate from £1 million upwards.

- Focus on process. When your business moves from the point that everyone knows what everyone else is doing all the time to a more mature structure where responsibility is clearly divided up, you will need to create clear procedures for communicating management ideas, decisions and operations.

- Learn about national excellence standards to enhance your processes.

- Focus on personnel. As you grow you will need to employ more people.

- Is your growth strategy acquisitive or organic?

- Will you try to expand your HR from within or externally?

- Have you established a management succession plan?

- Try to establish a growth framework early on, rather than cobble your exit plan together at the last moment.

Chapter Nineteen
More Management Accounting and Reporting Tools

As your business matures and you are again involved in detailed discussions with financial institutions or with shareholders for second-stage finance, the performance of the business will come under fresh scrutiny. You will want to prepare yourself by becoming familiar with the analytical tools that third parties will use to evaluate your company.

You will already be used to examining in detail your trading accounts, both the formal year-end profit and loss account and the monthly management accounts that are prepared internally. You may have less familiarity with the balance sheet and funds flow statement, which are food and drink to financial analysts.

The balance sheet

Whereas the profit and loss account covers a trading period and is therefore 'for the period ended...', the balance sheet relates to a moment in time, normally the end date of the trading period. It is a tally of what the business *owns* (including what is owed to the business, classified collectively as its 'assets'), and what the business *owes*, its short and long-term liabilities and provisions for debt. The balance between assets and liabilities is referred to as 'shareholders' funds'. Below as Figure 19.1 is a pro-forma balance sheet.

FIGURE 19.1 A pro-forma balance sheet

Assets	£	Liabilities	£
Fixed Assets		**Long-term liabilities**	– not due to be repaid within one year
Land and buildings		Bank loan	
Equipment		Taxation owed	
Vehicles			
Current assets		**Current liabilities**	– due to be repaid within one year
Stock = inventory		Bank loan	
Debtors = money owed by customers		Creditors = money owed to suppliers	
Cash includes bank deposit			
		Shareholders' funds	= 'equity capital'
		Issued share capital	= original contribution from shareholders
		Reserves	= retained profits + increases in value of business

Note that the assets that the company owns are grouped according to how 'liquid' they are – ie how quickly they can be converted into cash. The main division is between *fixed assets* – those assets which are likely to be owned by the business for at least a year before being turned into cash – and *current assets*: those that will be converted into cash inside a year.

The individual categories of asset are listed in order of liquidity under the fixed and current subheadings, with the most 'liquid' at the bottom and the most 'illiquid' at the top. So in the *fixed assets* category, Land and Buildings is at the top because they are not likely to be turned into cash anytime soon. However in the *Current Assets* category Bank and Cash are at the bottom because they are totally liquid. Liabilities that must be repaid within a year, are under *Current Liabilities*, while those that will remain unpaid for more than a year are *Long-term Liabilities*.

The difference between the total values of the assets and the liabilities is the value of the business, theoretically the amount for which it could be liquidated. This is the *net asset value* of the business, also known as its *net worth*. This figure is the same as the *equity capital* of the business, which is owned by the shareholders.

Capital

Capital is the money that finances the business long term. If all the capital belongs to the shareholders. it is called *equity capital* or *shareholders' funds*.

A frequently asked question is why equity capital (shareholders' funds), which finances the company, should be on the liabilities side of the balance sheet? The answer is that the money is not owned by the company but is *owed* by the company to its owners.

However, capital may be borrowed, often from a bank, in which case it is called *debt capital*. If money is borrowed, it's only called debt capital if it is for the long-term financing of the business. (A more technical name for debt capital is 'fixed interest bearing funds'.)

The formulas in Figure 19.2 are essential to understanding the capital architecture of corporate finance:

FIGURE 19.2 The architecture of corporate finance

Assets – liabilities = equity capital = net worth = net assets

Assets – liabilities (excluding long-term financing) = equity capital + debt capital

The equity capital or shareholders' funds consist of two elements:

- issued share capital (= money contributed by shareholders);
- reserves (= retained profit or increase in the value of the company since its start date, which also belongs to the shareholders).

Issued share capital may consist of *ordinary shares*, which entitle the holders to dividends but no certain return on their investment, and *preference shares*, which entitle holders to regular percentage returns on the face value of the shares but no other dividend, and rank ahead of ordinary shares for repayment in the event of liquidation. Both classes of shares rank behind repayment of all creditors.

There are more complicated classes of share that are hybrids of ordinary and preference shares and are often used by venture capitalists to improve the security on their non-debt investments or enhance their value if the company is sold. Of these, the most common are:

- preferred ordinary shares – a special class of ordinary share that gives them preference in liquidation;
- participating preference shares, which entitle holders to a share of dividends;
- convertible preference shares, which can be converted into ordinary shares on fixed terms within a specified time period.

Capital gearing

Capital gearing, called 'leverage' in the US, refers to the ratio of debt to equity in a company's capital. Generally, if the equity portion is less than half, the company is considered to be 'highly geared'. Conversely, if the ratio is more than half, the company is said to be 'low geared'.

Funds flow statement

The funds flow statement is also known as the 'Statement of Sources and Applications of Funds'. It is sometimes referred to as the 'cash flow statement', not to be confused with the cash flow spreadsheets that you use daily in running your company.

The funds flow statement shows the effect on cash of the operations of the business during the trading year. Simply stated, this will be the bottom line profit adjusted for any transactions that did not involve receipt or payment of money. Taking an elementary example: where no cash changed hands, of a company with sales of £100, cost of sales £70 and profit of £30, the funds flow statement would show the difference between the profit position of £30 and the cash position of zero as in Figure 19.3 below:

In practice, the bottom line profit is adjusted in constructing the funds flow statement in respect of two different things:

- Any line items in the profit and loss account that are non-cash items (for example depreciation of fixed assets or provision for debts that have not, or will not have to be paid).

- Any increase or decrease in the value of balance sheet items between the balance sheet at the start of the trading period, and the balance sheet at the end of the trading period. These increases or decreases are equivalent to payments or receipts of cash. For example:
  - an *increase* in equipment would represent *cash paid*;
  - an *increase* in debtors would represent *cash not received (= same effect as cash paid)*;
  - an *increase* in creditors would represent *cash not paid (= same effect as cash received)*.

Figure 19.4 offers a more sophisticated *pro-forma* funds flow statement.

FIGURE 19.3 Simple example of funds flow statement

Profit	30
add	
Increase in Creditors	70 *(unpaid)*
	100
deduct	
Increase in Debtors	100 *(not received)*
Total Cash Effect	0

FIGURE 19.4 Example of a 'pro-forma' funds flow statement

		£
Net Profit		
Add	Depreciation	
	Increase in provisions	
	Increase in creditors	___
Deduct	Increase in motor vehicles	
	Increase in debtors	
		___
	Total change in cash	___

In order to construct a funds flow statement, the changes in the values in the opening and closing balance sheets for the period to be analysed are required. The closing balance sheet must be completed first. If you are forecasting future cash flow, this means that you will have to prepare both a forecast profit and loss account and the end-of-period balance sheet. Only then can the change in the cash position be calculated.

Key external performance indicators

There are three frequently used key performance indicators, displayed in Figure 19.5, that have significant impact on how external investors perceive a company. You may be familiar with them already.

FIGURE 19.5 Frequently used key performance indicators

Earnings per share = $\dfrac{\text{net profit after tax}}{\text{number of shares in issue}}$

Return on capital employed (per cent) = $\dfrac{\text{profit after tax}}{\text{total equity capital}}$

Price/earnings ratio = $\dfrac{\text{market price of share}}{\text{earnings per share}}$

The first two items in Figure 19.5 are indicators of profitability. The third is a measure of how highly investors rate the profit that a company has produced. A fourth indicator, yield, is simply the reciprocal of price/earnings ratio expressed as a percentage.

Key internal indicators

Finally, let us return to the key internal indicators that measure the health and profitability of the business and to which you, as well as external financial institutions, will pay attention.

The first four are integral to cash management on which we have focused throughout the course of this book.

Liquidity ratio

The surplus of current assets over current liabilities, (net current assets), is known as working capital or liquidity and the 'liquidity ratio' is simply:

$$\frac{Liquid\ Assets}{Current\ Liabilities}$$

A company's liquidity ratio indicates how easily it can pay its day-to-day running costs. Normally liquid assets are cash and bank balances, other 'money' (for example in the form of bills receivable and quoted securities) and trade debtors. They are cash or items that can be turned into cash in the ordinary course of business and, in the case of debtors, within the company's normal credit terms. Stocks, which can be less easily converted into cash, are *not* included.

In effect, the liquidity ratio compares the balance sheet figure for liquid assets with the amount owing in respect of day-to-day running costs. If the ratio is less than 1.0, the company probably has insufficient liquidity.

Stock days

$$\frac{\text{Stock} \times 365}{\text{Purchases}}$$

The stock days ratio compares total cost of purchases for the year (used to generate sales) with the closing stock of purchased items held. For example, if purchases are 6,000 and closing stock 500, then the company has stock for 30 days or one month's operation.

Debtors payment period

Another simple time-related ratio

$$\frac{\text{Debtors} \times 52}{\text{Sales}}$$

In this ratio, the value of closing balance sheet debtors is compared to sales for the year. This is a measure of the number of weeks that the company takes to collect money from debtors.

Creditors payment period

This is the converse of debtors payment period.

$$\frac{\text{Creditors} \times 365}{\text{Purchases}}$$

This time, the closing value of balance sheet creditors is compared to total purchases for the year, measuring the number of days that the company takes to pay suppliers. If the number is less than 30 you may be paying some creditors more quickly than you need; if the number is more than 60, you are on dangerous ground.

Return on capital employed

This and the next ratio are favourites for all potential investors. Return on capital employed (ROCE) is calculated as:

$$\frac{EBIT \times 100\%}{Shareholders'\ Funds}$$

where EBIT is the acronym for 'earnings before tax and interest'.

The ratio compares the company's pre-tax and interest profit on operations for a year with the shareholders' investment, including any undistributed profits. If the calculated rate is less than the rate of interest paid on bank deposits, outside shareholders might prefer to invest their funds elsewhere. Conversely, if the rate is lower than the rate paid on debt borrowing, then, if the company borrowed more, the return for the shareholders would be higher.

Return on sales

This last ratio compares the same operating profit with sales over the period of one year:

$$\frac{EBIT \times 100\%}{Total\ Sales}$$

It shows how efficiently the directors are using the sales revenue to manage costs and overheads, and to drive the business forward. The higher the result, the stronger the company will be to handle problems such as price wars, increasing costs or reducing sales.

A final point relevant to the evaluation of an established company's performance is that external investors are more interested in relatively long-term activity and trends, the comparison of several sequential years' results, than in one year's results only.

Chapter Twenty
Managing Export Business

Market research

The initial decision to examine a specific export market will necessarily be based on incomplete information. You may be drawn to a particular market by its size, its rate of growth, your knowledge of the local competition or the experience of your competitors in entering that market. Perhaps you have limited experience of the market through sourcing supplies for your business from there, attending a trade show in the country or meeting a visiting delegation. Through any of these activities, you may have gained a first order that indicates market prices are favourable. Perhaps your inclination to enter this particular export market is no more than a perceived affinity with the country and its people.

Whatever the thought process or chain of circumstances that has persuaded you to consider a specific market, your first serious step is market research in at least the equivalent depth to the desk research you would carry out into any new niche market at home. The scope of the research will be wider, to include the legal and regulatory environment, the distribution chain and channels to market, and terms of business, as well as the current and potential market for your product or service, pricing structures, competitor activity and local promotional practices. In developed export markets, particularly those of Western Europe and the EU accession states of Central and Eastern Europe, there are many sources of information for you to tap into, from internet websites and published statistics to chambers of commerce, trade associations, inward investment agencies and the commercial officers at the local British Embassy.

Good starting points are the UK Trade and Investment country desks at the Department of Business, Innovation and Skills (BIS) and the London offices of the joint chambers of commerce that foster trade between individual foreign countries and the UK, such as the German–British Chamber of Commerce and Industry. From these sources and the further sources located in the market itself, you should be able to develop a 'long list' of potential customers to form the nucleus for a pilot marketing campaign.

Commissioning field research at this stage of your investigation is probably not a cost-effective exercise. It is more important for you or your marketing manager to gain personal exposure to the market. Attendance at relevant trade and industry exhibitions can be a valuable experience, provided that you use your time wisely. Some continental trade shows are so large that it is easy to become overwhelmed by the number of exhibitors and to be distracted from visiting the few stands that are most relevant to your business. A good way to avoid such confusion is to collect a copy of the catalogue on arrival before visiting the exhibition, to shortlist the most promising exhibitors' stands and to plan the optimum route between them.

Visiting potential customers on their stands at exhibitions is unlikely to yield immediate orders for your products or services – after all, their objective is to market their own products at the shows where they exhibit. However, in some industries, such as automotive, it is common for original equipment manufacturers (OEMs) to set up buying offices with the express purpose of meeting prospective new suppliers. From your point of view, this is better than 'cold calling' and may serve as a first step in the long process required to establish your company as a qualified supplier to the OEM. In any event, your attendance at trade shows should help you to firm up on a more refined 'shortlist' of potential customers for a direct sales approach.

Sales development

Hopefully, your follow-up campaign of direct approaches to potential customers you have identified in this way will yield a handful of first orders, and their service will provide you with a learning curve in the management of export logistics with the minimum of financial risk. Export logistics, documentation and the financing of exports are complex subjects requiring great attention to detail, and later sections of this chapter offer an introduction. Although they are not strictly a part of the marketing and sales function, logistics and export finance are an important element in most export customer relationships and may impact the terms of business significantly. Problems in these areas may be the deciding factor in whether or not to open a new account or service a particular order.

It is also time for you to decide how you are going to develop your business in the market you are now opening up, and foster the sales relationships you are establishing with new customers. For the easily accessible markets of Western Europe, you may be able to service your customers and develop new business by normal electronic and written communication, supplemented by visits from your export manager or yourself at regular intervals. Personal contact is as crucial in these markets as in those that are further afield or less developed, including the United States, which are difficult to manage from the home office, not least because the cost of visiting them regularly is high in terms of both travel costs and senior management time. If you want your business to develop from more than a trickle of sporadic orders, you will require representation. By now, you should have acquired sufficient market knowledge to make a reasoned judgement as to the kind of intermediary your business needs. Basically, the choice is between the appointment of one or more sales agents or, alternatively, distributors.

Sales agents

Working as an independent contractor on commission, the foreign sales agent's task is to gain orders for his principal's goods and convey them to the principal. Normally, the exporter retains responsibility for delivering the product to the customer, which it may delegate to the company's forwarding agent.

The agent is not normally restricted to selling one company's goods, but is restricted either to a well-defined geographic territory, or sometimes to a specific market sector within a geographical area – such as the retail trade or mail order houses – for consumer products.

Typically, the agent's characteristics and role can be defined as:

- The agent is a company, firm or sole trader, usually a local national, with some experience in the product area.
- Responsibility for:
  - research;
  - promotion;
  - selling;
  - order getting;
  - customer care;
  - problem solving, etc.
- In some cases, the agent has additional responsibility for:
  - calling orders off the forwarding agent's local warehouse;
  - confirming delivery schedules;
  - debt collection.
- The agent receives commission from the company on sales in its territory, usually of between 5 and 10 per cent, based on the exporter's ex-works price and payable only after customer payment in full.
- Usually, the agent does not have any authority to commit the principal contractually beyond accepting an order.

The benefits of an agent are the ability to start up quickly and the low cost to the exporter. The disadvantages are uncertainty about the strength of the agent's commitment, lack of control over its commercial actions, and the cost penalties of termination in many countries (particularly under EU law).

Distributors

In contrast to the sales agent, the foreign distributor acts as a principal, buying and selling manufactured product for its own account and on its own terms. In effect the distributor is the exporter's direct customer, although not the end-user. Delivery to the territory is made through the distributor, which manages the local customer relationship directly.

Distributors are usually incorporated, and their characteristics and role are definable as:

- They purchase goods from the manufacturer and resell into the territory, sometimes as a sole distributor, at a profit.

- They make their profits by marking up the discounted price at which they purchase goods from the exporter to the agreed market price.

- They perform all the agent's tasks plus:
  - stocking goods and spare parts;
  - pre- and after-sales service;
  - sales administration;
  - local deliveries;
  - installation;
  - credit control and debtor collection.

- Distributors' discounts vary from one product sector to another (industrial goods provide for 15 to 25 per cent mark-ups; consumer goods for mark-ups of 50 per cent or more).

- Higher distributors' margins also reflect the additional services they perform compared with agents, and their greater financial risk.

The advantages of exporting through a distributor are that it may be restricted from selling competitors' products under the terms of the distribution agreement, and its activities are easier to monitor than those of the sales agent. The distributor is usually a better channel to market than the agent for technically complex finished products requiring after-sales service and repair facilities.

Selecting sales agents and distributors

You should never appoint an intermediary without developing a clear specification of the role to be filled, and then checking thoroughly that the appointee has the necessary attributes to perform the role. For some national markets with strong regional characteristics, it may be sensible to appoint more than one distributor with clearly defined territories, or a single distributor with several supporting agents. Generally, when one or more agents are appointed for a territory serviced by an exporter's sole distributor, the latter's selling responsibilities are diminished accordingly, and the distributor's margin is reduced by the amount of the agent's commission.

In making your selection of individual distributors and agents, the following criteria are key:

- *Compatibility versus competition*: Familiarity with the same kind of product, bringing market knowledge and customer contacts, is an advantage, but appointing a sales agent or distributor that is already selling competitors' product would be a mistake, and replacing an existing competitor has its perils. Appointing an agent who is already selling complementary but non-competing products successfully may be a good solution, provided that the complementary products are not inferior in quality to your own.

- *Commercial capability*: Look for market knowledge, marketing skills and promotional expertise allied to administrative capability and, for distributors, logistical capability in terms of warehousing and transport facilities.

- *Technical capability*: Assess the technical qualifications of management and staff, and in-house training activity in new products.

- *Financial status*: Perform normal credit reference routines and reviews of trading history, balance sheets and capital adequacy where audited accounts are available.

Through your screening process based on these criteria you will aim to arrive at a shortlist of three or four candidates from which you can make the final selection. Final selection should be carried out by making a personal visit to each candidate's place of business; only at this stage should you allow subjective judgement to influence the decision.

However confident you may be in your final choice, be sure to grant only a trial period of representation (typically 12 months). Although the initial engagement is provisional, it should always be the subject of a full written agreement, not just for your company's protection but also to clarify, without ambiguity, for both parties exactly what is being agreed. The agreement should define all of the following:

- products;
- territories;
- duration of the agreement and provisions for termination;*
- quantitative definition of minimum performance levels;
- commission rates/discounts;
- credit and payment terms;
- the principal's duties and responsibilities;
- use of copyright and ownership of IPR;
- limits of the agent/distributor's authority;
- product and commercial liabilities to customers;
- indemnities and/or compensation on termination;*
- law governing the contract (jurisdiction);*
- provisions for dispute resolution.

*for territories within the Single Market, compliance with EU law is mandatory.

Export logistics

Until your export trade becomes substantial you will not want to consider staffing an export department within your business, with the additional fixed cost that would involve. Fortunately, the evolutionary changes of the information age have bred new logistics solutions, and the outsourcing of logistics management to specialist freight forwarders has now become an attractive option for many companies, both large and small. Even the administrative activities of arranging transportation, managing shipping and forwarding agents, arranging insurance, export documentation, customs clearance, and the payment of freight and other charges can be safely outsourced to the freight forwarder, as well as the physical functions of packing and labelling, warehousing and inventory management. Electronic (EDI) technology is already in common use in the freight industry, and freight forwarders can provide cargo tracking facilities online both for the client and for the forwarder.

Freight forwarders take the form of:

- Local companies that deal with clients in their immediate areas, or operate at sea ports or airports concentrated on particular types of traffic.

- National companies with offices in the major ports and airports and in the largest industrial conurbations throughout the country. They often have overseas agents or correspondents in the markets that they commonly service.

- International companies with their own offices overseas and offering worldwide services. All freight forwarders provide one or more of the following services:

  - road and rail distribution;

  - maritime intermodal services;

  - airfreight consolidation and forwarding;

  - trade facilitation, customs booking and consultancy;

  - logistics and supply chain management.

In selecting a freight forwarder for your export market, make sure that its range of services extends to the cheapest, quickest and safest routing and the best modes of transport. For example, if you are serving Asian markets you will require your freight forwarder to provide consolidation and groupage services – the ability to group together consignments from several exporters and present them to a shipping company or airline as a single large consignment. In this way, you will be able to benefit from a more competitive tariff for your small consignments.

International transport documentation

There are three basic types of international transport document:

- documents of carriage, including the airway bill, bill of lading and consignment note;
- documents for Customs and other regulatory bodies;
- commercial documents.

Bill of lading

The bill of lading is the central document of carriage for ocean shipment. It is a receipt for goods shipped, a document of title and evidence of the freight contract. Possession of a valid negotiable bill of lading constitutes effective legal control of the goods.

Airway bill

The primary document for the carriage of goods by air. It serves as the contract between the shipper and the carrier, as a receipt of goods for shipment, a form of invoicing, and a document for the import, export and transit requirements of Customs.

Road consignment note

The CMR Convention, a set of legal articles that form the contract between the carrier and shipper, governs the international carriage of goods by road.

Regulatory documents

International transport also requires regulatory documents, such as those for the declaration of goods to Customs authorities, import and export licensing, and the movement of dangerous goods.

Commercial documents

The commercial documents in a specific transaction will depend upon the nature of the consignment and methods of payment, and are likely to include invoices, insurance certificates, letters of credit and shipping instructions. Commercial contracts are usually phrased in 'Incoterms', the set of international rules for the most commonly used terms in foreign trade, produced and published by the International Chamber of Commerce (ICC), originally in 1936 and revised in 2000 and again in 2010.

A full explanation of commercial documents and their use is provided in *The Handbook of International Trade* (Sherlock and Reuvid, 3rd edn, Kogan Page, 2010).

Financing exports

Before engaging in any export market it is important, at the outset, to understand how the differences between international and domestic trade can affect the exporter financially. The key consideration is to minimize any funding gap generated by the company's export activity to a level that can be accommodated comfortably within the company's financing arrangements.

The following factors may have an effect:

- Transit times in the carriage of goods and documents are almost certainly longer.

- Different time zones, working-week cycles, holiday periods and languages may impact communications and payment schedules.

- Political risk, customs and excise routines, and local laws and business practices may cause problems to the payment mechanism or delays in the settlement of insurance or other claims.

- Debt recovery procedures differ, and will be costly and time-consuming to pursue from afar.

Methods of settlement

The following methods of settlement are all in current use and present differing degrees of risk for the seller.

Advance payment

The payment for goods in full before they are received, possibly when the order is placed, is the optimum method for the exporter, although some form of retention until the goods are received and checked is normal. However, except for mail order sales to consumers, it is unlikely that trade or industry customers in developed markets, especially the EU, will agree to advance payment. In undeveloped or risky markets advance payment may be the only safe basis for doing business if a customer is unable to offer documentary credits.

Open account

Under open account conditions the exporter dispatches both the goods and documents directly to the importer. The importer receives the goods, and in due course remits payment to the exporter according to the terms agreed between the parties. This procedure is common in the EU between supplier and customer, but in terms of risk it is at the other extreme to advance payment. You will be well advised to limit open account sales to importers of established high standing, or those with whom you have traded satisfactorily for a time.

Documentary collections

The normal alternative to open account, where an exporter wishes to secure payment from lesser-known importers, is to make use of the banking system to obtain payment or acceptance of a bill of exchange. Documentary collection procedures, subscribed to by almost all banks in the commercial world and national chambers of commerce, are covered by the International Chamber of Commerce (ICC) Uniform Rules for Collection that came into force in January 1996.

Under these procedures, an exporter normally hands the shipping and other appropriate documents to its bank after shipping the goods, with instructions that they be transmitted to the buyer's bank and be released against payment by the importer or against acceptance of drafts drawn on the importer. All instructions must be full, clear and precise. Before shipment the exporter should ensure that the importer possesses an import licence that is valid for a period sufficient for the goods to be cleared at their destination, allowing for any potential delay. The exporter should also confirm that current exchange control authorization has been granted to the importer, where applicable, enabling payment to be made immediately or at maturity of the usance drafts, in the currency of collection and as instructed.

There are two main categories of documentary collections – documents against acceptance (D/A) and documents against payment (D/P). D/A is an insecure procedure unless the documents, including documents of title (eg full sets of bills of lading), are retained by the bank until such time as the drafts have been accepted by the importer, and the collecting bank adds its 'per aval' endorsement to the acceptance.

We would recommend that you adopt the D/P procedure under which the relevant documents are released to the importer against payment. Assuming that full sets of documents of title are included in the collection, control of the goods is retained until payment is obtained and the seller is in a comparatively secure situation.

There is still the risk, as under D/A, that the goods are not taken up by the buyer, which can be mitigated by asking the collecting bank to store and insure them with a view to returning them to the seller (unless they are perishable) or to finding another buyer, perhaps at auction.

Documentary credits

There are four main types of documentary credit:

- *Revocable credits*: where the buyer's commitment can be withdrawn. They are rarely used and best avoided.

- *Irrevocable credits, unconfirmed*: the buyer is committed to pay and the seller has the undertaking of the issuing bank, but not the confirmation of a local bank. The risk to the seller lies in the standing of the issuing bank and in the country risk. You may mitigate the risk by demanding that the confirmation of an acceptable bank be added to the credit.

- *Irrevocable credits, confirmed*: the seller is assured of payment and the buyer, through the banking system that gives evidence that the goods have been shipped, is assured of receiving shipping documents. However, absolute clarity is essential in the terms of the credit and the specific documentation. You should scrutinize the credit on receipt and seek any necessary clarification or amendments immediately.

- *Revolving credit*: if you export regularly to a given customer as a pattern of trade emerges, you will find a revolving credit helpful to your cash flow. Revolving credits are reinstated automatically if they are stated as being 'revolving' according to the written terms and conditions. They may take one of two forms – those that revolve automatically and those that revolve periodically. Your bank will advise you on the detailed mechanisms.

Finance alternatives

In relation to the four methods of settlement there are a series of different finance alternatives for exporters, of which the following are the more common.

Bank overdraft

In cases where a manufacturer or trader agrees with its buyer to accept a documentary credit but cannot finance the manufacture or purchase of the goods covered by the documentary credit, a bank may be persuaded to provide the necessary pre-shipment finance in the form of a short-term bridging loan or overdraft facility to cover the period in question. The arrangements may provide for the bank to have control over the goods as soon as they are manufactured or bought, until such time as they are shipped and the proceeds received from the incoming letter of credit.

Bill finance

Finance can be obtained in the form of an advance, with recourse to the drawer, in respect of bills of exchange sent through the banking system on either D/A or D/P documentary collection. Progress is traceable through the banking system and the advance is liquidated on receipt of proceeds from the collecting bank. Of course, your bank will be more inclined to finance bills sent on D/P.

Forfaiting

Forfaiting is defined as the purchase, without recourse to any previous holder, of debt instruments due to mature at a future date that arise from the provision of goods and services. Most forfaiting transactions tend to relate to commodity trade and the sale of capital goods.

Export factoring

Available from specialist international factoring companies, many of which are owned by banks, export factoring allows the exporter to hand copies of all its invoices drawn on overseas buyers to the factoring company, which purchases the debts, often without recourse. Responsibility for credit control, debt collection and foreign exchange risk may be taken on by the factoring company under a variety of schemes offered. As your exports grow, you may find that factoring is the most efficient way of closing the gap in funding your trade.

Currency fluctuation

Any account of trade finance alternatives is incomplete without reference to currency fluctuations and the complex topic of currency management. Foreign trade in any currency other than the trader's own gives rise to the possibility that the rate of exchange of the foreign currency may fluctuate against the trader's own currency, resulting in either an unexpected loss or unrealizable profit.

This concern persuades many exporters and importers to insist on trading in their own currency only, which very often results in a loss of orders or less advantageous prices than trade in the counterpart's currency or a neutral currency, typically the US dollar, the Swiss franc or, of course, the euro. The currency exposure may be redressed by 'hedging' – the purchase or sale of a currency matching the trade contract in amount, currency and value date. If you are exporting to Eurozone members, there is now no practical alternative to quoting, invoicing and accepting payment in euros.

Checklist

- Before committing to an export market, carry out desk research in depth from all available published sources, trade associations and government agencies.

- Attend trade shows to give yourself market exposure. Plan carefully in advance to make best use of your time and help develop shortlists of potential customers.

- Use the servicing of your first orders as a learning curve in export logistics and the financial management of exports.

- Decide how you are going to develop your export business and on the appointment of intermediaries.

- The sales agent is an independent contractor working on commission to gain orders for its principal's goods. The foreign distributor acts as a principal, buying and selling manufactured product at a profit for its own account.

- In selecting individual distributors and agents, apply key criteria to screen them out but make final decisions face to face at their places of business.

- Be sure to grant only a trial period of representation, which should be defined in a full written agreement.

- When appointing agents and distributors in the Single Market, make sure that agreements comply with EU law.

- Consider outsourcing your export logistics to a specialist freight forwarder whose services extend to the cheapest, quickest and safest routing and modes of transport for your export markets.

- Plan to minimize any funding gap generated by export activity so that it can be accommodated within the company's financing arrangements.

continued

- Avoid accepting orders on open account except from well-established trade accounts with good payment records. Insist on confirmed irrevocable credits where possible, or documentary collections against payment.

- As your exports grow, consider the use of revolving credits and factoring.

Chapter Twenty One
Planning the
Endgame

When you started your business it is unlikely that you had a highly developed long-term strategic plan. It is more likely that your business plan was founded on a growth policy to achieve a certain level of market penetration within the first three years, defined by levels of turnover and market share. As your business starts to develop and demonstrates that it can continue to generate profits, you will need to plan how to manage it to grow further, and perhaps faster, and as an owner decide what your longer-term objectives are in terms of wealth creation and the release of capital from the business.

Plainly, the first issue in your strategic planning is to revisit your original growth policy and to decide what changes or refinements you should make to achieve sustained, longer-term growth. Some owners are satisfied with a certain level of profit and personal income and have no entrepreneurial urge to drive the business forward to higher levels of profitability; for them it is sufficient that turnover increases at the rate of inflation, provided that margins and profits are maintained. Effectively, such owners are opting for a 'zero growth' strategy, which sounds prudent but, in practice, is likely to prove highly risky. It is often said that a business either grows and prospers or declines and dies; in general terms, this view is supported by empirical evidence. Most of us can think of small and sometimes larger businesses, often family-owned companies, that seem to have adopted a zero growth strategy and are visibly 'withering on the vine'.

Organic growth versus growth by acquisition

Assuming that you have adopted a positive growth strategy as a means to generate increasing profits and add value to the net worth of your shareholding, you will need to consider how to achieve the necessary levels of annual growth to fulfil your objectives. We noted in Chapter 18 that, as a basic dynamic of business, growth can be either created organically or purchased by acquisitions.

Again, organic growth can be defined as growth through increased sales, which occurs through the development of the firm as an organism represented by its services and products. In this context, 'organic' means structured, organized, systematic, coordinated. Many of the chapters in Part Two and also Chapter 18 focus on the business areas that have to be addressed in order to stimulate and strengthen the organism.

An alternative and faster form of growth than organic expansion is through integration with another firm by merger or acquisition. Integration can be horizontal, that is, between the same type of business, or vertical, that is, between two firms operating at different stages of the supply chain in a business sector, offering complementary services or even operating in different markets.

The two forms of growth are not mutually exclusive, and good decision making by the entrepreneur requires that the horizon is constantly surveyed for both kinds of opportunity, which will better enable business objectives to be achieved. Your surveying activity should include spotting new investment opportunities and alternative means to finance the firm. As with the adoption of a zero growth policy, a company failing to seek opportunities is likely to become stale and run the risk of heading into decline.

Organic growth

Drawing on many of the key points from Chapters 7, 10, 13 and 20, we conclude that sales growth can be achieved by several routes:

- gaining market share relative to competitors;

- creating a new market through product innovation;
- adopting a strategy to expand the market;
- following a long-term trend of growth in a given market.

When firms expand they are usually responding to increased orders. At first they will use the same buildings, the same people and the same equipment. In the longer term, other decisions will need to be taken, such as capital investment and staff training.

In theory, organic growth should be less risky than acquisition, and is a route likely to be more favoured by lenders. However, the growth programme must be underpinned by a sound business plan with clearly articulated short-term, medium-term and long-term objectives.

Among many considerations, the entrepreneur must consider whether the existing staff are sufficiently trained, or of sufficient quality, to meet the growth demands, the most appropriate sales and marketing strategy, and the financial implications of the growth programme, notably in respect of cash flow.

Organic growth sometimes requires the investment of additional capital from an outside investor. This can be a further minefield, as the case study which follows demonstrates.

CASE STUDY: Venture capital at the second stage – a cautionary tale

Kevin and Helen built a business together from 2003 in the niche market of corporate business wear for women continuing to work while pregnant, which grew and prospered through to 2007. The highlight of the period was the February 2007 opening of their first shop in London's trendy King's Road, which has just the right demographic mix of local residents and service business employees. Retailing in their own premises proved rapidly to be more profitable than the previous formula of franchised boutiques in multiple outlets and pointed the way to opening more shops in carefully selected Greater London locations. However, this bolder strategy would clearly demand additional permanent capital in the business.

An angel passes

Out of the blue, Helen and Kevin were approached by a well-known figure in the retailing world as a substantial potential equity investor. He had a track record of successful business management and investment in the sector and convinced them of the benefits that he could bring to the business. After a period of detailed planning and careful negotiation, a deal was agreed in July 2007 and solicitors were instructed to prepare contracts. The incoming investor's funds were to be provided from the exit proceeds of another business investment that had matured and was in the process of being sold.

On the strength of the developing personal relationship and their 'handshake' agreement with the investor, Kevin and Helen negotiated leases for further premises in Notting Hill and Richmond that satisfied their expansion criteria. They were days away from signing the Notting Hill lease with the encouragement of their 'angel' when the blow fell. In a curt e-mail their prospective partner informed them that he was withdrawing. Apparently, his sale transaction had fallen through and he could not, or did not wish to, invest. A face-to-face meeting or even a telephone call to explain what had happened would have softened the impact.

Dire consequences

The loss of their investor proved disastrous. On the strength of the promised funding, Kevin and Helen had increased their working capital commitments and were unable to cover them. One of the top three firms of international accountancy practices was consulted and they were advised to negotiate a creditors' voluntary agreement (CVA). Under instruction from the accountants, they entered into a CVA with their creditors in October 2007. On the basis of the plan agreed with them, creditors could expect to receive 39.5 pence in the pound over four years, with a downside of 18 pence if targets were not achieved.

However, the CVA relief from their predicament was short-lived. Their advisers had neglected to warn them how critical service providers would react. As a matter of policy, BT declined to service the company's customer transactions by telephone because of its CVA status. By the same token, credit card companies refused to transfer payments from customers for goods purchased before despatch. In one case, appeals to the chief executive of the parent company bank were of no avail. Equally, another high street bank demanded a £50,000 deposit before agreeing to conduct business with the company – as good an example of 'catch-22' as any in recent commercial history.

The lessons from this story are clear. Don't extend commitments in the expectation of new funding until contracts are signed and the deal is closed. And, when a financial crisis arises, question professional advice closely and think through all the consequences of the action proposed. Of course, 20:20 hindsight is easy. For proactive entrepreneurs seeking to accelerate the growth of their businesses by bringing in venture capital, be very careful in your choice of investors. 'Beware of Greeks bearing gifts' may be sound advice.

Growth by acquisition

'Mergers' and 'acquisitions' are usually spoken of in the same breath, and the distinction between the two is mainly technical. In the case of a merger the shares of two companies are combined, either by one company (Company A) issuing new shares to the shareholders of the other company (Company B) in exchange for their shareholdings at an agreed ratio, or by forming a new holding company that issues shares to the shareholders of both Company A and Company B in agreed proportions. In the case of an acquisition, Company A makes an offer for the shares of Company B, with or without the consent of the board of Company B; the consideration may be cash, loan stock or shares in Company A or any combination of the three. Often a cash alternative is offered in place of the loan stock or share elements.

In practice, the result of most mergers or acquisitions is that the owners of one company, or directors in the case of public companies where the shares are widely held, gain a dominant, if not controlling, position in the combined and reorganized business. The term 'takeover' is often applied to merger and acquisition transactions, implying a victor and victim. Although used pejoratively, 'takeover' is usually an accurate enough description of what has happened or is about to happen. Equally, the term 'merger', which implies a meeting of minds, is more often than not a euphemism for takeover. Like marriages, few mergers are made in heaven.

Putting yourself in the position of an objective predator, a firm will wish to acquire when it sees an opportunity to make an investment with a positive incremental net present value. However, there are other supporting factors that may motivate an acquisition:

- elimination or reduction of competition;
- safeguarding sources of supply or sales outlets;
- access to economies of scale that a larger business can yield;
- recognition that the target company is undcrutilizing its asset base;
- risk spreading and reduction by diversification.

Acquisitions often provide a quick way to enter other markets and industries. Diversification can make the firm safer and reduce the risk of corporate failure, particularly when the markets in which you are operating show signs of stagnation.

However, diversification into areas where your firm lacks expertise can be risky and costly. You should also address the implications of issuing shares in your company as consideration for acquisition in terms of any potential loss of control.

In pursuing an acquisition policy it is important to keep in mind the motivations of the owners whose businesses you are targeting, as well as your own. As we identified in Chapter 1, entrepreneurs in small businesses tend to value one or more of the following:

- satisfaction in building up a business;
- a desire to lead a particular way of life;
- freedom to make management decisions;
- a desire to keep a tradition alive or perhaps ensure family succession.

While larger listed companies may have the incentive of generating increases in earnings per share by taking over companies at prices that reflect a lower price/earnings ratio, smaller companies are more likely to be sensitive to the vendor's motivations when structuring their deals. In any event, decisions that consistently ignore the question of wealth creation cannot be taken by either purchasers or vendors.

Exit and inheritance strategies

Your long-term strategic plan would be incomplete without the inclusion of your personal exit strategy. You may have been driven to consider the endgame already, with the introduction of private equity capital to fund the growth of the business (see Chapter 5). Just as private equity investors will be looking for a degree of certainty that they can realize their investment in your company within a three to five-year period, you should be looking at the opportunity to release a part of your capital within the same time frame.

Owners of most privately owned businesses seek to either pass the business on to the next generation, particularly if the company is a family company, or sell it to a third party, by either a straight trade sale or management buyout (MBO). The MBO concept can also be applied to the succession plan scenario.

Essentially the exit route alternatives are:

- succession plan;
- trade sale;
- MBO or MBI (management buy-in);
- a realization of assets;
- flotation.

Succession plan

Many owner-managers will work closely in a team environment over a long period of time. Therefore, it is natural to want to pass the business down to someone in the management team, particularly where there are younger members. The considerations are similar where there are younger family members, although in this case the business may be handed on for nominal or little consideration. In terms of providing for succession in a family company, the current UK capital gains and inheritance tax regime is still probably as favourable as it is ever likely to be.

Insurance policies can play a very useful role in succession planning:

- A 'key staff' insurance policy may be taken out to provide a much-needed cash sum for the company in the event of the death of an owner-director.

- Where there is more than one shareholder, there should be a formal shareholders' agreement ensuring that shareholder protection insurance is in place. This enables a director's estate to receive a fair value for his or her shareholding upon death, while ensuring that the relevant shareholding is passed on to the other shareholders.

Frequently, owner-directors continue to maintain control so that they receive a salary or dividend in retirement, sometimes because they don't trust their children/successors to provide them with a secure source of income. For this reason, the owners should plan to build up a substantial pension fund as well as making a sensible provision for savings.

In the event that the chosen successors have little capital, and provided that the company is sufficiently liquid, it can create cash for the departing owner by purchasing its own shares. With an effective current capital gains tax of 10 per cent (see Chapter 15), it is better to exploit this advantage wherever possible rather than receive sums subject to income tax.

Trade sale

In many cases a trade sale is the natural exit route. For third-party private equity shareholders, it will be the preferred route in the absence of a sustainable flotation within the time frame for the manager's planned exit. At the end of the day, most people have a price that they will accept, and the wealth can be passed down to family members.

A company sale can take one of two forms: a sale of shares or a sale of assets. It is highly preferable for a vendor to sell his/her shares. This ensures that business taper relief (see Chapter 15) and retirement relief, if applicable, can be claimed. It also avoids the potential double taxation charge arising from a sale of assets.

In an assets sale the company will sell the assets and make chargeable gains subject to corporation tax. The owner will then pay income tax when the profit is extracted. If an assets sale is unavoidable, the most efficient way forward is usually a pre-liquidation dividend. In practice, it is well worth encouraging the purchaser to purchase the shares in your company, even if it entails passing on a discount or giving indemnities and warranties that would not be demanded in an assets sale, provided that the latter are not too onerous.

However, a trade sale of your company's shares may not be quite so straightforward as it first appears. Perhaps the purchaser will ask you to accept shares in its company for a part or the whole of the consideration. If the purchasing company is listed on the London Stock Exchange you may be willing to accept a part of the consideration in shares, given that a share exchange does not attract capital gains tax until such time as the shares received are sold. Nevertheless, before accepting this alternative be sure that there is an active market in the shares and that you are free to sell them over a reasonable period. If you are in any doubt about your ability to convert the shares into cash, be sure to insist on arrangements for them to be placed in the market on your behalf.

Another quite common requirement in trade sales is for the purchaser to insist on an 'earn out' element in the payment of the purchase consideration. Under this kind of arrangement you will receive only a part of the purchase consideration on completion of the transaction, and the remainder in one or more instalments over a further period, with the price adjustable by reference to the audited net profits before tax.

This is a reasonable approach if the final reckoning relates to a financial year that has ended before the acquisition was completed and the audited accounts are not yet available. However, calculation of the outstanding consideration is often referenced to an accounting year that is not yet complete or to one or more financial years ahead, and such conditions give rise to a number of uncertainties.

You may be able to sell the company without some element of earn-out but, if not, there are several conditions that you should strive to include in the part of the sale agreement that refers to the earn-out period:

1 A sufficient part of the purchase consideration to be paid upfront in cash on signature of the agreement. This is your

'drop-dead' money of which you can be certain if the rest of the transaction is delayed or fails to be carried out.

2 Your continued employment by the company, if the deferred element relates to a future accounting period, as a director and on no less than the same terms that you enjoyed prior to the sale of the company. Your employment should be the subject of a written service agreement.

3 An undertaking from the purchaser in the form of a shareholders' agreement that for the financial periods to which the earn-out provisions apply, no parent company management charges will be levied, no additional senior management appointed, no capital expenditure incurred, no loan capital introduced, no new share capital issued and no dividends paid without your express written consent.

The third set of provisions is necessary to ensure that neither pre-tax profits nor shareholders' funds are deflated during the earn-out period, and your remaining shareholding is not diluted by actions of the new controlling shareholder unrelated to normal trading.

If the purchaser requests that you remain with the company as a salaried director for a minimum or indefinite period of time, irrespective of any earn-out arrangements that may be agreed, do not be deceived into thinking that your trade sale is anything other than a takeover of your business. Whatever the intentions of the parties at the time of the transaction, and however flattering an invitation to stay on may seem, it is extremely unlikely that you will still be employed or play any active part in your company's affairs 18 months after the sale. Of course, there are recorded cases of vendors who have gone on to take increased responsibilities and senior positions in the group of which their company has become a part, but such cases are few and far between. More commonly, the vendor finds it difficult to adjust to a new situation where he or she is unable to take decisions unilaterally, or where the management ethos or business practices of the group are incompatible. Moreover, there is likely to be a band of thrusting young managers to whom the vendor is now exposed, who are confident that they can run the business better.

A service contract will help to ensure that the final parting is financially acceptable, but with the gift of hindsight, you might wish that you had negotiated a higher drop-dead element in the purchase consideration, if there is still an earn-out payment outstanding. As a general recommendation, you should try to ensure that at least two-thirds of the total purchase consideration in a trade sale is paid in cash on completion.

MBO or MBI

A management buyout (MBO) is often a good way of exiting from a business. In fact, an MBO may not involve the existing management at all, and could be a scheme led by institutional investors, involving the insertion of a new management team into the business, thereby creating a management buy-in (MBI).

Similar considerations apply as with a trade sale. However, earn-out provisions and service contracts for the vendors are less likely, as are earn-out provisions. In raising institutional financial backing, the new management team will probably have developed a business plan of its own that involves ambitious growth targets and major changes to the way in which the business has been run previously. You are unlikely to be a welcome guest at the feast that follows.

Realization of assets

A realization of assets is often a scenario forced on the owner because of poor trading, and takes the form of a receivership or liquidation. In cases where there are difficulties in making a trade sale on the best terms or there are peculiarities in the business, such as a total dependence on the continuing presence of the original owners, the owner-director(s) may decide to wind up the company voluntarily, following either a sale of the assets and ongoing trade, or a planned closure of the business. In any event, good timing and prompt decision making will help to maximize the outcome.

Flotation

A public flotation on the Alternative Investment Market (AIM) of the London Stock Exchange, or even a full listing for larger companies, can be the ultimate exit route over time, and entrepreneurs may be attracted by the prestige of leading a quoted company. However, the listing process is fraught with complicated pre-flotation requirements, and the post-flotation maintenance of the listing is a continuing burden.

The actual process of flotation is expensive, and involves the appointment of an accredited nominated adviser or sponsor, solicitors to the issue, reporting accountants, a corporate broker and financial public relations consultants. The decision whether or not to go public should be appraised long before the decision is finalized, after evaluating carefully the alternative strategies and contrasting them with the flotation model. For a step-by-step account of the flotation process and post-flotation management issues, you may wish to consult *Floating Your Company: The essential guide to going public* (Reuvid, 3rd edn, Kogan Page, 2007).

If all goes well, new capital can dramatically increase your company's potential growth in many different ways, and is the stepping stone to substantial financial rewards through future share sales. However, the best-laid flotation plans can be blown off course by market developments beyond the influence of your advisers or yourself, such as the 2001/02 'bear' market, which caused a number of companies to defer or break off their flotations, or the present plunge in the financial sector following the 'credit crunch' of 2008 that has caused companies to defer their independent public offerings (IPOs).

The main disadvantage of flotation is its inadequacy as an exit strategy for the owner-managers of the company. There will be restrictions on the disposal of the owner shareholdings for several years, and invariably the owner-managers will be required to remain in office for an extended period following flotation.

Bowing out

In Chapter 1 we introduced the SWOT analysis as a planning tool and suggested that the same assessment exercise to which you subjected your business start-up plan and your own capabilities as an entrepreneur could be carried out at any time in the life of a business. One time when the SWOT tool is certainly appropriate is if you have reached a point when you have to question the future direction and prosperity of the business or, indeed, its ability to survive. However unwelcome an experience this may be, it is better to carry out the analysis as soon as you begin to have serious doubts rather than wait until poor trading forces you into an assets realization programme under an administrator or receiver.

There are many external reasons, probably beyond the control of its owners/directors, why a previously healthy business may fall into decline. All too often the deterioration occurs because the management has failed to anticipate changes in the business environment or to plan and manage the internal change and development programmes necessary for continuing growth. The hardest lesson for any entrepreneur to learn and accept is that he or she can no longer make a useful contribution or that his/her continuing management presence may be a liability to the business. If you find yourself in that unhappy position, take a deep breath and get out.

Checklist

- As your business grows profitably, revise your original growth policy to achieve sustained, longer-term growth. Zero growth strategies are risky.

- Growth can either be created organically or purchased by acquisition.

- In theory, organic growth should be less risky than acquisition, and is a route more likely to be favoured by lenders. Consider whether existing staff are of sufficient quality to meet growth demands, and the cash flow implications of the growth programme.

- Where a merger or acquisition results in the owners or directors of one company gaining control or dominance of another, in reality the transaction is a takeover.

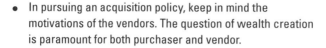

continued

- In pursuing an acquisition policy, keep in mind the motivations of the vendors. The question of wealth creation is paramount for both purchaser and vendor.

- Succession plans can provide for exit payments to owners through the company's purchase of its own shares, which are subject only to capital gains at the current preferential rate.

- Owners should plan for retirement by building up pension funds rather than expect to continue drawing salaries or dividends subject to income tax.

- Trade sales through the sale of a company's shares are preferable to a sale of assets for the vendor. The latter is subject to double taxation charges.

- Trade sales can involve 'earn-out' elements in the payment of the consideration. Take care to secure a substantial cash payment on completion and written undertakings to ensure that neither pre-tax profits nor shareholders' funds are deflated, and your shareholding is not diluted during the earn-out period.

- MBOs and MBIs involving institutional investors are an acceptable variation on trade sales. If you remain an employee after any kind of trade sale, do not expect your employment to continue beyond the short term.

- Asset realization through a voluntary winding-up of the company may be appropriate following a sale of the assets and ongoing trade. Good timing and prompt decision making will help to maximize the outcome.

- Public flotation of your company may be the stepping stone to substantial financial rewards, but there will be restrictions on the disposal of owner shareholdings for several years, while owner-managers must stay on post-flotation.

- When you can no longer contribute usefully to the business, plan your exit.

Appendix One
Further Reading

Kogan Page titles

Kogan Page publish a wide variety of helpful titles for people in business. Information on the full range of titles is available from the Kogan Page website: www.koganpage.com.

Business communication
Effective Internal Communication, 2nd edition (2008), Lyn Smith and Pamela Mounter
Marketing Communications, 4th edition (2004), Paul Smith
Secure Online Business Handbook (2006), ed Jonathan Reuvid

Finance, accounting and fund-raising
Accounting for Non-Accountants (2008), Graham Mott
Essential Management Accounting (2008), Belinda Steffan
Practical Financial Management, 7th edition (2008), Colin Barrow
How the City Really Works, 3rd edition (2010), Alex Davidson
How the Global Financial Markets Really Work (2009), Alex Davidson
How to Understand Business Finance, 2nd edition (2010), Bob Cinnamon and Brian Helweg-Larsen
Venture Capital Funding, 2nd edition (2008), Stephen Bloomfield

Strategy
Bids, Tenders and Proposals, 3rd edition (2009), Harold Lewis
Floating Your Company, 3rd edition (2007), ed Jonathan Reuvid
The Growing Business Handbook, 12th edition (2009), ed Adam Jolly
Mergers & Acquisitions (2008), ed Jonathan Reuvid

Strategic Planning (2008), Robert Wittmann and Matthias Reuter

Law and company secretarial
The Company Secretary's Handbook, 5th edition (2008), Helen Ashton
The Employer's Handbook, 7th edition (2010), Barry Cushway
Essential Law for Your Business, 13th edition (2009), Patricia Clayton
Health and Safety at Work, 9th edition (2010), Jeremy Stranks

Management
How to Be an Even Better Manager, 7th edition (2008), Michael Armstrong
The 30 Day MBA (2009), Colin Barrow
The New Boss (2008), Peter Fischer
Successful Interviewing and Recruitment (2010), Rob Yeung

Sales, marketing and advertising
Develop Your PR Skills (2010), Lucy Laville and Neil Richardson
Effective Customer Care (2010), Pat Wellington
How to Market Your Business, 6th edition (2008), Dave Patten
A Quick Start Guide to Online Selling (2010), Cresta Norris
Winning New Business: Essential selling skills for non-sales people (2007), Richard Denny
How to Write a Marketing Plan, revised 3rd edition (2010), John Westwood

Start-ups, business plans and new directions
Forming a Limited Company, 10th edition (2008), Patricia Clayton
How I Made It, 2nd edition (2010), Rachel Bridge
How to Be a Successful Entrepreneur (2009), Helga Drummond
How to Write a Business Plan, 3rd edition (2010), Brian Finch
Working for Yourself, 26th edition (2009), Jonathan Reuvid

Working from home
Starting a Business from Home (2008), Colin Barrow

Other sources of information

Official information
Leaflets from government offices provide a further source of information. They are normally available either from the government department concerned or from The Stationery Office.

Information on employment issues
IRS Employment Review (published fortnightly), Industrial Relations Services, London

Legislation is available from the Department for Business, Innovation and Skills website (www.bis.gov.uk). Relevant Acts include:

> Asylum and Immigration Act 1996
> Data Protection Act 1998
> Disability Discrimination Act 1995
> Employment Act 1989
> Employment Act 2002
> Employment Equality (Religion or Belief) Regulations 2003
> Employment Rights Act 1996
> Race Relations Act 1976
> Rehabilitation of Offenders Act 1974
> Sex Discrimination Acts 1975 and 1986
> Sexual Orientation Regulations 2003
> The Children (Protection at Work) Regulations 1998 and 2000
> Trade Union Reform and Employment Rights Act 1992
> Transfer of Undertakings (Protection of Employment) Regulations 1981 (TUPE)

Appendix Two
Useful Contacts

Government

The Adjudicator's Office
(For complaints against rulings by HM Revenue & Customs)
Haymarket House, 28 Haymarket, London SW1Y 4SP
Tel: 020 7930 2292
Web: www.adjudicatorsoffice.gov.uk

Business Link
Tel: 0845 600 9006

Signpost line: 0845 756 7765/freephone 0800 500200
Web: www.businesslink.org

Business Eye (Wales)
Tel: 0845 796 9798
Web: www.businessconnect.org.uk

Business Gateway (Scotland)
Tel: 0845 609 6611
Web: www.bgateway.com

Invest Northern Ireland
Tel: 028 9023 9090
Web: www.investni.com

CCTA Government Information Service
A gateway to all Government Department websites:
www.open.gov.uk

Central Office of Information
Web: www.coi.gov.uk

The Data Protection Registrar
Wycliffe House, Wilmslow, Cheshire SK9 5AF
Tel: 01625 545745
Web: www.dpr.gov.uk

Department of Business, Innovation and Skills
Ministerial Correspondence Unit, 1 Victoria Street, London SW1H 0ET
Tel: 020 7215 5000 or 020 7215 6740
Web: www.bis.gov.uk

Department of the Environment, Food and Regional Affairs
Nobel House, 17 Smith Square, London SW1P 3JR
Tel: 020 238 6951
Web: www.defra.gov.uk

Department for Business, Enterprise and Regulatory Reform
Enquiries: 1 Victoria Street, London SW1H 0ET
Tel: 020 7215 5000
Web: www.berr.gov.uk

Export Credits Guarantee Department (ECGD)
PO Box 2200, 2 Exchange Tower, Harbour Exchange Square, London E14 9GS
Tel: 020 7512 7000
Web: www.ecgd.gov.uk

Her Majesty's Treasury
The Public Enquiries Unit, 1 Horse Guards Road, London SW1A 2HQ
Tel: 020 7270 4558
Web: www.hm-treasury.gov.uk

HM Revenue and Customs
Formerly the Inland Revenue, HM Revenue and Customs has a number of helplines for enquiries, a listing of which can be found on its website at www.hmrc.gov.uk.

Local Enterprise Companies
These have different titles and forms in different areas. Details can be obtained from regional Business Link offices.
Tel: 0845 600 9006
Web: www.businesslink.org

Office of Fair Trading
Fleetbank House, 2–6 Salisbury Square, London EC4Y 8JX
Tel: 0845 722 4499
Web: www.oft.gov.uk

Office for National Statistics
Cardiff Road, Newport, Gwent NP10 8XG
Tel: 0845 601 3034
Web: www.statistics.gov.uk

Revenue Customs and Excise
Addresses of regional/advice centres are available by phone.
Tel: 0845 010 9000
Web: www.hmrc.gov.uk

Start-up advice

National Federation of Enterprise Agencies
Tel: 01234 354053
Web: www.nfea.com

England and Wales

Local Enterprise Agencies
Business in the Community, 137 Shepherdess Walk, London N1 7RQ
Tel: 0870 600 2482
Web: www.bitc.org.uk

The National Assembly for Wales
Industry and Training Department, Crown Buildings, Cathays Park,
Cardiff CF10 3NQ
Tel: 029 2082 5111
Web: www.wales.gov.uk

Welsh Development Agency
Plas Glyndŵr, Kingsway, Cardiff CF10 3AH
Tel: 01443 845500
Web: www.wda.co.uk

Scotland

Scottish Business in the Community
PO Box 408, Bankhead Avenue, Edinburgh EH11 4HE
Tel: 0131 442 2020
Web: www.sbcscot.com

Scottish Enterprise
5 Atlantic Quay, 140 Broomielaw, Glasgow G2 8LU
Tel: 0141 248 2700
Web: www.scottish-enterprise.com

The Office of the Scottish Executive
Enterprise and Lifelong Learning, Meridian Court, 7 Cadogan Street,
Glasgow G2 6AT
Tel: 0141 248 2855
Web: www.scotland.gov.uk

Highlands and Islands Enterprise
Cowan House, Inverness Retail and Business Park, Inverness IV27GF
Tel: 01463 234171
Web: www.hie.co.uk

Northern Ireland

Invest Northern Ireland
44–58 May Street, Belfast BT1 4NN
Upper Galwally, Belfast BT8 6TB
and
17 Antrim Road, Lisburn BT28 3AL
Tel: 028 9023 9090
Fax: 028 9049 0490
Web: www.investni.com

National associations representing small firms

Association of Independent Business
34 Bow Lane, London EC4M 9AY
Tel: 020 7329 0219

The British Chambers of Commerce
Manning House, 22 Carlisle Place, London SW1P 1JA
Tel: 020 7565 2000
Web: www.chamberonline.co.uk

British Franchise Association
Thames View, Newton Road, Henley-on-Thames, Oxon RG9 1HG
Tel: 01491 578050
Web: www.british-franchise.org.uk

Confederation of British Industry (CBI)
Centre Point, 103 New Oxford Street, London WC1A 1DU
Tel: 020 7395 8247
Web: www.cbi.org.uk

Federation of Small Businesses Ltd
Sir Frank Whittle Way, Blackpool Business Park, Blackpool, Lancs
FY4 2FE
Tel: 01253 336000
Web: www.fsb.org.uk

The Forum of Private Business Ltd
Ruskin Chambers, Drury Lane, Knutsford, Cheshire WA16 6HA
Tel: 01565 634467
Web: www.fpb.co.uk

Smaller Firms Council (CBI)
Centre Point, 103 New Oxford Street, London WC1A 1DU
Tel: 020 7395 8247
Web: www.cbi.org.uk

The Work Foundation
(formerly The Industrial Society)
Peter Runge House, 3 Carlton House Terrace, London SW1Y 5DG
Tel: 0870 165 6700
Web: www.theworkfoundation.com

Forming a company

Companies Limited/Rapid Refunds
For purchasing an off-the-shelf company.
376 Euston Road, London NW1 3BL
Tel: 020 7383 2323
Web: www.limited-companies.co.uk

Industrial Co-operatives UK
Advice on setting up worker cooperatives.
Holyoake House, Hanover Street, Manchester M60 0AS
Tel: 0161 246 2900
Web: www.cooperatives-uk.coop

Institute of Directors
116 Pall Mall, London SW1Y 5ED
Tel: 020 7839 1233
Web: www.iod.co.uk

The Law Society
Lawyers for your business.
113 Chancery Lane, London WC2A 1PL
Tel: 020 7242 1222
Web: www.lfyb.lawsociety.org.uk

The Patent Office
Concept House, Cardiff Road, Newport, South Wales NP10 8QQ
Tel: 01633 814000
Web: www.patent.gov.uk

Registrar of Companies
Companies Registration Office, Crown Way, Cardiff CF14 3UZ
For Scotland: 37 Castle Terrace, Edinburgh EH2 2EB
For London: Companies House Executive Agency, 21 Bloomsbury
Street, London WC1B 3XD
Tel: 0870 333 3636
Web: www.companies-house.gov.uk

Banks

Abbey National plc
Abbey National House, 2 Triton Square, Regent's Place, London
NW1 3AN
Web: www.abbey.com

Barclays Bank plc Business Direct
Octagon House, Gadbrook Park, Northwich CW9 7RB
Tel: 01606 844033
Web: www.barclays.co.uk

HSBC plc
8 Canada Square, London E14 5HQ
Tel: 020 7991 8888
Web: www.banking.hsbc.co.uk

Lloyds TSB Bank plc, Small Business Advice
PO Box 112, Canons House, Canons Way, Bristol BS99 7LB
Tel: 0117 943 3433
Web: www.lloydstsb.com

National Westminster Bank plc, Business One Stop Shop
PO Box 4114, 120–126 High Street, Hornchurch, Essex RM12 4DF
Tel: 0800 028 2677
Web: www.natwest.com/startup

Raising capital

3i plc
91 Waterloo Road, London SE1 8XP
Tel: 020 7928 3131
Web: www.3i.com

British Insurance Brokers Association (BIBA)
BIBA House, 14 Bevis Marks, London EC3A 7NT
Consumers helpline: 0870 950 1790
Fax: 020 7626 9676
Web: www.biba.org.uk

British Venture Capital Association
Tower 3, 3 Clements Inn, London WC2A 2AZ
Tel: 020 7025 2950
Web: www.bvca.co.uk

EU Money Service
2 Gallands Close, Swanland, Ferriby HU14 3GE
Tel: 01482 651695
Web: www.europeangrants.com

Factors and Discounters Association
Boston House, The Little Green, Richmond, Surrey TW9 1QE
Tel: 020 8332 9955
Web: www.factors.org.uk

Finance and Leasing Association
Imperial House, 15–19 Kingsway, London WC2B 6UN
Tel: 020 7836 6511
Web: www.fla.org.uk

Institute of Patentees and Inventors
Suite 505a, Triumph House, 189 Regent Street, London W1R 7WE
Tel: 020 8541 4197

The Prince's Trust
18 Park Square East, London NW1 4LH
Tel: 020 7543 1234
Web: www.princes-trust.org.uk

The Prince's Scottish Youth Business Trust
Tel: 0141 248 4999
Web: www.psybt.org.uk

Venture Capital Report Ltd
7 Old Park Lane, London W1K 1QR
Tel: 020 7072 2410
Web: www.vcr1978.com

Premises

English Partnerships
St George's House, Kingsway, Team Valley, Gateshead, Tyne and Wear
NE11 0NA
Tel: 0191 487 6565
Web: www.englishpartnerships.co.uk

Estates Today
Online commercial estate agency
Web: www.estatestoday.co.uk

Royal Institution of Chartered Surveyors
12 Great George Street, Parliament Square, London SW1P 3AD
Tel: 0870 333 1600
Web: www.rics.org

Marketing and sales

Chartered Institute of Marketing
Moor Hall, Cookham, Maidenhead, Berkshire SL6 9QH
Tel: 01628 427500
Web: www.cim.co.uk

Chartered Institute of Public Relations
The Old Trading House, 15 Northburgh Street, London EC1V 0PR
Tel: 020 7253 5151
Web: www.cipr.co.uk

Direct Marketing Association UK Ltd
DMA House, 70 Margaret Street, London SW1W 8SS
Tel: 020 7291 3300
Web: www.dma.org.uk

Institute of Direct Marketing
1 Park Road, Teddington, Middlesex TW11 0AR
Tel: 020 8977 5705
Web: www.theidm.com

Marketing Society
1 Park Road, Teddington, Middlesex TW11 0AR
Tel: 020 8973 1700
Web: www.marketing-society.org.uk

Safety and standards

British Safety Council
70 Chancellor's Road, London W6 9RS
Tel: 020 8741 1231
Web: www.britishsafetycouncil.org

British Standards Institution
389 Chiswick High Road, London W4 4AL
Tel: 020 8996 9000
Web: www.bsi-global.com

Health and Safety Executive
Rose Court, 2 Southwark Bridge, London SE1 9HS
Tel: 020 7717 6000
Web: www.hse.gov.uk

Managing finance

Association of Chartered and Certified Accountants (ACCA)
29 Lincoln's Inn Fields, London WC2A 3EE
Tel: 020 7396 7000
Web: www.acca.global.com

Chartered Accountants Directory
Datacomp, 4 Houldsworth Square, Reddish, Stockport, Cheshire
SK5 7AF
Tel: 0161 442 5233
Web: www.chartered-accountants.co.uk

Chartered Institute of Taxation
12 Upper Belgrave Street, London SW1X 8BB
Tel: 020 7235 9381
Web: www.tax.org.uk

Institute of Certified Book-Keepers
12 St James' Square, London SW1Y 4RB
Tel: 0845 060 2345
Web: www.book-keepers.org

Institute of Chartered Accountants in England and Wales
PO Box 433, Chartered Accountants Hall, Moorgate Place, London
EC2P 2BJ
Tel: 020 7920 8100
Web: www.icaew.co.uk

Institute of Chartered Accountants of Scotland
ICA House, 21 Haymarket Yards, Edinburgh EH12 5BH
Tel: 0131 347 0100
Web: www.icas.org.uk

Institute of Financial Accountants and The International Association
of Book-Keepers
Burford House, 44 London Road, Sevenoaks, Kent TN13 1AS
Tel: 01732 458080
Web: www.ifa.org.uk and www.iab.org.uk

Labour relations and personnel management

Advisory, Conciliation and Arbitration Service (ACAS)
Brandon House, 180 Borough High Street, London SE1 1LW
Tel: 020 7210 3613
Web: www.acas.org.uk

Chartered Institute of Personnel and Development
151 The Broadway, London SW19 1JQ
Tel: 020 8971 9000
Web: www.cipd.co.uk

Chartered Management Institute
Management Information Centre, Management House, Cottingham
Road, Corby, Northants NN17 1TT
Tel: 01536 204222
Web: www.managers.org.uk

Export

The British Chambers of Commerce
Trade Partners UK Support for Export Marketing Research Scheme,
4 Westwood House, Westwood Business Park, Coventry CV4 8HS
Tel: 024 7669 4484
Web: www.britishchambers.org.uk/exportzone

British Exporters Association
Broadway House, Tothill Street, London SW1H 9NQ
Tel: 020 7222 5419
Web: www.bexa.co.uk

British International Freight Association
Redfern House, Browells Lane, Feltham, Middlesex TW13 7EP
Tel: 020 8844 2266
Web: www.bifa.org

Commission of the European Communities
Jean Monnet House, 8 Storey's Gate, London SW1P 3AT
Tel: 020 7973 1992

Euler Trade Indemnity plc
1 Canada Square, London E14 5DX
Tel: 020 7512 9333
Web: www.eulerhermes.com

Export Credits Guarantee Department
PO Box 2200, 2 Exchange Tower, Harbour Exchange Square, London
E14 9GS
Tel: 020 7512 7000
Web: ww.ecgd.gov.uk

Institute of Export
Export House, Minerva Business Park, Lynch Wood, Peterborough
PE2 6FT
Tel: 01733 404400
Web: www.export.org.uk

SITPRO Ltd
(formerly Simpler Trade Procedures Board)
Oxford House, 8th Floor, 76 Oxford Street, London W10 1BS
Tel: 020 7467 7280

Technical Help for Exporters
British Standards Institution, 389 Chiswick High Road, London
W4 4AL
Tel: 020 8996 9000
Web: www.bsi-global.com

UK Trade & Investment
Export Control Enquiry Unit, Kingsgate House, 66–74 Victoria
Street, London SW1E 6SW
Tel: 020 7215 500
Web. www.uktradeinvest.gov.uk

Information and communication technologies

British Telecom
Advice on communications and information technologies for business.
Web: www.britishtelecom.co.uk

Exploit
Web: www.exploit.com

Liszt
Description of most mailing lists and joining details.
Web: www.liszt.com

Nominet
To register internet names.
Web: www.nic.uk

Submitit
These companies will submit your website address to online search
engines.
Web: www.submitit.com

WebCounter
Adds visitor counter to your website.
Web: www.digits.com

Sector information

Construction

Federation of Master Builders
14–15 Great James Street, London WC1N 3DP
Tel: 020 7242 7583
Web: www.fmb.org.uk

Crafts

The Crafts Council
44a Pentonville Road, London N1 9BY
Tel: 020 7278 7700
Web: www.craftscouncil.org.uk

Design

British Interior Design Association
3–18 Chelsea Harbour Design Centre, Lots Road, London SW10 0XE
Tel: 020 7349 0800
Web: www.bida.org

Design Council
34 Bow Street, London WC2E 7DL
Tel: 020 7420 5200
Web: www.designcouncil.org.uk

Estate Agents

National Association of Estate Agents
Arbon House, 21 Jury Street, Warwick CV34 4EH
Tel: 01926 496800
Web: www.propertylive.co.uk

Farming

Agricultural Development Advisory Service
Oxford Spires, The Boulevard, Kidlington, Oxon OX5 1NZ
Tel: 01865 842742
Web: www.adas.co.uk

Farming & Agricultural Finance Limited
(part of Royal Bank of Scotland Group)
PO Box 4115, Hornchurch, Essex RM12 4DS
Tel: 01453 767644
E-mail: philip.coysh@rbs.co.uk

Gardening and landscape architecture

Institute of Horticulture
14–15 Belgrave Square, London SW1X 8PS
Tel: 020 7245 6943
Web: www.horticulture.org.uk

The Landscape Institute
33 Great Portland Street, London W1W 8QG
Tel: 020 7299 4500
Web: www.l-i.org.uk

Hospitality

British Beer and Pub Association
Market Towers, 1 Nine Elms Lane, London SW8 5NQ
Tel: 020 7627 9191
Web: www.beerandpub.com

Hotel and Catering International Management Association
Trinity Court, 34 West Street, Sutton, Surrey SM1 1SH
Tel: 020 8661 4900
Web: www.hcima.org.uk

IT

Association of Computer Professionals
204 Barnett Wood Lane, Ashtead, Surrey KT21 2DB
Tel: 0137 2273442
Web: www.acpexamboard.com

British Computer Society
1 Sanford Street, Swindon, Wilts SN1 1JH
Tel: 01793 417214
Web: www.bcs.org

Management consultancy

Institute of Management Consultancy
3rd Floor, 17–18 Haywards Place, London EC1R 0EQ
Tel: 020 7566 5220
Web: www.imc.co.uk

Tourism

VisitScotland
23 Ravelston Terrace, Edinburgh E14 3TP
Tel: 0131 332 2433
Web: www.visitscotland.com

Wales Tourist Board
Brunel House, 2 Fitzalan Road, Cardiff CF24 0UY
Tel: 0870 121 1251
Web: www.visitwales.com

Transport management

Association of Car Fleet Operators (AFCO)
Rivendell House, Winton Road, Petersfield GU32 3LL
Tel: 01730 260162

British Vehicle Rental and Leasing Association (BVRLA)
River Lodge, Badminton Court, Amersham, Bucks HP7 0DD
Tel: 01494 434747
Web: www.bvrla.co.uk

Glass's Information Services Ltd
1 Princes Road, Weybridge, Surrey KT13 9TU
Tel: 01932 823823
Web: www.glass.co.uk

Specialist libraries

Business Information Service
British Library, Lloyds TSB Business Line, 96 Euston Road, London NW1 2DB
Tel: 020 7412 7454/9799
Web: www.bl.uk/bis

Chartered Institute of Marketing Library
Moor Hall, Cookham, Maidenhead, Berks SL6 9QH
Tel: 01628 427500
Web: www.cim.co.uk

Chartered Management Institute Management Information Centre
(for members only)
Management House, Cottingham Road, Corby, Northants NN17 1TT
Tel: 01536 204222
Web: www.managers.org.uk

Export Market Information Centre Library
Kingsgate House, 66–74 Victoria Street, London SW1E 6SW
Tel: 020 7215 4555

Frobisher Crescent Library at City University
Contact numbers for various departments are given on the website
www.city.ac.uk/library

London Business School Library
25 Taunton Place, London NW1
Postal address: London Business School, Regent's Park, London
NW1 4SA
Tel: 020 7262 5050
Web: www.lbs.lon.ac.uk/library

London Metropolitan University Library
School of Business Studies, 84 Moorgate, London EC2M 6SQ
Tel: 020 7320 1000

Monopolies and Mergers Commission Library
New Court, 48 Carey Street, London WC2A 2JT
Tel: 020 7324 1467

Office of Fair Trading Library
Field House, 15 Bream's Buildings, London EC4A 1PR

Office for National Statistics
Government Buildings, Cardiff Road, Newport, South Wales NP9 1XG
Web: www.statistics.gov.uk

UK Trade and Investment
Kingsgate House, 66–74 Victoria Street, London SW1E 6SW
Tel: 020 7215 8000
Web: www.uktradeinvest.gov.uk

Websites of interest

CBI 'Fitforthefuture'
New site from CBI on National Best Practice.
Web: www.fitforthefuture.org.uk

Electronic Telegraph
Access to full text of *Daily Telegraph* and directory listing of British business.
Web: www.telegraph.co.uk

Financial Times
Business directory and up-to-date financial information.
Web: www.ft.com

Keele University Management Web Resources Database
Well-resourced database of business and management websites with good links.
Web: www.keelc.ac.uk

Kogan Page
Extensive list of publications for start-ups and SMEs.
Web: www.koganpage.com

Strathclyde University Business Information Sources on the Internet
Thoroughly recommended website with extensive listings of sites and general sources of business information.
Web: www.dis.strath.ac.uk

WhoWhere
E-mail address, telephone number and street address directory.
Web: www.whowhere.com

Yahoo!
Search engine with extensive business directory.
Web: www.yahoo.com

Yell
Online version of the Yellow Pages.
Web: www.yell.co.uk

Transport-related publications

Business Car
Tel: 01733 578458

Fleet Car Business
Tel: 01733 467000

Fleet Management
Tel: 01733 578458

Fleet News
Tel: 01733 467048

Fleet Operator
Journal of AFCO
Tel: 01730 260162

Motive
Journal of BVRLA
Tel: 01494 434747

Index

NB: page numbers in *italic* indicate figures or tables

Index of Advertisers